UNPATHED WATERS

UNPATHED WATERS

Account of the life and times of

JOSEPH HUDDART, FRS

At one time a Captain in the service of
the Honourable East India Company and
later an Elder Brother of the Corporation
of Trinity House.

WILLIAM HUDDART

Foreword by
Dr R. S. Porter

Quiller Press
London

First published 1989 by
Quiller Press Limited
46 Lillie Road
London SW6 1TN

ISBN 1 870948 36 X

Designed by Hugh Tempest-Radford Book Producers
and printed in Great Britain by Butler & Tanner Ltd,
Frome and London

CONTENTS

FOREWORD

by Roy Porter

Eighteenth-century Britain had due cause to celebrate its giants: Lord Chatham and his son, Pitt the Younger; Marlborough and Nelson; Samuel Johnson and Joshua Reynolds—men without peers in politics, in arms and in the arts. But what secured Britain's phenomenal rise to greatness under the Hanoverians was a kind of strength in depth. These small islands, perched on the North West extremity of Europe, boasted enviable numbers of literate, numerate, energetic, and self-reliant people, adept at turning a penny and fired with the spirit of enterprise. Foreigners visiting these shores for the first time marvelled at the multitudes of these middling folk and their unsurpassed business.

Britain's yeomen and farmers pioneered advances in agricultural techniques. Her craftsmen were constantly making innovations in technical processes, her industrialists boldly placed their faith in inventiveness and in the heavy machinery, factories, and steam-power necessary to make inventions pay. British merchants scoured the globe, seeking new outlets for exports and buying up exotic wares to grace comfortable British homes and hearths. And, not least, her doughty mariners—in the Royal Navy and the merchant marine alike—made the world safe for British trade. History books have often told us that it was the Victorian age which saw the triumph of the middle classes; but if that is so, their glory was built upon the backs of their grandfathers.

In this eye-opening biography, we see unfolding the life of one of these many unsung heroes of eighteenth-century England, Joseph Huddart. Born into a family neither rich nor poor, in a Cumbria which was beginning to play a major part in the booming North Atlantic economy, Huddart lived a full and busy life; his skills and resourcefulness gained him a deserved personal prosperity (though one tinged with frequent family tragedies), but they also helped to contribute to the transformation of his country into a great imperial nation and the world-leader in advanced technology.

Not least, as Mr Huddart's detailed researches amply document, Joseph Huddart was a versatile man, eager to apply his mind and energies to whatever challenges and opportunities afforded themselves. Like so many Cumbrians, he went to sea, and developed a maritime career which culminated in years of faithful service with the East India Company. Retirement from the service, however, by no means meant idleness. Huddart became a major surveyor of Britain's coasts. As a Fellow of the Royal Society, he investigated colour-blindness and mirages. He was active in improving lighthouses and harbour facilities. He threw himself into fen drainage. He was one of the leading lights in promoting and designing London's docks. And, not least, it was he who must largely take the credit for the mechanization of rope manufacture. No mere sea-captain, Huddart was a visionary engineer and expert technocrat at precisely the moment when such skills were required for Britain's industrialisation. Huddart and his ilk helped build the infra-structure without which none of those vital activities of the 'middling sorts' mentioned above would have been possible.

Huddart was no James Boswell or William Hickey. He had no great vices, no exotic adventures. He was, rather, a sober, gentle, modest fellow, attached to his family, esteemed by his friends, and universally respected for his honesty, devotion to duty and public service. As his prose makes so clear, he was candid and direct, entirely without affectation. Readers of William Huddart's affectionate and eye-opening life may wish that some of those Georgian virtues were more in evidence today.

Roy Porter

The Wellcome Institute for the History of Medicine, London
August 1989

INTRODUCTION

In writing this book I have attempted to thread into the rich tapestry of Georgian England the shreds of information which survive about an individual sufficiently outstanding to earn a place in the *Dictionary of National Biography*, yet not known well enough for his name to be enshrined in the history books.

Joseph Huddart made no single contribution to eighteenth-century England by which he might be remembered, but seafaring, that life-blood of Britain, benefited considerably by his endeavours to improve navigation, by his charts, by his twenty-five years of active service at Trinity House and by his invention of the manufacture of cordage. Nevertheless, a memory of his dedication to unpathed waters lingers on.

The sources from which my information is drawn are:

A memoir of the late Captain Joseph Huddart FRS by his son Sir Joseph Huddart (1821).

A Brief Memoir of the late Captain Joseph Huddart FRS and an account of his invention in the Manufacture of Cordage as contained in a letter to James Walker by William Cotton (1855).

The Autobiography of Sir John Rennie (1875).

Lives of the Engineers, Samuel Smiles (1874).

The First Edition of the *Encyclopaedia Britannica* (1771).

A Treatise on Shipbuilding, by Mungo Murray (1754).

A Memoir on the origin and incorporation of the Trinity House of Deptford Strond by Joseph Cotton (1818).

The Wealth of Nations, Adam Smith (1776).

A Tour through the whole Island of Great Britain, Daniel Defoe (1727).

The Logs and Wage Payment Books of the *Royal Admiral*.

The Letters Patent of 24 May 1793 and 19 September 1799 and such family papers as are relevant to Captain Joseph Huddart.

Letters and papers in possession of the Senhouse family, now in the archives at Carlisle.

The reference to an Indiaman, the *Grosvenor*, is taken from an account published in 1791.

The Report and Survey of Boston Harbour is reproduced with the courtesy of the Boston Corporation.

The Report and Survey of Hull Docks is reproduced with the courtesy of the Corporation of Kingston-upon-Hull.

The copies from the Senhouse papers are reproduced with the courtesy of Mr J. Scott-Plummer.

Copies of correspondence between Huddart & Co. and the Navy Board have been obtained from the Record Office.

Plans of London in 1813 have been supplied by the Guildhall Library.

I wish to acknowledge my indebtedness to Mr T. R. B. Williams-Ellis for the loan of the original log of the *Royal Admiral*'s fourth voyage; information on other voyages has been gained from the India Office Library and Records; to Mrs L. A. Dennison, the Information Officer of Trinity House, for her assistance and details of lighthouses; and to the City Archivist of Swansea for information on Swansea Harbour. And, finally, I am indebted to Dr J. C. F. Barnes for information on Allonby in the eighteenth century and for her exhaustive research into contemporary issues of the *Cumberland Pacquet* and other records which have brought to light interesting details of the early life of Joseph Huddart; I am also grateful to her for the interest she has shown in reading through my manuscript and the encouragement she has given me in writing this book.

CHAPTER I

His Early Years

'THIS PRECIOUS stone set in the silver sea' was never more true of England than in the eighteenth century. While European countries were spilling their blood and pouring out their treasure in defending their frontiers or extending them the British shores remained inviolate so long as mastery of the sea was maintained. This situation left the British population free to develop their trade, increase their wealth at home and extend their colonies abroad, particularly where other colonial powers were involved in wars on their own soil.

At the beginning of the eighteenth century Marlborough had established the English as a power to be reckoned with: his four famous victories had put England on the map and by the end of the century Britain emerged the most powerful country in Europe or, in fact, the western world.

Joseph Huddart's part in the mastery of the sea was not in confronting foes but in charting the trackless deep where hidden rocks and shoals took a toll of British shipping far in excess of any enemy fleet; in surveying for Trinity House to guide our shipping with sea marks; and in his invention of patent cordage which greatly increased the strength of rope and made it easier to handle.

Even when Britain had the biggest sailing fleet ever afloat a revolution in laying up rope was not an epoch-making event to enshrine the name of Joseph Huddart in the history books, but nevertheless he deserves to be remembered as one whose outstanding efforts contributed to the advancement of technology and the ascendancy of the British nation in the nineteenth century.

A tribute was, however, paid to him by W. Walker & Son who, in June 1862, published an engraving designed by Gilbert grouping the well-known scientists and inventors of the eighteenth century, the names of many of whom are familiar. Joseph Huddart is shown in the centre as portrayed by John Hoppner. In fact, all the scientists who make up the engraving are taken from contemporary portraits and many of them were members of the Royal Society. A number of these engravings exist today.

Joseph Huddart was born in the Cumberland village of Allonby on 11 January 1741 (or 31 December 1740 OS). His father was William Huddart, a farmer at Allonby living on the coast overlooking the Solway Firth, born in 1704 the son of John Huddart and Mary Watson, who married on 8 February 1699. His farm lands extended along the north side of the road leading to West Newton, in which parish the farm was situated. The freehold of the farm belonged to his elder brother Joseph, born in 1702, a

3

successful London tradesman living in Eaton Street,[1] near Pimlico, who had two daughters both of whom married rich men associated with the East India Company. Apart from his brother Joseph, William had another brother, John, born in 1710, who had two daughters, Patience and Anne, and a sister, Hannah, born in 1715, with four children, two boys and two girls, but these we leave in obscurity. His wife Rachel survived him by thirty years and continued to live at Allonby until her death on 25 May 1792 by which time she was 87 years old. This accounts for Joseph Huddart's visits to Allonby with which he never lost contact, although after his retirement from the sea he set up home in London.

A century later the descendants of the family still owned a small piece of land at the point where Allonby Beck turns through a right angle and starts to run parallel with the shore.

According to a contemporary writer Allonby was a small, neat, pleasant market town and a bathing place of some popularity. It was also a fishing town, but actually it was very much a village with about three hundred and twenty inhabitants. It was said that shoals of herrings frequented the area for ten years and then stayed away for ten years. This is borne out to some extent for the period from 1755 to 1763 and the shoals did return about ten years later. There were those who could remember three successive decades of this occurrence.

At one time the majority of Allonby's population were Quakers but by the time that Joseph was born, the Quaker population was probably only a quarter of the village; nevertheless, they still had a meeting house whereas there was no church.

In 1743 the Rev. Dr Tomlinson, Rector of Wickham and a Prebendary of St Paul's cathedral in London, offered to assist the inhabitants of Allonby in building a chapel. Dr Tomlinson belonged to the Tomlinsons of Blencogo, a neighbouring village, and his brother as Lord of the Manor was prepared to dedicate land for the purpose.

There was opposition from the Quakers, but the Prebendary went ahead with acquiring the site which was at the western end of the village and built a chapel at his own expense assisted by gifts from others. The chapel was built in the style prevailing in the mid-eighteenth century, being 54 feet in length and 21 feet in breadth, and containing thirty-one pews with a faculty pew for the Lord of the Manor, who had the right of presentation, and pews for the curate and clerk.

The Chapel of Ease was consecrated by Bishop Fleming in 1745 and at Dr Tomlinson's request was dedicated to Christ. Dr Tomlinson and his heirs were declared its patrons. An inscription was placed over the door which read: 'This chapel was built by the Rev. Dr. Tomlinson Rector of Wickham and Prebendary of St. Paul's London 1744'.

A school house adjoined the chapel, built largely by contributions and the curate was under an obligation to teach there. The foundation of this school at a time when Joseph was arriving at school age was a matter of profound importance in the start of his career. Although he had exceptional qualities these had to be developed. Joseph was an only child and it is said that he inherited from his mother Rachel a vigorous constitution and a strong and determined spirit and moreover imbibed from her frugal habits and those correct moral principles which he maintained throughout his life and which

---

[1] Eaton Street has since been rebuilt and is known as 'Grosvenor Gardens'.

rendered him an upright man and essentially a gentleman. Whatever their origin these were certainly qualities he possessed. But he could not be regarded as acquisitive or ambitious for his advancement. When offered the position of a Fourth Officer in the service of the East India Company, his first inclination was to decline it, looking at the initial loss of income and prestige, being master of his own brig, rather than any possible gain that might be achieved from shaking the Pagoda Tree.

When his accumulated wealth enabled him to purchase a country estate he never established himself there or even went and visited it, leaving the management to his son while he continued his experiments and astronomical observations in London. It was late in life before he acquired a carriage and even then he preferred to walk. Good character and intelligence always earned his respect even in those in the humblest station in life, and he would make such people feel at home. In an age much addicted to the excesses of alcohol he was abstemious and, in fact, was never known to have been drunk.

Those few who have written about Joseph Huddart, like Samuel Smiles, have portrayed his life as one of rags to riches: this, of course, suited Samuel Smiles' theme of self-help. But actually, with Joseph Huddart the lot had fallen unto him in a fair ground. Due to the incumbent of Allonby and his son he gained a good education to which he was able to add as a boy his own study of the principles of navigation. Due to his father's investment in fishery he was able to start a career at sea very much on his own terms. If the coastal trade was the nursery of navigation, off-shore fishery was its cradle.

At the age of twenty-two he was master of a brig: at twenty-eight with the money he inherited from his father and the help of his uncle and friends, he had built his own brig of which he was shipowner and master, trading with North America. Later it was his uncle in London, whose elder daughter had married Sir Richard Hotham, who brought him in contact with the East India Company. Eventually he was given the command of the *Royal Admiral*, an Indiaman.

If we turn back the pages of history for two centuries or even for quarter of a millenium what sort of world do we find? In the realms of art and craftsmanship by the end of the eighteenth century the zenith had been reached though music and literature had still some way to go. The rarer the artifacts of the eighteenth century become today the more they are prized, particularly those of the leaders in the field such as Josiah Wedgwood, Matthew Boulton and Chippendale. The architecture of the eighteenth century likewise is unmatched today and many houses built at that time are still lived in provided that they are on a modest scale. Indeed, with the addition of plumbing and electricity a soundly built house of that period is as good as anything built today.

If on the other hand we look at technology, at the beginning of the eighteenth century it was non-existent and by the end of the century it was still in its infancy. Mechanisation had begun but the technological achievements of today would then have been in the realms of Gulliver's travels.

Against what sort of economic background did Joseph start his life? Daniel Defoe, writing in 1709, divided the population into seven income groups, starting with the Great who lived profusely and finishing with the Miserable that really pinched and suffered want: the situation had probably not changed a generation later. Farmers, he thought, fared indifferently as against skilled artisans and journeymen who felt no want.

Joseph's father, having his own farm and no doubt grazing as well off common land, which was the practice before the Enclosure Movement, can hardly have suffered any want. The difficulty with farming was that those who farmed land surrounding a market town or on waterways got a good price for their produce whereas those in remote places had little chance of selling what they produced. Consequently cattle rearing rather than crops paid best in Cumberland: beef on the hoof could be driven to market.

This was an age of cottage industries and Joseph's father supplemented his income with shoemaking. Probably he had been apprenticed to this trade before he took over the farm. No doubt keeping cattle he was his own fell-monger, but even so he would require the services of a tanner. Tanning in the eighteenth century was a lengthy process involving liming, baiting, oozing and finally currying the fell. Shoes cost about five shillings a pair and in England only the very poorest went unshod but this was not the case in most countries. Shoemaking was probably more remunerative than farming and so far as Joseph assisted in the trade it taught him the use of his hands and after retirement from the sea he was back at his bench making his own instruments.

Although a good deal is known about Daniel Defoe's 'Great who lived profusely', as one descends the scale of income groups less and less is known about those who swelled the ranks of the lower echelons, but one can pick up records of lower class economics. In 1767 a London clerk's daily menu cost about one shilling and two pence (or six new pence in modern currency) out of earnings of £50 a year. That would give him bread and cheese and small beer for breakfast; a chuck of beef or scrag of mutton, sheep's trotters or pig's ear soused with cabbage, potatoes or parsnips, bread and small beer with half a pint of porter for dinner and a supper of bread and cheese etc. and half a pint of porter:[1] in modern terms, a 'ploughman's'.

To be 'clothed in the plainest and coarseth manner' in 1767, a suit of second cloth would be £4 10s and a complete wardrobe for a fifty-pounds-a-year clerk would come to £13 15s.[2] It was a labour-intensive age for clothing; Arkwright had not yet invented his Spinning Jenny, the first step in mechanisation, which eventually enabled suits in the 1930s to be sold for fifty shillings. Henry Fielding indicates the value of clothes in the episode when two ruffians set upon poor Joseph Andrews and, not content with his money, knocked him senseless and stripped him naked – much to the embarrassment of the lady passengers in a passing stagecoach.

Looking at education at this time, it was obviously much a matter of chance. George III is said to have been the first monarch to have a proper education although Henry VIII and Queen Elizabeth I were both well read. Grammar Schools introduced in the reign of Edward VI were undoubtedly the backbone of education in England and though intended for all classes they gradually became the prerogative of the Well-to-do; but they existed only in towns. Country lads had little chance of schooling unless their parents were able to afford a private tutor or could afford a public school: not that these were any better than Tom Brown's School Days, and the

[1] *London Life in the Eighteenth Century*, Dorothy George.
[2] *Ibid.*

only subject that mattered was classics.

Even writing at the beginning of the nineteenth century Sir John Rennie, the son of the famous engineer, says:

> I therefore made little progress in anything but classics in which I had become tolerably proficient and had Homer, Thucydides, Euripedes, Sophocles, Virgil, Horace etc. at my fingers ends whilst I could scarcely demonstrate the Pons Asinorum of Euclid in fact in those days a knowledge of Greek and Latin was considered as including everything else and anything like science or physics was considered of secondary consequence.
>
> *The Autobiography of Sir John Rennie*

Indeed there was no lack of school text books at that time to pave the way to Parnassus.

Joseph Huddart was fortunate as, although living in a remote village, shortly after his birth a school was built there and the Reverend Thomas Wilson, appointed as the first incumbent of the Chapel, took charge of it and his son assisted. Wilson and his son had both been educated at Glasgow which was then a college rather than a university and astronomy was one of the subjects in which they had both gained considerable knowledge. Surprisingly, however, they had little knowledge of mathematics though Glasgow had a Chair in Mathematics and Dr Robert Simson, a celebrated Professor of Mathematics, had been elected to the Chair in 1711 and held it till 1768.

Much of our knowledge of Joseph's boyhood has been handed down by his schoolfriend Joseph Senhouse, who was two years his junior and the son of Humphrey Senhouse, an influential man in Maryport and High Sheriff of Cumberland in 1742. Joseph Senhouse was a joint owner with his brother of plantations in Barbados and Dominica. Having retired, in 1782 he was elected Mayor of Carlisle and in the following year he was knighted. He was still alive when the Memoirs of Captain Joseph Huddart were written and was able to give first-hand information on those early days at Allonby.

Joe, as his family called him, was a boarder at Mr Wilson's school in 1752 for which his father paid annually for schooling and boarding £6 18s and 2s 6d cockpenny. Cockpennies, a peculiarity of schools in the North, were paid at Shrovetide to the schoolmaster rather like the Easter offering made to the parish priest, originally intended to defray the cost of cock-fighting. It was not long, however, before Joe joined his brother William at Cockermouth School run by the Reverend Joseph Ritson.

Although Joseph Huddart was an intelligent school boy his interests did not end there. He took the opportunity to learn singing from an itinerant music master who visited the village in his boyhood, and not content with that, he made himself familiar with the theory of music and when the music master returned after some interval he found that Joseph had taken it upon himself to teach music to some of his young friends. He could play the violin, harpsichord and flute, and his love of music remained with him throughout his life. At the age of seventy he was delighted to listen to a lady performing on the organ in Limehouse Church.

Like boys today, model-making was one of his hobbies, but this was not the world of model kits: the materials had to be found, cut to scale and shaped. When a flour mill was being constructed in the village Joseph observed the workmen as they proceeded, making his own scale model as the work progressed and finishing his model when the mill was finished.

When he was in a rowing boat he noticed the effort put in by the oarsmen: this turned his mind to the idea of a boat that could be propelled without manual labour and he proceeded to make a model impelling the boat with a coiled spring.

The construction of ships and the peculiarity of their hulls was something that absorbed Joseph Huddart throughout his life, and so also did the making of astronomical observations to which he was first introduced by John Wilson. Joseph certainly proved himself to be the Wilson's most promising pupil and being an only child he had little to distract him from any studies he wanted to pursue beyond the help he was expected to give his father in herding his cows on the hills which commanded a view of the Solway Firth. In the days before the Enclosure Movement much of the countryside was common land which farmers took advantage of for grazing, though this necessitated a herdsman.

Joseph realised that the precious hours of daylight were not to be wasted by idly gazing at his surroundings as most boys would have done. He made himself a desk in which to carry his books and writing materials. One imagines that this was similar to those bible boxes that were popular at the time, with a hinged lid on which he could write and a space inside for his books etc. With the aid of this he could carry on his studies in the open air. In later life he carried a quill in a shagreen case which also had a receptacle for ink so that he had all the facilities of a fountain pen.

One has to realise the importance of daylight and the difficulty in the eighteenth century of working after dark. The only form of illumination was candles. The use of lamps had not been introduced. In fact, the only lamps known at that time were those of ancient Rome consisting of a wick floating in oil, and although attempts had been made to produce a serviceable lamp, it was not until 1784 that a Frenchman named Argand conceived the idea of the type of oil lamp that became the *sine qua non* of every Victorian household. By having a hollow cylindrical wick which induced a draught up the middle of the flame, with the aid of a tall glass chimney he was able to produce a bright, smokeless flame.

Only the wealthy could afford to make extensive use of candles and even they often chose to be careful, as we can tell from the candelabra of the period which could be dismantled so as to reduce the number of candles they held. In London cheap candles were a halfpenny a pound but on farms they were probably made from a mixture of animal fats from sheep and cattle which were melted down and poured into water to dissolve out the impurities and then the liquid fat was poured through a horse-hair sieve to remove any solids. Wicks were then dipped repeatedly into the molten fat until a sufficient coating of fat was achieved to make a candle. But these fell a long way short of the candles we know today. The wicks were not corded and therefore had to be snuffed periodically and tallow was a much softer wax than its modern equivalents.

Once the Wilsons had introduced Joseph to the study of astronomy he pursued it throughout his life. Not only did it play an important part in his life at sea, but it became his hobby on retirement. It was the basis by which he determined the longitude of many places on his charts: it was by astronomy that he calculated the true north and the magnetic variation of his compass as it changed during his voyages: it was by lunar distance tables that he checked the accuracy of his chronometer at sea. It would not be out of place therefore to take a close look at the science of astronomy as it was understood in the eighteenth century.

Astronomy was no longer the hobby of stargazers, it had become a science of great importance in the accurate charting of the globe, which depended upon fixing the position of places on the terrestrial sphere by their relation to bodies on the celestial sphere. But man's ability to study the heavens depended upon the development of the telescope.

The telescope was introduced at the beginning of the seventeenth century, but optical glass was of poor quality and lack of technology resulted in distortion. It was not until John Dollond invented the chromatic telescope in 1754 that an efficient refracting telescope became available, capable of a magnification of two hundred times. In the meantime, Isaac Newton had solved the difficulty of getting a clear image with a reflecting parabolic mirror which avoided chromatic aberration.

With these limitations the study of the behaviour of stars could not be carried much further than Ptolemy had achieved, but the number of stars visible was vastly increased.

On the other hand, the knowledge of the Solar System and its behaviour was well advanced. The existence of the planets had been established and their size and their distance from the sun, though admittedly Uranus was not discovered until 1781, whereas it took succeeding centuries to discover Neptune and Pluto.

The size of the Sun, of which astronomers wrote in the masculine gender as if it were a deity, was calculated at 763,000 miles in diameter, whereas modern astronomers put it at 865,000 and its distance from the Earth at 95,000,000 miles: modern estimates are 93,000,000 miles. The period it took each known planet to revolve round the Sun was known with absolute accuracy. The period of rotation of Mars and Jupiter was accurately known but there was no certainty over the rotation period of the other planets. Except for Saturn the inclination of the path of each planet to the ecliptic had been correctly observed: the calculations of the sizes and distances of the planets were within a marginal error of about ten per cent of present day calculations. But after the observation of the transit of Venus across the Sun on 3 June 1761 (an event which occurred twice at close intervals in a period of over a century) more accurate calculations became available. At the transit the Sun's parallax was observed to be 8.69″ instead of 10″ on which previous calculations had been based.

Kepler's laws were the foundation of the knowledge of the movement of the planets and these laws are all accepted today. All sorts of speculations had been made about the Moon by the Ancients, but by the middle of the eighteenth century a fairly precise knowledge had been achieved. Her diameter was calculated at 2,180 miles (now corrected to 2,160 miles): the Moon filled a feminine role. Although it was known to have no atmosphere the possibility of inhabitants was not ruled out. Indeed, this thought continued into the nineteenth century. A number of charts had been prepared in the seventeenth century of the Moon's surface and many of the names given to mountains and what were thought to be oceans survive today. There was an exaggerated idea of the height of the Moon's mountains, which were erroneously thought to far exceed the height of any mountains on the Earth.

The idea of anyone travelling to the Moon and safely returning would have been as fantastic as the legendary Icarus flying too near the Sun with a disastrous landing.

Newton had explained how the movement of the Moon caused the tides and that spring tides were caused by syzygies, that is, the combined attraction of the Sun and the Moon when they were in a straight line, particularly at the equinoxes. It remained for Joseph Huddart in his later life to translate these theories into the practical effect of the movements of tides along the coastlines. It was he who in 1800 fixed the high-water mark of ordinary spring tides upon the Hermitage Lock entrance to the London Docks. One of the fixed permanent stone marks was there 150 years later, built into the river wall by him in front of the Prospect of Whitby Inn, near the Pelican Stairs at Shadwell. Section 309 of the Port of London (Consolidation) Act 1920 reads:

> The high water mark of ordinary spring tides at one mile below London Bridge shall be taken as level with the mark fixed by the late Captain Huddart in the year 1800 upon the Hermitage entrance lock of the London Docks commonly called 'Trinity Standard'.

The Reverend Wilson regarded Joseph as a possible candidate for the Church: his father hoped he would join him as an apprentice in the shoemaking trade. But the shoemaker's bench had become cut with geometric figures which showed where Joseph's inclinations lay. If there is a destiny that shapes our ends, in Joseph's case it was the great shoal of herrings that came to the Solway Firth in 1756. This determined William Huddart and his 'respectable' neighbours to form a Company to exploit the windfall. Respectable was a word our forefathers used to denote those of some standing. Indeed, to Dr Samuel Johnson the word meant venerable: it had not acquired the condescending overtones it has today.

To carry out the project they built a fish-yard on the shore at Allonby, which is still standing today and is now used as a riding school.

Twenty-one years later the premises were sold off and the following advertisement appeared in the local press on the 10th of February, 1788, from which we can judge the scale of the operation, as the fish-curing yard covered about two-thirds of an acre.

HERRING HOUSE at ALLONBY

> To be sold on Thursday 5th March (1778) at Mr. Younghusband's at the Ship in Allonby to the highest bidder. All that large and convenient FISH-YARD or FISH CURING CONVENIENCE consisting of a Square enclosed with a high wall 67 yds long and 45 yds broad, with a building the whole length and ten yards broad, and on another range, hewn stone cisterns that will hold in first pickle 500 barrels of herring: with salt houses and other offices suiting the premises. Also 5 Smoak [sic] Houses for drying Red Herring, on a good situation that will hang at one time 500 barrels: with two dwelling houses, all held on a lease of 999 years, 21 of which are expired, paying a rent of 18s a year. To be sold in one lot. Days of payment and other conditions to be exhibited at time of sale.
>
> The premises at any time before the sale will be shown to any person by Mr. Amos Beety or John Hodson of Allonby.

Attempts had been made by both Charles I and by Charles II to establish a fishing industry to take advantage of the plentiful supply of fish in the seas around Britain particularly in the North West, but both kings had more pressing problems to face and it was not until after the Union that the Royal British Fishery was established. In 1750 a more practical approach was made to encourage the white herring fishery by granting a charter to form a corporation by the name of the Society of the Free British Fishery. The corporation was to continue for twenty-one years and be under the direction of a Governor, President, Vice-President and Council who continued in office for three years with power to make by-laws and raise capital of £500,000 by subscription. Any number of persons in any part of Great Britain could subscribe £10,000 in the stock of the Society under the name of the Fishing Chamber and carry on their own business on their own account.

On the question of the fishery industry requiring the support of a bounty, Adam Smith points out that a bounty upon production of a commodity had a more direct operation than one on exportation and would impose only one tax upon the people, that which they must contribute in order to pay the bounty. As it would tend to lower the price of the commodity it would in some respects repay those who had contributed. He regarded the tonnage bounty given to the white herring fishery as this sort of bounty. Though the bounty did not contribute to the wealth of the nation it might be thought to contribute to its defence by augmenting the number of its sailors and the amount of its shipping. This certainly was the case with Joseph Huddart because here was a training ground for seafaring literally on his doorstep.

Adam Smith however considered the nation was grossly imposed upon by the grant of these bounties, because they were too large, and not proportionate to the fish caught; and that it encouraged the buss fishery as opposed to the boat fishery and thereby did not lower the price of fish. A buss was a two-masted fishing vessel which was decked in and therefore enabled fishing on a much more extensive scale.

The bounty to which those entering the scheme were entitled was fifty shillings a ton to be paid yearly for fourteen years with the addition of a three per cent return on the money subscribed. In 1771 the bounty was reduced to thirty shillings a ton.

The Act set out regulations as to the nets to be used, the marks to be adopted on herring barrels, the number of hands and the quantity of salt to be used.

At this point we must draw some threads together. We know that Joseph as a teenager visited his uncle in London and to travel some three hundred miles by coach or make the journey by sea was too expensive an expedition to be undertaken without some compelling reason. It is not unreasonable to suppose, therefore, that Joseph and his father went to London together to seek the assistance of the uncle who was in the business of money-lending, in putting up capital to obtain the bounty and erect a fish-yard. No doubt they took with them any gold that the respectable neighbours were prepared to put into the scheme.

An anecdote has survived of this visit, that while walking through St James's Park with his uncle a day or two after his arrival in London, a man having the appearance of a tradesman touched his hat to Joseph. His uncle was surprised and said, 'You surely cannot know that man.' 'Yes,' Joseph replied, 'he belongs to Westminster Abbey, I gave him sixpence yesterday to show me the works of the great clock.' Joseph's fascination with clocks remained with him throughout his life and he made himself a longcase clock with the novelty of showing the time of high water. He was quite adept at taking clocks and watches to pieces, cleaning and repairing them and putting them together again with all the skill of a clockmaker who had served his apprenticeship. Late in life, he made the pendulum of an astronomical clock for his observatory to enable him to make accurate observations.

It was probably during Joseph's visit to London that he obtained a copy of Mungo Murray's *Treatise on Shipbuilding and Navigation*, as this was available only in London, either in the Strand or Exchange Alley or St Martin's Lane or at Union Stairs. Indeed, how else would a youth living on the shore of the Solway Firth obtain such a book, which had only recently been published? It cost eighteen shillings and if one allows a factor of fifty to bring eighteenth-century prices to the level of today's prices we are talking about £45 – an expensive textbook. No doubt his uncle bought it for him to give him a comprehensive work on mathematics and a knowledge of seafaring.

There were a number of textbooks at that time on mathematics but probably they would not include tables of logarithms and the tables required for trigonometry. There were also a number of treatises on navigation. John Roberts, a mathematical teacher at Christ's Hospital and later at the Royal Academy at Portsmouth, published his *Elements of Navigation* in the same year as Murray – 1754. As far back as Charles II's reign, the Royal Hydrographer John Seller had written his *Practical Navigation*, also the *Sea Atlas* and the *English Pilot*. Seller was a maker of compasses and also published charts. Another eighteenth-century authority was Patoun.

No doubt Murray hoped to make his the official textbook and the forerunner of the *Admiralty Manual of Navigation*, as his book is dedicated 'To the Right Honourable the Lords Commissioners for Executing the office of the Lord High Admiral of Great Britain Ireland and His Majesty's Plantations abroad with the utmost submission by their Lordships Most dutiful most humble and most obedient servant Mungo Murray'.

Mungo Murray was a shipwright at Deptford and was certainly an authority on shipbuilding and on mathematics. 'Mathematicks was expeditiously taught at his home in Deptford from six to eight every day except Wednesdays and Saturdays.' He published a further work on the 'Rudiments of Navigation' in 1760.

Part I of his treatise is devoted entirely to instruction in mathematics and covers extracting square roots and cube roots, proportions or the Rule of Three as it was called, Geometry, Trigonometry and Logarithms. Added to this there were tables of Logarithms, Sines, Tangents and Secants.

Part II is devoted to the 'orthographick' projection of solids on a plane; the variation of the compass; how to keep a reckoning at sea and the Metonic Cycle. The Metonic Cycle is the nineteen year period it takes the phases of the Moon to return to the same day of the year.

From the information given in Part II of Mungo Murray's treatise we are told that Joseph 'commenced building a model of a seventy four gun ship exactly according the rules and directions therein laid down with all the ribs, planks, bolts, rigging &c. &c. of a real vessel: this model he completed with indefatigable labour and perseverance'. It remained in the possession of the family for a long time and was much praised by any navigator that saw it.

Actually Mungo Murray was a shipwright and not a rigger and he confined the information in his treatise to hulls: these he dealt with in detail giving every measurement. It follows that Joseph who had not, at this time, even seen a man o' war must have completed the rigging at a later stage. In fact, anyone attempting a model of a third rate man o' war, which in real life would have a gun deck of about 150 feet in length and 40 feet in breadth, would require detailed information of about 183 items which go to make up the rigging of such a ship. Knowing the ropes meant knowing where each rope was made fast.

Murray set out the measurements of the various timbers which constituted the hull of a man o' war from the first rate to the sixth rate, and the same of an Indiaman of 630 tons, the Bonetta 398 tons, a Thames barge of 340 tons, a French Privateer of 372 tons, a ship of 162 tons, a fishing smack of 114 tons and a sloop of 50 tons.

There was added to his treatise by way of an appendix, 'An English abridgement of another treatise on Naval Architecture lately published at Paris by M. Du Hamel a member of the Royal Academy of Sciences, F.R.S. of London, and Surveyor General of the French Marine'. At this time the French were regarded as leading in the field of shipbuilding and the principles laid down by Du Hamel were quoted by contemporary writers on the subject. At various points in his life we find Joseph Huddart carrying out experiments on the resistance of water to various types of hulls, and there can be little doubt that he based his knowledge of hull construction on the following principles laid down by Du Hamel.

> All the rules we have hitherto laid down, collected from the principal dimensions of ships built by the most eminent masters, should only be so far regarded as they may assist the artist in forming the body in such manner as to produce effects answerable to the service for which the vessel is designed.

> In order to qualify a builder for such an undertaking, it is necessary he should understand the nature of fluids, and of such bodies as will float in the water; when he has made himself acquainted with these, I would recommend him to M. Bouger's treatise on shipbuilding.

The principal Qualities belonging to Ships

> 1st. To be able to carry a good sail, not only because, in forming the body, the water lines are all supposed to be described when a ship is upright in the water, but likewise for doubling a cape, or getting off a lee shore, which will be impossible to be done when a ship lies over in the water, this will likewise render her lower tier, if not all her guns useless.

> 2nd. A ship should steer well, and feel the least motion of the helm.

> 3rd. A ship should carry her lower tier of guns four feet and a half, or five feet out of the water, otherwise a great ship, that cannot open her ports upon a wind, but in smooth water, may be taken by a small one, that can make use of her guns or she must bare away before the wind, to have the use of her guns; on which account it will be proper to raise the ports higher before than in midships, because the fore part of the ship is often pressed into the water by carrying sail.

> 4th. A ship should be duly poised, so as not to drive or pitch hard, but go smooth and easy through the water, rising to the sea when it runs high, and the ship under her courses, or lying to under a mainsail, otherwise she will be in danger of carrying away her masts.

> 5th. A ship should sail well before the wind, large, but chiefly close hawled, keep a good wind, not fall off to the leeward.

> Now the great difficulty consists in uniting so many different qualities in one ship, which seems indeed to be impossible; the whole art therefore consists

in forming the body in such a manner, that none of these qualities shall be entirely destroyed, and in giving the preference to that which is most required in the particular service for which the vessel is built; in order to which, it will be necessary to know, at least nearly, what form will give the vessel one of these qualities, considered abstractly from the rest.

To make a Ship carry a good Sail

A flat floor timber, and somewhat long, or the lower futtock pretty round, a straight upper futtock, the top timber to throw the breadth out aloft; at any rate to carry her main breadth as high as the lower deck. Now, if the rigging be well adapted to such a body, and the upper works lightened as much as possible, so that they all concur to lower the center of gravity, there will be no room to doubt of her carrying a good sail.

To make a Ship steer well, and quickly answer the Helm

If the fashion pieces be well formed, and the tuck carried pretty high; the midship frame carried pretty forward; a considerable difference of the draught of water abaft more than afore; a great rake forward, and none abaft; a snug quarter-deck and forecastle, all these will make a ship steer well; but to make her feel the least motion of the helm, it will be necessary to regard her masts. There is one thing not to be forgot, that ship which goes well will certainly steer well.

To make a Ship carry her Guns well out of the Water

It is plain, that a long floor timber, and not of a great rising; a very full midship frame, and low tuck with light upper works, will make a ship carry her guns high.

To make a Ship go smoothly through the Water without pitching hard

A long keel, a long floor, not to rise too high afore and abaft, the area or space contained in the fore body, duly proportioned to that of the after body, according to the respective weights they are to carry; all these are necessary to make a ship go smoothly through the water.

To make a Ship keep a good Wind

A good length by the keel, not too broad, but pretty deep in the hold, which will occasion her to have a short floor timber, and great rising.

As such a ship will meet with great resistance in the water, going over the broad-side, and little when going ahead, she will not fall much to leeward.

Now, some builders imagine that it is possible to make a ship carry her guns well, carry a good sail, and to be a prime sailer, because it would require a very full bottom to gain the first two qualities, whereas a sharp ship will best answer for the latter; but when it is considered that a full ship will carry a great deal more sail than a sharp one, a good artist may so form the body as to have all these three good qualities, and likewise steer well, for which purpose I would recommend somewhat in length more than has been formerly practised.

After what has been said upon this head, I believe it will not be thought impossible to unite all these different qualities in one ship so that all of them may be discerned in some degree of eminence; but when it happens otherwise, the fault must be owing to the builder, who has not applied himself to study the fundamental rules and principles of his art.

Excepting some ancient builders, who were happily born with a natural genius, and our moderns, who being instructed in the principles of the mathematicks, have truly laboured very hard to make a progress in the art of shipbuilding, one may, without violating the truth, affirm that the greatest part satisfy themselves with copying such ships as they esteem good sailers, and it is these servile mechanick methods, which, to the great reproach of the art, are but too common, that have produced all these pretended rules of proportion, all these methods of describing the mid-ship frame, and forming the rest of the timbers, which every builder endeavours if possible to conceal, and keep wholly in his own family.

How low and mean is this? It is as if a great architect should endeavour to conceal the proportions of the different orders of architecture; whereas they are published everywhere, and so well known that many can raise a very beautiful porch or triumphal arch; but tho' the methods of describing the midship frame, and forming the rest of the timbers, be known to most apprentices, yet we have but few good master builders; This requires more than those mechanick rules; they should at least have such a knowledge of the mathematicks, physicks, mechanicks, of the nature of solids and fluids, as to be able to discover what figure would procure some good quality, without hazarding or putting a bad one in its place.

Let us suppose one to have a collection of draughts of a vast number of ships, and whose good and bad qualities have been remarked with all possible exactness, such a valuable treasure would be of great service to a person who could calculate precisely by the draughts where the fault lay, and how it might be rectified. For instance, suppose a ship sails well, but carries her guns too low, a builder who is not acquainted with these principles would raise her deck, in consequence of which she would not sail well; whereas, one that could scarcely calculate how much the resistance of the fluid is diminished upon the prow, would take great care to add no more to any of the other parts than he could find by exact calculation might be done without augmenting the resistance in the fluids.

Clearly, Mungo Murray's Treatise, which Joseph must have read, marked, learnt and inwardly digested while his herd of cows grazed in the fields, was the first step on young ambition's ladder. In this book he had the theoretical knowledge he required to become a Master of a ship though some gaps had to be filled in. Murray gives Hadley's quadrant, by this time an important navigational instrument, scant mention, while explaining the use of the out-dated Analemma. The third part of Murray's Treatise deals with navigation and enables us to see how ships determined their position at sea.

Part III sets out the theories of Plain Sailing, Parallel Sailing, Middle Latitude Sailing and Mercator Sailing. Joseph had every opportunity not only to study Murray but also to put theory into practice while still a lad. By the middle of the eighteenth century, navigation had become an exact science, but there were no aids for the incompetent. In mid-ocean one wave looked like another: it was water, water everywhere and once the ship had lost account of her position she was at the mercy of any rocks that lay in her path.

One could not, of course, say that by this time the seven seas had been charted. James Cook was still making discoveries; but the established sea routes and their hazards were known. To illustrate the accuracy with which Huddart could navigate, at noon on 10 March 1787, he reckoned that the island of Trinidad, off the coast of South America, was at a distance of 56 leagues from the position of the ship on a bearing of South 57° West. At noon the following day when by account the ship had travelled 53 leagues the island is sighted at a distance of three leagues: the extremes bearing South 64° West to South 54° West. No land had been sighted since the previous 13 February when the ship was off the coast of Africa. Strictly speaking, leagues at that time were defined in Britain as three Statute Miles while distances at sea were calculated in minutes which were slightly more than a Statute Mile.

Of course, Huddart was an outstanding navigator and there were those who were not so successful. Captain Barrow, from whom he took over the command of the *Royal Admiral*, lost his previous ship, the *Royal Captain*, homeward bound on her maiden voyage on the rocks off Pelowar on 17 December 1773. There have been several graphic accounts of the loss of the *Grosvenor* on 4 August 1782 off the coast of Pondoland, South Africa, with an enormous treasure on board. Although Captain Coxon in command had been heard to say the night before that they were a hundred leagues from the nearest land, he cannot have known his position. The ship had left Trincomalee on the 13 June without sighting land and had seen only one sail some weeks earlier and, added to this, owing to the cloudy weather, Coxon had made no observation for some days: then on a passage for St Helena and reaching latitude 29°, she was 5° off course.

The third officer, who was officer of the watch at the time, should have heeded the words of the men aloft striking the main topgallant mast, of 'breakers ahead', and given orders to wear ship. This would have allowed soundings to have been made to check the ship's position. Even if he thought the ship could not be near land, no one in those days could be certain that there were no uncharted rocks.

As it was, by the time Coxon had been alerted and given the order to wear ship it was too late: she had struck the rocks splitting the vessel fore and aft. The ship's company managed, with one exception, to get ashore but on that inhospitable coast even on shore there was only a slim chance of survival: in fact, after 117 days only a very few of the 135 managed to reach a Dutch farmstead.

Returning to the principles of navigation, there were basically four methods by which a ship determined her course. The first was called Plain Sailing, an expression which has passed into our everyday language, meaning taking a course that presents no problems: but in the language of the eighteenth century it meant treating an area of the globe as a plane for the purpose of navigation. Plane sailing might have been a more appropriate spelling and indeed this spelling is adopted by the pedantic.

If the Earth is regarded as a plane, then the parallels of latitude and the meridians form a rectangular pattern like graph paper. The ship is then regarded as steering a Rhumbline, that is, sailing on a fixed bearing across this rectangular pattern. The word 'rhumb' was usually applied to any of the thirty-two points of the compass. The difference, calculated in nautical miles from the equator, between one parallel and another was referred to as the Difference of Latitude or, alternatively, the Northing or Southing. The difference in miles between meridians, which for this purpose were as running parallel, was called Departure. Therefore, using trigonometry the ship's course across a rectangular pattern could be resolved into Northings or Southings representing the difference in latitude and Eastings or Westings giving the ship's departure.

When several courses were stemmed in a twenty-four hour period each course would be so resolved and the result set out on a traverse table in the Log book, which for this purpose was divided into five vertical columns. In the first column would be set out the course and the distance travelled; in the next two would be set out the north and the south differences of latitude; and in the fourth and fifth columns the departure east and the departure west would be entered. It has to be realised that in twenty-four hours the wind could change many times and the course of the ship had to change accordingly.

Nautical almanacs contained printed tables resolving traverses, a page being devoted to each degree between zero and forty-five degrees. On the page for any particular bearing there would be tables of distances each resolved into difference of latitude and departure. These figures were entered in the appropriate columns of the Log book or traverse table and the totals over a twenty-four hour period arrived at, that is from noon on one day to noon on the next day. The differences between the total Northings and Southings gave the change of latitude, and the difference between the total Eastings and Westings gave the ship's departure from which the change of longitude could be calculated. This fixed the ship's position at noon each day which, when possible, was checked by observation.

The second method of determining a ship's position at sea was called Parallel Sailing and consisted of stemming a course along the same parallel of latitude, so that from the distance travelled could be calculated the change in longitude. At the equator each degree represents a difference of sixty nautical miles and therefore it is trigonometrically possible to calculate the difference between two meridians in nautical miles at any degree of latitude. In the eighteenth century the corollary was expressed as follows:

Because the circumference of circles are as their radii hence it follows that the circumference of any parallel is to the circumference at the equator as the cosine of its latitude is to radius.

i.e. the Earth's radius. What is true of circumferences is true of their proportional parts, so that to arrive at the change of longitude in minutes one has to divide the number of nautical miles in a ship's departure by the cosine of the parallel latitude along which it travelled.

Middle Latitude Sailing was a variation of Parallel Sailing. If two places lie on different latitudes the calculations are based on an intermediate parallel arrived at by adding the two latitudes and halving the result. The method was feasible for distances of 450 miles between the equator and latitude 30° or 300 miles between latitude 30° and latitude 60°, but in latitudes above that only for a run of not more than twenty-four hours.

The fourth method of determining a course at sea was called Mercator Sailing. Mercator's projection, which is a familiar page in most atlases of the world, was published in 1568 and in 1590 improvements were introduced by Edward Wright and by 1630 the chart was in general use. To be able to obtain correct bearings on a flat surface the globe had to be treated in a cylindrical pattern, so that instead of meeting at the pole, meridians ran parallel and parallels of latitude instead of decreasing in proportion to the cosine of the latitude became equal.

To keep this chart in proportion the meridians had to be extended proportionately the further north or south they went. All calculations were made in minutes and according to the eighteenth century corollary – since the length of every intermediate minute, between the equator and any parallel is equal to the secant of the latitude, the sum of all these lengths will be equal to the sum of all the secants to every minute contained between such parallel and the equator. Tables of meridional parts were printed in nautical almanacs to enable distances to be calculated from charts on Mercator's Projection converting the extended distances to the actual distances for every minute, working from the equator.

It was no easy task for a lad to master geometry and trigonometry and be able to work in three dimensions without the aid of a tutor, though Huddart had the advantage of peace and quiet with a chance to think things out without interruption. It was unlike midshipmen huddled together in the cuddy trying to take instruction from a short tempered captain with all the distractions of a working ship and a tempestuous sea. Fortunately, textbook writers were fairly generous with their explanations backed up with copious examples realising the difficulty in getting across to an innumerate world. There were, of course, more involved applications of mathematics to be mastered than those used in charting a course, such as calculating the magnetic variation of the compass, which involved fixing the Sun's true azimuth. This had to be done at frequent intervals on a long voyage. Another conundrum was calculating the longitudinal position of a ship by applying Maskelyne's Lunar Distance Tables. This was quite beyond James Cook, who had relatively no education and, in fact, he did not start to study trigonometry until he was thirty. The lunar distance calculations were done by his purser.

As a youth Joseph was not only mentally alert but also physically so, no labour or exposure was too much for him. He is said to have been tall and muscular and judging from the spacing on the holes on his flute he had unusually large hands. No doubt he was capable of more physical effort than the average person. William Cotton writes:

> Even when a youth of about sixteen, he gave a striking proof of self command and of a superior mind. For while his companions, after the fatigues and exposure of the night, were indulging themselves in the alehouse, he was generally found occupied in making nautical observations, in examining the set of the tide and currents, and taking bearings of the coast. His superiority in conduct and ability was soon acknowledged by his fellows, and they yielded to him a deference which early in life prepared him to direct others.
> *A Brief Memoir of Captain Joseph Huddart F.R.S.*
> by William Cotton, 1855.

Huddart spent seven years in the White Fishery trade, first as a seaman and then as a master; he probably commanded small vessels while still in his teens. In 1762 he took command of the sloop *Allonby* to convey fish cured by the Company to Cork and other parts of Ireland for the supply of the West Indian markets. In this year, on 16 February, Joseph's father William Huddart died, leaving him his sixteenth share in the 'Fishing Conveniency' which belonged to the company at Allonby of which William Huddart was a member and his one-fourth share in the fishing boat called the Fellowship, together with all his fishing gear, shoemaking lasts and tools. He also left him a hundred pounds in cash and his silver watch. Rachel his wife did not do so well; her son had to enter into a bond to pay her four pounds a year half at Candlemas and half at Lammas, possibly this represented the rent she had to pay to Uncle Joseph for the house.

During his voyages to Ireland be became aware of the inadequacy of the charts of St George's Channel and this eventually led him to make a complete survey of the sea and publish his own chart. Some twenty years later he was depicted as holding this chart in a portrait painted in Macao. Any leisure moments he had were devoted to studying ship-building and improving his knowledge of astronomy. Whenever an opportunity arose to make a survey of the coasts and roadsteads in his trips to Ireland he would use them to build up his knowledge of St George's Channel. In this same year he married Elizabeth, the younger daughter of a yeoman called Johnston living at Coupar in Abbey Holme. There were five sons of the marriage, two of whom died in infancy; of the others, William was born in 1763, Joseph in 1768 and Johnston in 1771 – they will be mentioned again later.

By 1763 the shoals of herrings had deserted the Solway Firth and in 1764 Huddart was offered by a relative the command of a brig named *Glory*, which he held for two years and then decided to fulfil his ambition to build his own brig at Maryport according to a model of his own. Maryport was then a town of growing importance: at the beginning of the century it consisted of little more than fishermen's huts, but chiefly due to Humphrey Senhouse, who was the local coal owner, a considerable shipping trade was built up with Ireland. The ships were laden in the River Ellen which runs through the town whence they carried their cargo to Ireland. There was also an established shipbuilding yard carried on by John Wood and his son William and it was here in 1767 that Huddart decided to realise his ambition to build a ship of his own, which was to be a collier of about 190 tons burden rigged as a brig.

To meet the cost of this Huddart had to think in terms of £10 for each ton burden, tonnage in those days being based on carrying capacity and not on displacement. The only cash Huddart had to put down was £300, but the ownership of ships was traditionally divided into sixty-four shares, so that he had to find a number of partners or co-owners to take up the shares. In fact, he found fourteen friends who were prepared to take up two shares each for a sum of £49: the names of these were William Birkbeck, Anthony Stephenson, Robert Bird, John Horn, Samuel Carleton, Joseph Stainten, John Beeby, Thomas Bleamire, Thomas Temple, Thomas Bouch, William Litt, William Port, Joseph Harrison and John Hodgson, who took up four shares.

Who were these angels, to use the parlance of the theatrical world? Painters often fill the background of their canvas from their own imagination rather than from life, and to do the same, these names may well be identified with the holders of the fifteen shares in the fish-curing enterprise, William Huddart having had the sixteenth share. They would have seen Joseph Huddart proving himself as a promising youth ten years earlier and now grown into a master mariner of outstanding ability and reliable temperament such as would have inspired their confidence.

The value of one share has only to be multiplied to establish the cost of the ship as £1,568, which is well below what might be expected; but as Huddart worked on the ship himself, providing the design, moulding the timbers and obtaining discounts where possible, economies were made. Everything in the eighteenth century bore the imprints of the hands that fashioned it – nothing to the smallest fitting was punched out by machinery. To meet the current expenditure the co-owners put up their cash by instalments; even so, there was still a balance to be found by raising a loan which no doubt was provided by Huddart's uncle. If so, the fact that the ship had the same name as his aunt was no coincidence. The brig was launched in 1768 and although it had already traded, it was surveyed in 1770 in London for a debenture which suggests finance by the uncle.

Some grains of information on the colliery trade can be gleaned from the records made at the time such as the entry into Cork Harbour on the 19 October 1769 with a cargo of 150 tons of coal priced at £52 13s 4d. When it came to the *Patience* making her first passage to North America, Huddart's shareholding friends became apprehensive of his ability to cross the Atlantic and persuaded him to engage a sailing master; but the sailing master proved to be something of a broken reed although he had frequently made that voyage. Huddart knew the course he was taking and had every confidence in himself, his reckoning and the observations he had made, and was determined to hold his course for the port to which the ship was bound. The sailing master mistook the appearance of the first landfall they sighted and insisted that they were off course. To settle the matter Huddart allowed the sailing master to go ahead in a boat to reconnoitre, while he maintained the course he had set which took him straight into the river of their destination. His guide had to acknowledge his mistake.

Annual voyages were made to North America until 1773 and the coal trade with Ireland was carried on for the rest of the year. Evidently Huddart took a cargo of coal to Massachusetts in May 1773 and this was his last voyage across the Atlantic. The manifest for the cargo of timber brought back to Whitehaven reads as follows:

> The following Manifest is proper to give to the Officers to prepare your certificates Manifest of a cargo to be shipped on board the Patience of Maryport   Joseph Huddart Commdr.

> Burthen One hundred & Twenty Four Tuns Mounted with two Guns Navigated with Ten Men British built & bound for Whaven &c as in foregoing folio.

> Port of Falmouth New England

> These are to certify that proof has been made to us by affidavit agreeable to the Act of the 5th Geo. cap 45 the following quantity Deal Planks boards & Timber now shipped on board the Patience whereof Jos. Huddart is Mastr. bound for Whitehaven are truly and bona fide of the growth and produce of His Majesty's Plantation in North America

> Two hundred pieces of pine plank from one & a quarter to three inches thick from ten to eighteen inches wide and from ten to fifteen feet long Quantity Two and a half thousand feet
> Sixty pieces of pine timber from ten to twenty inches square and from fifteen to seventy feet long containing One hundred and fifty tons Forty pieces of Oak Timbr from ten to twenty inches square and from Twenty to fifty feet long containing Forty three Tons
> Twelve pieces of Maple Timber from Ten to Fifteen inches square and from ten to thirty feet long containing Twelve Tons

> Given &c. 29 May in the thirteenth year of &c. &c. 1773

One overriding problem with navigation which was not solved until the second half of the eighteenth century was that of fixing the longitude of a ship at sea. Calculating a ship's longitudinal position from its departure was hardly viable except for short periods. A Board of Longitude had been established in Queen Anne's reign to find a solution to the problem. Owing to the rotation of the Earth the position of any celestial object depended on the time of day. James Ferguson, who published his 'Astronomy explained on Sir Isaac Newton's Principles' in 1756 explained the matter as follows:

> To every place 15 degrees eastward from any given meridian it is noon one hour sooner than on that meridian, because the meridian comes to the sun

an hour sooner: and to all places 15 degrees westward it is an hour later because their meridian comes an hour later to the sun and so on: every 15 degrees of motion causing an hour difference in time. Therefore they who have noon an hour later than we, have their meridian that is their longitude 15 degrees westward from us: and they who have noon an hour sooner than we, have their meridian 15 degrees eastward from us: and so for every hour difference of time 15 degrees difference of longitude. Consequently if the beginning or ending of a lunar eclipse be observed suppose at London to be exactly midnight and in some other place at 11 at night that place is 15 degrees westward from the meridian at London; if the same eclipse be observed at 1 in the morning at another place that place is 15 degrees eastward from the said meridian.

But it was not easy to determine the exact moment either of the beginning or ending of a lunar eclipse, because the Earth's shadow through which the Moon passes is faint and ill defined about the edges, therefore recourse had to be made to the eclipses of Jupiter's satellites which disappear so instantaneously as they enter Jupiter's shadow, and emerge so suddenly out of it that the phenomenon may be fixed to half a second of time. The first or nearest satellite to Jupiter is the most advantageous for the purpose, because its motion is quicker than the motion of any of the rest and therefore its immersions and emersions are more frequent. To quote from a writer at the time:

English Astronomers have calculated tables for shewing the times of eclipses of Jupiter's satellites to great precision for the meridian of Greenwich. Now let an observer who has these tables with a good telescope and a well regulated clock at any place of the earth observe the beginning or ending of an eclipse of one of Jupiter's satellites and note the precise moment of time that he saw the satellite either immerge or emerge out of the shadow and compare that time with the time shown by the tables for Greenwich: then 15 degrees difference being allowed for every hour's difference of time will give the longitude of that place from Greenwich as above; and if there be any odd minute of time for every minute a quarter of a degree east or west must be allowed as the time of observation is later or earlier.

Huddart used the eclipse of Jupiter's satellites to determine the longitude of Bombay with greater precision than had been done before. Maps at that time showed it too far to the west.

The second method of determining longitude was by the Lunar Distance method. Work on providing the data to make this possible started with the foundation of the Royal Observatory at Greenwich in 1675: John Flamsteed was appointed the first Astronomer Royal. He died in 1720 having spent the rest of his life in calculating data on the movement of stars to make lunar distance calculations possible. Halley furthered the work by recording the movements of the Moon; but in fact the first lunar distance tables were produced in 1755 by Professor Mayer of Gottingden and this was followed by Neville Maskelyne who brought out his edition in 1770. Maskelyne also held the appointment of Astronomer Royal and was a dominant figure on the Board of Longitude. He can hardly have welcomed the chronometer which gave an effective answer to the problem astronomers had spent a century resolving.

W. A. Falconer, in the *Dictionary of the Maritime*, gives the following explanation. Lunar Distance is the apparent distance of the Moon from the Sun or a fixed star at the time of making the observation for finding longitude, the reduction of which from the effect of parallax and refraction to the true distance requires some tedious calculations.

The Nautical Almanac may be considered a perpetual observer, that communicates universally and instantaneously certain celestial appearances as they take place at Greenwich Observatory. Here the distances are between the moon and the sun and certain remarkable stars in or near the zodiac, for every three hours; and any intermediate distance or time may be thence found by rule of proportion with sufficient accuracy.

If therefore under any meridian a lunar distance be observed the difference between the time of observation and the time in the Almanac when the same distance was to take place at Greenwich will show the longitude.

Of course, by the time Maskelyne had published his lunar distance tables chronometers were available, but the tables were still useful for correcting chronometers at sea as there was no other method. Huddart's log of the *Royal Admiral* for 27 March 1787 when taking his departure from Tristan da Cunha records 'Chronometer corrected by means of 15 lunar obs.' Apart from this, chronometers were very expensive in comparison to the cost of a ship. As late as 1804 the Regulations of the East India Company read:

That such officers as have not been already instructed in the method of finding longitude of a ship at sea by lunar observations do immediately perfect themselves under Mr. Lawrence Gwynne at Christ's Hospital previous to their attending the Committee to be examined for their respective stations; and that they do produce to the Committee a certificate from that gentleman of their being qualified in the method.

The third method of determining longitude and the only one in use today was by use of a deck watch. The eighteenth-century clockmakers could make accurate pendulum clocks but they needed adjusting for changes of temperatures. A pendulum 39.1392 inches in length will take a second to swing in the latitude of London but its length is constant only so far as the temperature is constant. Apart from this the movement of a ship precluded the use of a pendulum.

The need to fix the position of a ship at sea became so imperative that a statute was passed in 1714 establishing the Board of Longitude and offering prizes of £20,000, £15,000 and £10,000 for anyone who could come up with an effective method of determining longitude at sea within 30 miles, 40 miles or 60 miles respectively. A certain Major Holmes made a voyage along the coast of Guinea using two pendulum watches and then a M. Huygens improved upon this but variations in temperature had to be calculated.

Their efforts were followed by John Harrison, who was the son of a Yorkshire carpenter. His first chronometer was completed in May 1736 and he replaced the pendulums with two spring loaded dumb-bells. It was a somewhat clumsy device weighing 72 lbs. This was put on board a man o' war and by its exact measurement of time in its return journey from Lisbon corrected an error of almost a degree and a half in the reckonings of the ship.

In 1739 Harrison completed a second machine which came up to the requirements of the Act of Parliament for finding the longitude at sea. He overcame the variations in temperature by using two metals with different coefficients of expansion. In 1741 Harrison embarked upon a third machine which was not completed until 1758. This machine weighed 102 lbs and was intended to be stowed near the waterline. He introduced a balance wheel instead of the dumb-bells making the rim of two metals with different coefficients of expansion so that as the spokes of the wheel expanded the rim bent inwards owing to the different expansion of the two metals used to compensate the expansion. As the clock was intended to be stowed at the waterline he made a pocket watch on the same principle to be used on deck and checked with the master clock.

He applied to the Board of Longitude for a trial in the West Indies and he received an order for his son to proceed from Portsmouth to Jamaica in November 1761 taking the third instrument in a man o' war.

The result of the experiment was that the difference of longitude found by the time piece and that calculated at Jamaica in 1743 by the transit of Mercury was five seconds – a little more than a geographical mile. The return journey was a tempestuous one and the accuracy suffered but not so as to fail to come within the requirements of the statute. In the whole journey the chronometer lost one minute and fifty-four seconds which in the latitude of Portsmouth is about eighteen miles. The deck watch proved a more accurate instrument than the master clock.

Huddart used a chronometer made by John Arnold who was a celebrated maker of chronometers. He was born in 1744 and served his apprenticeship at Bodmin, later setting up in London. When only twenty years old Arnold made the smallest repeating watch ever attempted which was set in a ring. He gave it to George III who was so delighted with it that he gave him 500 guineas. Arnold also made improvements in chronometers for which the Board of Longitude posthumously rewarded him with £5,000, which was paid to his son J. R. Arnold who followed him in the business.

One may say that the obsession with latitude and longitude did not end with the sea. Every mansion had its library lined with hide-bound volumes and no library was complete without matching terrestrial and celestial globes mounted in Chippendale pedestals which answered questions such as the places in the southern hemisphere which had the same latitude as those in the northern hemisphere, the distances between places, the time at any place when it is noon at Greenwich and so on. With the celestial globe, astronomical questions were answered, such as the time when a star will rise or be upon the meridian. Geography was related to the behaviour of the Earth as a planet rather than the nature of individual countries. In fact, outside Europe and the Mediterranean not a lot was known of what went on beyond the coast lines of the continents.

In places where there was a British presence the longitude had been fairly accurately established by transits and eclipses, comparing the time of occurrence with Greenwich, but in other places the recorded longitude was approximate or unknown. Until the voyages of Captain Cook, Australia appeared on the globe as a distorted outline under the name of New Holland. Terres Australes was the name applied to the polar regions of Antarctica.

CHAPTER II

The Honourable Company

IN 1771 Joseph Huddart visited his paternal uncle, who was also named Joseph and who was a wealthy tradesman living in Eaton Street in Westminster: it was he who had assisted his nephew with money to build the brig *Patience*. So far as is known the uncle was a successful pawnbroker. Pawnbroking in the eighteenth century was not the back-street trade accommodating the down-at-heel, which it became in the twentieth century; pawnbrokers were the fringe bankers of the day, doing bill broking as well. People tended to put their savings into silver and jewellery, which were useful as status symbols in times of affluence and easily hypothecated when times were hard.

There were, in fact, not many other avenues for investment. There were only five stocks quoted on the Stock Exchange of which one was the South Seas Company, in whose stocks many had lost their fortunes earlier in the century. The alternative was to lend money on mortgage, where an attorney not only had to match borrower with loan but carry out an expensive investigation of title. In short, these were securities only for long-term investors with sizeable sums to invest. As the uncle had financed his nephew in building a brig, it is likely that advancing money to ship owners was part of his trade and that gave him a connection with the shipping world. Be that as it may, his elder daughter had married Sir Richard Hotham, a prominent ship owner, husbanding two ships in the East India Company's service, so Lady Hotham and Joseph Huddart, about whom we are writing, were first cousins. Huddart accompanied Sir Richard to Dudman's yard at Deptford to see a ship he was building there, and at the same time inspected other Indiamen. The yard was situated in Grove Street and led down to the Thames.

Huddart obviously made a lasting impression on Sir Richard, who was struck by his knowledgeable observations and saw in him material for an officer in the Honourable Company's service. Sir Richard tried to persuade Huddart to drop his present pursuits and enter a field where there was a chance of much greater reward. But Huddart had always been his own master and owned his own brig, whereas the Company could not, under its existing regulations, offer a higher position than the rank of Fourth Officer on entry to their service, and so he declined the proposal.

Nevertheless, from then on, much of Joseph Huddart's life centred round the East India Company. Its place in the history of the British Raj fills history books with a century of epic stories from Clive at Arcot to the Indian Mutiny, but in Georgian England the Honourable Company was not concerned with empire building, it was a commercial enterprise and one of the few multi-nationals of the day, others being the South Seas Company, the Hudson Bay Company and the Royal African Company. These companies were established by Royal Charter or Act of Parliament and were joint stock companies. All other commercial enterprises not so founded were partnerships with the partners owning a share of the common stock and being jointly liable for the partnership debts.

The English East India Company was established in the year 1600 by a charter from Queen Elizabeth I. In the first twelve voyages which they fitted out for India, the merchants traded with their separate stocks but in ships belonging to the Company. In 1612, they united into a joint stock company. The Company first established itself at Deptford in 1607 and up to that time England had not really had an ocean going mercantile fleet. Undoubtedly the Venetians were the first to undertake sea-borne trade on any scale and this had reached its zenith before Shakespeare wrote his *Merchant of Venice*. It is not surprising that a community who originally settled on a mudbank in a lagoon to escape their enemies should devote their attention to the sea, originally to survive but later to become a state renowned for its wealth and stability. But England's green and pleasant land was self-sufficient and fishery, coastal trade, and trade with the Continent were all the country needed.

In 1494 Portugal made its historic discovery of a route to the East round the Cape and brought back spices from the Orient at a fraction of the cost for which the Venetians obtained them from caravan routes, with the result that the much prized trade with the East went to Portugal and Spain.

To compete in this foreign trade England required ships which were sturdy enough to weather the storms round the Cape of Good Hope and sail across the Indian Ocean, which were stalwart enough to fight off attacks from the Portuguese, who regarded this route as their own particular preserve, and which had the capacity to carry not only a big cargo to justify the voyage but victuals and water for a crew which would be many months at sea. Such ships could not be purchased at a reasonable price – they had to be built. The first two ships were the *Trades Increase* and the *Peppercorn* of 700 tons costing £10 a ton to build. These were built at the newly established yard at Deptford. This yard expanded quickly and by 1615 it was employing 500 hands and owned twenty-one seaworthy ships: within the next six years it had a total tonnage of 10,000 and employed 2,500 seamen.

The East India Company was presided over by a Court which was the equivalent of a Board of Directors with a Governor who acted as Chairman and it had its own rules of procedure.

> Every man speaking in the Court shall stand up and be bareheaded and shall address his speech to the Governor or Deputy in his absence.
> Quoted by E. Keble Chatterton in *Old East Indiamen*

The man responsible for each one or more ships was a salaried official called the 'Ship's Husband'. When the Court met to decide on voyages the Husband attended to find out what shipping would be required and then prepared a list of the victuals for each ship and got the necessary stores together in the Company's warehouses. Apart from victuals he was responsible for the ship's stores and for the supervision of the clerks and for keeping account books. The warehouses in London were under the care of the 'Clerks of the Stores'. At the Deptford yard there were large stocks of timber and carpenters and caulkers who had the job of plugging between the planks to make a watertight joint.

The yard, which continued until 1626, developed into an elaborate organisation with its own 'Master Pylot to pilot down the Company's ships to Erith and Gravesend attending them until they be despatched into the Downs'.[1] The Downs was the point of departure for all the Company's ships.

The Company's charter conferred an exclusive privilege of trade in the East which for many years went unchallenged and unquestioned. The Company's capital was originally £369,891 5s divided into shares of £50 each. In 1676 there was what would be called in these days a one for one: the shares were doubled in value as a result of accumulated profits and became £100 shares, making a total capital of £739,782 10s. By 1685 a further £963,639 was added from the profits, making the total value of the stock £1,703,402.

By Charles II's time the exclusive privileges of the Company, unsupported by Act of Parliament, were becoming the subject of litigation with varying results. There was no longer a Divine Right of Kings and passive obedience of subjects: Parliament was now supreme, and anything resting on royal patronage was open to scrutiny. The Company had to establish its position with the government of the day. In 1698 a proposal was made of advancing two millions to the government at eight per cent by a new East India Company in return for exclusive privileges, the money being sought from new subscribers. The old and existing East India Company made an alternative offer of £700,000 at four per cent. But the government needed money whatever its price and the new East India Company was incorporated, the old East India Company being given the right to trade until 1701. However, the old Company took advantage of the situation by purchasing £315,000 stock in the new Company in the name of their treasurer. The present-day practice of one company holding stock in another was not then acceptable.

A confused situation arose in which private traders claimed the privilege of trading separately upon their stocks totalling £7,200. The old East India Company had the privilege of separate trade upon their stock until 1701 and after that as private traders, so that a competition grew up within the Company which nearly brought it to ruin, because of the Indians raising prices to the highest bidder and thereby making their goods unprofitable to sell on the English market, resulting in the market becoming overstocked.

This problem was resolved by a coalition under a tripartite indenture of the 22 July 1702 made between the Queen and the two Companies, and in 1708 the Companies were consolidated by Act of Parliament (6 Anne Cap 17) into the United Company of Merchants trading into the East Indies. Into this Act a clause was inserted allowing separate traders to continue their trade until Michaelmas 1711, but at the same time empowering the directors, upon three years' notice, to redeem the capital of £7,200 and convert the whole of the Company's capital into a joint stock. By the same Act, the loan to the government was increased from £2,000,000 to £3,200,000. On a renewal of the Company's charter in 1730 a further sum was lent to the government and the interest payable was reduced to three per cent. This became the India three-per-cent annuities which remained

[1] Quoted by E. Keble Chatterton in *The Old East Indiamen*.

in existence throughout the period of the British Raj. Now the Company enjoyed an established monopoly and carried on successful trade for several years.

The East India Company had three main settlements in India. The first was Madras, founded at the end of Charles II's reign, the second was Bombay which was originally part of the Gujarat Kingdom and ceded to the Portuguese in 1523. When Catherine of Braganza married Charles II in 1661, Bombay formed part of her dowry and in 1668 was leased to the East India Company for ten pounds a year. In 1687, Bombay became the centre of the administration of Western India. The third settlement was Calcutta, which originated with a factory set up by Job Charnock in 1686. This presence gave rise to hostilities with the Moguls and after the settlement of these hostilities Fort William was built on the banks of the Hooghly in 1694, which became the nucleus of Calcutta.

As the Moguls had ceased to be a force in India, it left a power vacuum in which the Indian princes of the Carnatic became independent. The French had established a settlement in Pondicherry and in 1741 Dupleix, its governor, hit upon the idea of entering into a military alliance with Chanda Sahib to support him as a candidate for the position of Nawab of the Carnatic and, at the same time, to raise a sepoy army under the command of the French to force the British out of Madras. The British supported Mohammed Ali as a rival candidate.

Dupleix succeeded in capturing Madras, the oldest and principal British settlement in 1746, which was later restored to the British at the treaty of Aix-la-Chapelle. Robert Clive, who was a writer in the service of the East India Company, escaped from Madras to Fort St David and learnt the skills of a professional soldier under Major Stringer Lawrence, which gave him the appointment of an ensign in the Second Company of Foot Soldiers. Chanda Sahib blockaded Trichinopoly which was held by the British, but Clive had the brilliant idea of creating a diversion by successfully attacking Arcot, Chanda Sahib's capital, which resulted in the death of Chanda Sahib and the installation of Mohammed Ali as Nawab. Clive then returned to England and married.

Two years later, he returned to India as governor of Fort St David only to be confronted at Madras with the news of the capture of Calcutta by the Nawab of Bengal, Siraj-ud-Daula, and the disaster of the Black Hole of Calcutta. Clive and Admiral Watson then set off for Calcutta which they retook without difficulty. On 21 June 1757 Clive defeated Siraj-ud-Daula in the amazing battle of Plassey with 3,200 men and nine guns against a force of 68,000 men and fifty-three guns.

On 12 August 1765 the Emperor Shah Alam granted the Company the right to collect the revenues of Bengal, Bihar and Orissa, which made the Company *de facto* rulers with a revenue of £4,000,000 sterling. In 1767 these rights were claimed on behalf of the Crown and the Company agreed to pay the government £400,000 a year compensation. The Company had raised their dividend by degrees from six per cent to ten per cent: but by two Acts of Parliament (7 Geo III Cap 47 and 8 Geo III Cap 11) the Company was restricted from further increases in their dividend owing to the large debt it had accumulated amounting to six or seven million pounds.

In 1769 the Company renewed its agreement with the government for a further five years with a provision for being allowed to increase the dividend to twelve-and-a-half per cent but not increasing it in any one year by more than one per cent. In 1768 by an account brought back by an East Indiaman, the *Cruttenden*, the net revenue clear of all deductions and military charges was stated to be £2,048,747. There was stated to be a further revenue arising from established customs of £439,000 and the profit of their trade, according to the evidence given by their chairman before the House of Commons, amounted to at least £400,000 a year or, according to their accountant, £500,000 a year. So great a revenue would certainly have justified an increase of £608,000 in annual payments and allowed a large sinking fund to reduce the Company's debts. But by 1773 their debts were increased by arrears of £400,000 to the Treasury, by unpaid duties to the customs-house, by a large bank overdraft and by bills drawn upon them from India, amounting to £1,200,000.

At this stage, the Company had to throw itself on the mercy of the government and seek a release from the annual payment of £400,000 and a loan of £1,400,000. The tremendous wealth that had come into the possession of the Company led to gross mismanagement, carelessness and no doubt misappropriation. Parliament demanded an enquiry.

Lord North's government was determined to put an end to the abuses that had arisen in India and passed the Regulating Act (13 Geo III Cap 63) which provided first for the appointment of a Governor-General with a council to be established at Fort William, Calcutta, with power of superintending the presidencies of Madras and Bombay. The latter was to have no power of declaring war or entering into treaties with the Indian princes and were subject in all respects to the authority of the Governor-General. Secondly, the whole civil and military government, the management of the territorial acquisitions and revenues in Bengal, Bihar and Orissa were vested in the Governor-General assisted by four councillors. Thirdly, instead of the Mayor's Court at Calcutta the jurisdiction of which had been gradually extended, a Supreme Court was set up at Fort William consisting of a Chief Justice and three Judges appointed by the Crown to deal with all cases both civil and criminal. The powers of the Mayor's Court were restricted to local mercantile cases. Fourthly, in England, the qualifications entitling a proprietor of shares to vote at the Company's General Court was raised from £500 to £1,000 which must have been held for one year unless inherited. The Court of twenty-four directors were no longer to be chosen annually but had to serve for four years.

At this point, therefore, the government of the Indian provinces rested with the Crown through its Governor-General and the commercial enterprise remained with the Company's Court of Directors.

This was the Company that Huddart was to serve from the age of thirty-three for the rest of his active days at sea, except for a twelve-month interlude. It did an immense trade in the East, having a complete monopoly; it was powerful, dictatorial and exacted as strict a discipline as the Royal Navy; but there were big prizes to be won in its service by those who were fortunate and had a head for business. The Company was respectfully referred to as the 'Honourable Company' or by those who were less respectful as the 'John Company'.

In 1773, Joseph Huddart, on his return from one of his voyages to North America, received a pressing invitation from Sir Richard Hotham to revisit London, which he did. Sir Richard proposed to him that he should enter the Company's service as Fourth Officer in the *York*, then nearly ready for launching and bound for St Helena and Bencoolen. To induce him Sir

Richard promised that he should succeed to the command of the ship upon the resignation of Captain Hayter without purchase. Huddart saw little advantage in this offer as many captains and officers were losing money by private trade and he, after all, had his own brig with which to trade. For profit-making much depended on the business acumen of the captain, his connections and his knowledge of the market. Neither Joseph Huddart nor his son William had much inclination to business and were apt to come out on the losing side.

The highest command that could be obtained in the Company's service on the first voyage was that of Fourth Officer and the pay was not sufficient to support a junior officer without some £500 capital of his own. It was not until the position of Second Officer was reached that the pay and allowances would support an officer. Huddart was persuaded possibly by his uncle or his cousin, Lady Hotham, to try one voyage and he entered the service of the East India Company in October 1773. In order to do this he put a Master in command of his own brig, so that if he did not like the Company's service he had his own ship to return to.

He sailed from the Downs on Christmas Eve 1773 and his leisure time was given to making scientific observations and nautical surveys, including a survey of the west coast of Sumatra rather than making a financial profit. The *York* returned in October 1775 after what was a successful journey for the owners but a bad one for the private trade of the officers and Joseph Huddart found he had lost £120. Once the ship was cleared he returned to his family at Allonby and resumed command of his brig.

Much of his trade with the brig had been with the American colonies and by the end of the Seven Years' War the French flag had ceased to be flown in America, so that the colonies no longer felt the need for British protection. The taxes England imposed for the support of the army had been reduced to a nominal tax on tea, more to maintain the principle of taxation than to provide revenue. However, even this caused resentment and led to the famous episode of the Boston Tea Party. British retaliation only made matters worse, breaking out in hostilities at Lexington in April 1775. In fact, relations had soured to such an extent that Huddart could no longer make his annual voyage to that country and confined himself to the coal trade between Maryport and Ireland.

Hostilities were not confined to the other side of the Atlantic. American privateers were active on the Cumberland coast, a certain Paul Jones burnt a large part of Whitehaven in 1778 compelling boats to sail in convoys. The *Cumberland Pacquet* of 15 September 1777 reports as follows:

> Captain Harris of the Success, from this port to Dublin on 3rd, encountered a cutter, two miles SW from the Calf of Man, pierced for ten guns and a number of men aboard.
>
> The cutter hailed him – whence came you? – from Whitehaven – Whither bound? – To Dublin – What is loading? – Coals – Are all vessels to leeward of you colliers? – All Colliers. – When did you sail? – Yesterday.
>
> Captain Harris in return hailed the cutter; From whence came you? – After a long pause he was answered – From a cruze. Captain Harris asked where he was bound – but no reply. The cutter filled her sails, stood to the SE., and night coming on was soon out of sight . . . . the cutter is strongly suspected of being an American Privateer.

In October 1776 he undertook for Sir Richard Hotham to superintend the curing of provisions at Cork for Sir Richard's ships in the Company's service and when these were ready he shipped them on his own brig to London arriving in December.

At the time Huddart was in London, Sayer, a well-known chart seller of Fleet Street, having heard of the surveys made of the Sumatra coast, obtained his permission to publish them and, at the same time, engaged him to complete a survey of St George's Channel of which no accurate chart existed. Huddart had already worked on this survey as and when opportunities arose. For this purpose he procured a small vessel, the *Liberty*, having put a Master again into his own for a voyage to Memel and on 26th April 1777 he sailed from Maryport to the Channel.

As there was no accurate chart to build on, the survey required indefatigable energy, perseverance and considerable self-confidence; not to mention a careful choice of crew and assistants. The chart proved a masterpiece of accuracy and had the sanction and approbation of all navigators who used the Channel. The chart was not only very profitable but it made Huddart's name as a hydrographer. He completed his survey during the summer, although the original work was dated 31 March 1778 on board the *Royal Admiral*.

On 26 August 1777 the *Patience* was put up for sale and the *Cumberland Pacquet* contains the following advertisement:

The ship PATIENCE

late under the command of

JOSEPH HUDDART

Burthen about 190 tons with all her materials as she came from the Sea. She was built at Maryport, not nine years Old. Of a moderate draught of Water, takes the ground with safety, is properly constructed for the Coal Trade or the Baltick Trade: and now in turn for loading Broughton Coals. The Purchaser to pay Twenty Guineas in hand, and to give satisfactory security for payment of the Remainder of the consideration Money in Equal portions at Three and Six Months from Day of Sale, in conformity with the conditions which shall then be produced.

NB. Inventories of her materials may be seen on Board and at the Place of Sale. Whoever has any demands on the said Vessel are requested, as soon as possible, to render Account to Mr. Joseph Sibson in Maryport, or the partners thereof.

After completing his survey Huddart sailed in the *Liberty* for Dublin on 2 September, returning from Drogheda on the 15th, and by 10 October 1777 he had re-entered the service of the East India Company.

CHAPTER III

The Royal Admiral

THE *Royal Captain*, the vessel spoken of earlier as being built in Dudman's yard, was lost on her maiden voyage when homeward bound having struck the rocks on the coast of Pelowar on 17 December 1773. One Indiaman, that is, a ship flying the flag of the East India Company, was said to be built on the bottom of another. That is to say that when a ship was lost or had to be scrapped the owner claimed the right to build another to replace it and a custom of hereditary bottoms, as it was called, arose which continued until 1796. Therefore, Sir Richard petitioned the Court on the loss of his ship for leave to build another in its place. The Court in this case was not willing to accede, although they did eventually through the influence of John Dingwall. Patience Dingwall, his wife, and Lady Hotham were sisters, and Dingwall himself was a wealthy stockholder in the Company with an influential vote in the Court of Directors.

The difficulty with the Court of Directors was probably due to a recent Act of Parliament (12 Geo III cap 54) which was designed to preserve timber for the Navy. Timber for the wooden walls of England had been running into short supply for the past century. By this Act, after 12 March 1772 the East India Company was prohibited from building or allowing to be built for their service any new ships until their total shipping, or the total they employed, was reduced to 45,000 tons. This did not preclude ships being built in India where, of course, local timber was used. At that time the Company had fifty-five ships abroad aggregating 39,836 tons and at home, including ships being built for their service, there were 22,000 tons, making a total afloat of 61,836 tons.

As has already been pointed out, the Court consisted of twenty-four directors, retiring in rotation each year. At least, this was the position until 1773, when the directors were required to serve for four years. Out of their number the directors appointed a chairman with a salary of £200 per annum and a deputy chairman: the directors received £150 per annum. Meetings were held once a week or more frequently if necessary. The directors formed themselves into sub-committees consisting of a correspondence committee; a buying committee; a treasury committee; a house committee; a committee for law suits; a shipping committee; an accounts committee; a committee for private trade, etc. Each committee had its secretary, cashier, clerks and servants.

Apart from the Court of Directors which corresponded with the board of a modern company, there was a General Court or a Court of Proprietors who elected the Directors and this gave a substantial stockholder a good deal of influence over the Company. Share holding was open to all men and women, British or native, and a £500 share or later a £1,000 share gave the owner one vote in the General Court. The qualification to stand for election as a director was £2,000 of stock. Some bought stock merely to influence their friends to jobs in India, and to restrict this, a provision, as we have seen, was introduced requiring a share to be held for twelve months, unless inherited, before the holder was eligible to vote.

No doubt, therefore, John Dingwall was able to sway the committee into bending the rules, which required a commander to have made two previous voyages to India, not only to give Huddart succession to a command he would not normally have obtained, but to add a condition with the concurrence of Sir Richard that he succeeded to the command of the new ship without having to purchase the first vacancy. Service in the East India Company was wholly unprofitable for junior officers and it was not until they reached the position of second officer that they made a living, but it was worth subsisting on a pittance for a man in his early twenties, particularly an unmarried man, to succeed to the rich pickings which went with a command. After all, barristers were in the same position, to say nothing of writers, actors and painters.

The Company realised that if it gave captains a vested interest in the ship they were more likely to bring it safely to harbour, hence captains, and indeed all officers, were allotted a proportion of the cargo space to use for their own profit. Captain Barrow, who lost Sir Richard's ship the *Royal Captain* on the rocks at Pelowar, was entitled to the command of the new ship built on its bottom. But Sir Richard must have lost faith in Captain Barrow as a commander and the best thing he could do was to engage the services of a first officer in whom he had every confidence. Captain Barrow was in declining health which was a considerable advantage from Huddart's point of view as the Captain was unlikely to survive another voyage, so that Huddart would have every opportunity of taking over the command.

We have to remember that by this time Huddart was in his mid-thirties and as a first officer he could be as young as twenty-three, so he was getting senior for the rank; and he had about twenty years of experience behind him, for most of which time he had been a master, and latterly master and owner of his own brig. Therefore, unless he saw the chance of a command he was unlikely to be interested. One factor that undoubtedly influenced him to join the East India Company's service was the collapse of the trade with America, but another factor was possibly the death of his uncle in London in the summer of 1777 who left him the farm at Allonby. This gave him and his family some financial security if the venture proved unprofitable or he was lost at sea as voyages to India were considerably more hazardous than coastal trade.

The will so far as it relates to Captain Huddart reads as follows:

> This is the last Will and Testament of me Joseph Huddart of Eaton Street near Pimlico in the Parish of St. George Hanover Square in the County of Middlesex Esquire. First I will and direct that all my just Debts and Funeral Expenses shall be paid and discharged by my Executrix hereinafter named as soon after my decease as conveniently may be. And I give and bequeath unto my dear Wife Patience Huddart All that my Leasehold Messuage or Tenement and premises with the Appurtenances in Eaton Street aforesaid &c. &c.
>
> And I give devise and bequeath unto my Nephew Joseph Huddart son of

my late Brother William Huddart and to his Heirs and Assigns for ever All my Freehold Messuage or Tenement Lands and Hereditaments at Allanby in the Parish of Bromfield in the County of Cumberland . . .

Subject to the interests of his widow the rest of his estate was left to the Dingwalls from which it must be assumed that Lady Hotham had predeceased her father. The Will is dated 14 July 1777 and was proved on 30 October 1777.

In short, Huddart was satisfied with the arrangements made with the Company and accepted the position of chief officer. Having completed the sale of his brig *Patience* and settled his other affairs in Cumberland he returned to London.

By this time travelling by road had greatly improved. The Carlisle and London New Post now boasted steel springs and was able to make the journey from Carlisle to London in three days by way of Ripon, Harrogate, Leeds and Sheffield, setting out from Beck's Coffee-house in Carlisle every Monday, Wednesday and Friday at 4 pm and arriving at 5 pm at the Cross Keys in Wood Street, near the Guildhall in the city of London, with a return journey starting at 7 pm and arriving at Carlisle at 9 pm. The fares were £3 4s 9d inside or £3 0s 3d from Penrith and £2 2s 0d outside or £1 19s 0d from Penrith where the coach stopped at Mr George Rickard's. Only 14 lbs of luggage was allowed free of charge, above that it was 4d a pound.

Huddart took up his lodgings at Deptford, where the *Royal Admiral*, the ship built on the bottom of the *Royal Captain* was still under construction. He made it his business to keep a close inspection of the finishing and fitting out of the ship and in fact devoted his whole time and attention to seeing that the work was carried out to his satisfaction.

The *Royal Admiral*, which was a ship of 914 burthen tonnage and 914 chartered tonnage, was a hundred and twenty feet and two inches in length and thirty-seven feet ten inches in width. Merchant ships were estimated by their burden, that is to say, by the number of tons they were capable of bearing, each ton being reckoned at 2,000 pounds weight, and the estimate was based on the size of the hold. Records of tonnage of Indiamen were misleading because between 1743 and 1772 the Company's regulations required ships of over 500 tons to have a chaplain on board and therefore the tendency was to keep the tonnage below 500. Ships were often registered as 499 tons when in fact they far exceeded that burden. The hull and rigging followed very closely on that of a man o' war, though more emphasis was given to carrying capacity and less to speed. Operating a monopoly trade, ships did not have to race to get business.

The *Royal Admiral* was chartered for Bombay and on 27 April 1778 sailed from the Downs with the following officers: Captain Barrow in command, Joseph Huddart, first mate; Charles Gregorie, chief mate; Christopher Sampson, second mate; Charles Moore, third mate; Edward Harriman, fourth mate; Thomas Hodgson, fifth mate; and Thomas Parkin was the Purser. It seemed that the ranking of the officers was arranged in anticipation of the early demise of Captain Barrow. Among the seamen was one Richard Holiday, who not only could spell accurately, an uncommon gift in those days, but wrote with the perfection of an expert scrivener. In later voyages he is singled out as the Captain's clerk.

Captain Barrow's health was deteriorating before the ship put to sea and soon he was dying so the ship put into Portsmouth where he died. This gave Huddart the opportunity of command he had been seeking and the

Court of Directors was petitioned to give him this command but there was some difficulty over the Company's regulations, which required a captain to have made two previous voyages to India in their service and Huddart had made only one. However, in the circumstances, the objection was brushed aside – Huddart was, after all, an experienced navigator; but he could not reap the pecuniary advantages due to a captain, because he was, in fact, taking charge of Captain Barrow's investment and had to account to the executors for the profits which Barrow would have made had he lived and any other benefits due to a command. He could enjoy only the profits from private trade as a chief officer. Needless to say, he carried out his obligations to Barrow's executors in an exemplary manner and to their complete satisfaction.

He took his eldest son William with him as a midshipman who was then fifteen years old. William had previously sailed as an apprentice in his father's brig *Patience* for just over a year.

On the outward bound passage to the Cape at about 11.30 am on 24 August 1778 the *Colebrook*, one of the ships of the convoy being on the lee bow of the *Royal Admiral* and a bit ahead, struck a rock, which went unnoticed on the *Royal Admiral* until the *Colebrook* was on her lee beam and hoisted the ensign union downwards. The *Royal Admiral*, having increased her water from twenty-six fathoms to twenty-eight fathoms, decided it was safest to stand on for about two miles making regular soundings and then lay to. Moore, the third officer, was sent in the pinnace to assist the *Colebrook*, but the leak was found to be so bad that the ship could not be kept afloat with the result that she sunk in about six hours on a rock, the existence of which was hitherto unknown. This did, however, allow time to save the passengers and crew although twenty lives were lost. Unknown rocks were a hazard that haunted all shipping in the eighteenth century and it was fortunate at least for those on board if ships were available to rescue them. Even in cases where it was possible to get ashore from a wreck the chances of survival on the African coast were minimal.

On his arrival the next day at Simons Bay, Cape Town, Huddart lost no time in taking steps to ascertain the exact position of the fatal rock, which was unknown even to the Dutch. To achieve this he got a Dutch pilot and a boat from the Resident, which was attended by his own pinnace with his son and a few officers on board. To carry out the survey it was necessary to land on the rock, in order to get bearings on the headland and some adjacent rocks which showed above the water. The surf was running high so they rested on their oars until it appeared safe to land. When they attempted to pull in, to quote Huddart, 'without the least warning a high breaker towering up in less than three seconds upset the pinnace'. Huddart and his son, who was steering, both jumped out and Huddart swam with the surf for some fifty or sixty yards with his son on his back until he felt the ground under his feet and landed safely. The other seven managed to save themselves but the instruments and firelocks were lost.

On 12 October the *Royal Admiral* made her departure from Cape Town arriving at Anjengo on 17 January 1779 where she anchored, and thence to Bombay arriving there on 7 February. Captain Barrow's private trade was sent ashore together with the Company's cargo of copper, lead and coals. The cargo taken on board for shipment to England consisted of 1,174 bags of saltpetre, 120 bales of Surat Goods and 31 bales of other goods, the main cargo being 7,575 bags of pepper. It is difficult to determine the exact size of a bag of pepper as measures in the eighteenth century varied with different trades and different localities, but a bag was probably three hundredweight. The extensive use of pepper at this time can be judged from the size of the pepper pots, many of which rivalled a sugar castor in size.

The ship weighed anchor on 8 May, arriving at St Helena on 21 August, where she lay at anchor off St James's Valley until 25 October when she weighed anchor arriving at the Downs on 13 January 1780, and anchored on the 15th in the Lower Hope a reach of the Thames.

Huddart did not remain long in England and now in command of the *Royal Admiral* he took his departure on 4 June with the same officers as on the previous passage apart from Charles Gregorie, the chief mate. This gave him the opportunity of promoting all his other officers leaving the position of fifth mate vacant for the promotion of his son William from midshipman.

The ship was bound for Bombay, the first port of call being Rio de Janeiro. To take advantage of the wind, ships made a southwest passage across the Atlantic and then an eastern passage to the Cape once in the southern hemisphere.

The *Royal Admiral* anchored at Rio de Janeiro on 22 August and took her departure on 19 September, passing Tristan da Cunha on 12 October and reaching the Malabar coast on 10 January 1781, where the British fleet was stationed, and the ship was put under the orders of Admiral Sir Edward Hughes.

The British fleet was engaged in the reduction of two Dutch settlements at Jagginaultporam and Negapatam. On 20 January the *Royal Admiral* hoisted Dutch colours in response to a signal from another ship: she was evidently now in the war zone. On 14 February boats from the men o' war took twenty of the ship's men, and the passengers and recruits on board were sent ashore. There was a naval presence of several ships of the line: *Superb*, *Exeter*, *Eagle*, *Worcester*, and *Coventry*. On 26 April the *Royal Admiral* was engaged in taking stores for the garrison at Tillicherry together with gun carriages, shot and 632 troops with four officers and on 26 May she anchored in Tillicherry Roads, sending the sepoys ashore.

On 11 May at 10 pm the enemy sent two fire boats into the Roads which burnt for two hours but did no damage. At daylight on 15 May Admiral Hughes weighed anchor with the *Superb*, *Exeter*, *Eagle*, *Worcester* and *Coventry*, ships of the line, and the Company's ship the *Royal Charlotte* and various country ships, that is local ships which had not sailed from England, with one of these sailing under the Dutch flag, arriving at Negapatam on 4 June. On 12 July the *Royal Admiral* gave chase to what appeared to be an enemy ship and ordered it to the Commodore, but it proved to be a Danish ship from Madras.

On Sunday, 15 July the Union Jack was hoisted on the flagstaff at Jagginaultporam with a general discharge of artillery as the Dutch Governor surrendered.

The practice of sailing under Dutch colours to deceive the enemy gave rise to a good deal of confusion. On 29 July a schooner was seen sailing with Dutch colours and the *Royal Admiral* manned a pinnace to board her when it proved to be the *Grampus* under the command of Captain Dixon. On 7 August the *Royal Admiral* anchored at Masulipatam and then on the 28th at Madras Roads. On 12 October she joined the fleet at Negapatam which was at anchor under the command of Admiral Hughes.

On 21 October Colonel Nixon attacked a redoubt at Negapatam on which the Dutch had mounted some guns and being unable to approach it by coming up the river, the position was carried by troops, some mounted and some on foot, fording the river higher up. Two hundred of the enemy were killed and a number taken prisoner.

Jagginaultporam and Negapatam were not isolated skirmishes. Rivalry with the Dutch over domination at sea and in trade with the East had led to a series of wars; the fourth war with Britain was waged between 1780 and 1784 starting with the Battle of the Dogger Bank when Zoutman attempted to convoy merchantmen through the English Channel and culminating in the peace of Fontainebleau in May 1784 when Negapatam was ceded to the British, and it was only the French under De Suffren that saved Cape Colony from a similar fate.

On 16 April 1781 De Suffren, conveying troops to the Cape, sighted a British convoy under the command of Commodore Johnston which had put into Porto Praya on the Island of St Jago for water and he decided to attack. The *Essex* and the *Hinchinbroke* were captured, but when the French engaged the *Monmouth* and the *Hero* they withdrew after an hour's action leaving their prizes. Johnston delayed following the French and by the time he arrived at the Cape on 2 July the French had safely landed their troops.

War had been declared between France and Great Britain in March 1778 which was really the outcome of the war over the American colonies. On 17 December 1781 the French fleet sailed to India and owing to the death of his superior, De Suffren assumed command. Not only was De Suffren a very able admiral, but his force was superior to that of the British. Nnevertheless, he was handicapped by having no shore base.

The *Royal Admiral* had left the fleet after the Negapatam incident, arriving at Bombay on 31 December 1781 where she remained until October 1782, thus escaping any involvement with De Suffren. When De Suffren reached Madras on 15 February 1782 he found Hughes with nine ships of the line under the guns of the forts and decided not to attack.

The threat to Hughes was that he might seize Pondicherry and co-operate with Hyder Ali, who was at war with the British, in attempting to capture Trincomalee. Hughes came out during the night of the 16th and gained a position from which he was able to attack the French convoy on the morning of the 17th thereby capturing five ships as prizes and a transport of 300 soldiers and some military stores. But, although the French flagship was badly damaged and some thirty killed, the engagement was indecisive.

On 12 April 1782 De Suffren overhauled the British squadron off Trincomalee and forced an engagement which became a close action by 1 pm. De Suffren directed his fire against Hughes's flagship, the *Superb*, and the next ahead, the *Monmouth*, with the result that a bloody conflict ensued. The *Monmouth* was reduced to a wreck and the *Superb* lost fifty-nine killed and another ninety-six wounded, but the failure of the French captains to press home the attack robbed the French of a victory. De Suffren's flagship was so damaged that he had to transfer his flag to the *Ajax*, and a violent squall then brought the engagement to an end much to the relief of the British.

De Suffren was short of men, provisions, spares and rigging as a result of his engagement, but by 5 July he had refitted from convoys and came in sight of the British at Negapatam: then, owing to a sudden squall, the *Ajax* was partly dismasted. The British were not anxious to move too far from port owing to the weather and the battle was delayed until 11 am the next day. De Suffren was again let down by his captains and the battle ended in Hughes's favour with the result that the French then left the British unchallenged.

The following year Huddart arrived back in the Downs on 25 August 1783. He had taken no active part in the skirmishes with the French and had lost the opportunity of trading. In fact, looking at his affairs, he found that in the ten years he had been with the Company he had barely increased his capital.

The two voyages which were to follow, however, offered much brighter prospects. The Court of Directors had the sole right of appointment of the voyage and the Chairman had the first nomination: in this case it was Sir Henry Fletcher who occupied the chair and he decided to appoint Captain Huddart to the Bombay and China passage, which was the most lucrative one. Sir Henry, who was a friend of Huddart's, had Cumberland connections as his mother Isabella was the daughter and co-heiress of John Senhouse of Netherhall, Maryport. It was not in Huddart's nature to solicit favours and we may take it that the appointment, which was well deserved, was not the result of any approach on his part but gained on merit. On his return Captain Huddart offered Sir Henry a pipe of choice wine which he purposely selected at Madeira but could not prevail on Sir Henry to accept it.

Accordingly Huddart joined the *Royal Admiral* in December 1783 and sailed for the Downs on 27 March 1784, returning to England in April 1786. His officers on this voyage were: Charles Moore, chief mate; Edward Harriman, second mate; Henry Bond, third mate; James Hutchins, fourth mate; Thomas Hemmings, fifth mate; and William Buchanan, sixth mate. Thomas Parkin again was the Purser, and Edward Watson the Surgeon, with John Brydon as his mate. The voyage was very successful and he was known to have observed that 'this was the first moment that he could say he had benefitted by entering the Company's service thirteen years before'. On this voyage he had the opportunity of fixing the position of the 'Basses de India', a reef the true position of which had not so far been determined. When he reached the latitude in which he expected to find the reef he sent a pinnace ahead to reconnoitre, and it was about eight o'clock on a fine clear morning when he got the signal for soundings he had been anxiously waiting for. He was then able to carry out an accurate observation and establish the exact position of the reef and record his survey.

On his return to England his joys were mingled with sadness, as he received news that Elizabeth his wife had died just before he reached England after a long and painful illness. He had taken his youngest son Johnston, which was his mother's maiden name, on this voyage while he was still thirteen. He was signed on as a seaman but promoted to a midshipman before the ship reached China, and he must have been kitted out as a midshipman before the ship sailed. He was given the position of coxswain, that is to say, put in command of the Commander's pinnace. Johnston accompanied his father on the next voyage by which time he was seventeen and given the rank of sixth officer.

In 1786 Captain Huddart made his last voyage, which was very much a repetition of the voyage he had returned from and the survival of his own log enables this voyage to be followed day-by-day, but a voyage that is successful is liable to be uneventful. In fact, Huddart had an unblemished career as a navigator due largely to his care and expertise, but good fortune must have gone along with him as well. He must often have said to himself 'but for the Grace of God there go I' when ships foundered on uncharted rocks covered by the waves. This voyage, then, is no epic tale like Lieutenant Bligh's voyage to Tahiti which took place in the same year and ended in the ill-fated mutiny but one of the humdrum events that contributed to Britain's wealth as a trading nation. Nevertheless, the voyage gives us an insight into the everyday workings of a sailing ship in the days when sailing was for real and not for play. This means taking a look first at the Ship's Company, secondly at the ship itself and finally the process of getting it ready for the voyage and departure from the Downs.

The Ship's Company consisted of the Commander Joseph Huddart and the following six officers: Charles Moore, chief mate; Edward Harriman, second mate; Thomas Hemmings, third mate; Edward Manby, fourth mate; William Adderly, fifth mate; and Johnston Huddart, sixth mate. There were four midshipmen, Robert Poultney, Jonathan Young, Edward Fairfax and Samuel Otterly. The age of midshipmen was normally between fourteen and eighteen but those who joined late or failed to get promotion would be older. In the Navy there was no commissioned rank below that of Lieutenant and a man had to be twenty-one years of age to hold a commission even though he had passed all his examinations at a much earlier age. Johnston at this time was just seventeen and already an officer.

In addition to the officers there was the Surgeon, John Durham, the Purser, Thomas Parkin, who had been on all the voyages of the *Royal Admiral*, the Captain's clerk, Richard Holiday, and the Surgeon's mate, John Brydon. The Petty Officers consisted of the boatswain, James Roach, who died in November of the following year and his two mates, a gunner and mate, the Captain's steward and the ship's steward and six quartermasters. The tradesmen consisted of a carpenter with a first and second mate, a caulker and mate, a sailmaker, a cooper and mate, a butcher and an armourer. There was a Captain's cook and a ship's cook and seven servants, one each for the Captain, the chief mate, the second mate, the surgeon, and the carpenter, the boatswain and the gunner.

The crew numbered seventy-two seamen or foremast men. It seems that the commander might have two servants or a clerk and one servant. The total complement was the Commander and 120 men, which was the Company's rule for ships of up to 1,000 tons: the *Royal Admiral* was 914 tons. Commanders were paid ten pounds a month, but there were rich pickings to be made out of private trade which, needless to say, required some entrepreneurial skill; like any form of trade it was easy to make a loss. On a passage to China a Commander could take up to £3,000 in bullion as few European goods were marketable in China and bring back thirty-eight tons of merchandise or possibly more, except raw silk and poisons. Similarly, the chief mate could take £300 in bullion and bring back eight tons of merchandise. The privilege extended to midshipmen and petty officers and some tradesmen who were allowed to take fifty pounds and bring back a ton of merchandise; midshipmen, who after all were boys, did not usually indulge in trade and sometimes the captain used their space in the hold.

Those availing themselves of the privilege had to pay customs on returning to England and had to pay the Company a percentage for warehousing space until the goods were sold. Tea could be brought back up to 9,336 pounds avoirdupois for the Commander down to 246 pounds for a tradesman. The Commander could also bring home two pipes of Madeira wine and, as has been seen, Huddart offered one pipe to Sir Henry Fletcher. The scale of pay for the mates was five pounds a month for the chief mate, four pounds a month for the second mate, three pounds ten shillings for the third mate, and two pounds ten shillings for the fourth mate. The junior officers, midshipmen and foremastmen were all paid the same, two pounds five shillings a month.

Tradesmen for the most part had higher rates of pay than seamen; the carpenter was the most important tradesman, getting four pounds ten shillings. He was responsible for the seaworthiness of the ship and had to be a competent shipwright. If the ship was damaged he had the responsibility of carrying out repairs to make it seaworthy and of supervising repairs in a foreign port. The surgeon got about the same as the third mate and his mate no more than a seaman. The pay of the ship's carpenter was at this time rated higher than that of the surgeon, perhaps his services were more valuable; but as the years went by surgeons' pay improved. Pursers seemed to come at the bottom of the scale with two pounds a month, but they had other opportunities of making money. A ledger was kept bound in parchment, the traditional material for account books at that time, with a folio for each of the ship's company: a two months' advance of pay was allowed as soon as the ship set sail.

There was a strict rule against Commanders increasing the numbers of midshipmen above four, breach of which could involve a Commander in three years' suspension. The reason for this was that families with money might offer a commander a substantial sum to gain a place for their son at sea as a midshipman. The crew having been signed on, preparations for the forthcoming voyage started on 6 November 1786. The work of setting up the rigging and fitting out the ship was recorded daily in the Harbour Journal by the Captain's clerk and this included a daily weather report as even at anchor there could be trouble from storms. While the work on board proceeded lighters arrived daily with cargo, victuals and casks of water to be stowed in the ship's hold. On 9 November the Company's surveyor arrived to trim the ship. This involved levelling the kentledge, which was pig iron laid on the keelson as permanent ballast, and sweeping the hold. While stowing the holds proceeded, a daily check was kept on the draught of the ship fore and aft.

Indiamen and men o' war were barques in the eighteenth century, that is to say, they were three-masted ships with square rigging on each mast apart from staysails. Each mast could be built up with a top mast and above that a gallant, which sailors pronounced 'garn' as the word derived its origin from the garland or rope collar which originally secured it to the topmast. There is a reference in the harbour journal to fidding on 21 November. The heel of the topmast rested on a trestle tree being a sort of shelf near the top of the mainmast where it was secured by a fid or bolt. The word seems to have survived in nautical circles as a name for a paper fastener. The cap of the mainmast was made with an iron ring which held the topmast above the fid. A corresponding system operated with the gallant. To support the masts laterally there were ropes called shrouds and these were held by lanyards to the chains. To give the shrouds more purchase a wooden platform was built on the sides of the ship called a channel (chain wale) the outer edge being held down with chains secured to metal plates bolted to the sides of the ship which took the strain of the shrouds. The lanyards were thin pieces of cord rove several times through dead eyes on the shrouds and on the chains, and these were slackened off when the ship was out of commission to avoid damage to the ropes through shrinkage. When the rigging was set up, that is to say, everything tightened to bear its proper strain, the lanyards were swayed meaning that they were pulled tight.

The stays took the strain of supporting the masts fore and aft. The bowsprit, as the word implies, was a boom extending over the bows of the ship and held in place by gammoning, that is, ropes lashing it to the prow, and the forestay would be fastened to the forward part of the bowsprit with the bobstay below it taking the strain back on to the hull of the ship at the water line. The bobstay was set up on 15 November. On 23 November the lower masts were scraped and payed, which meant that after scraping they were coated with tar or pitch. The nautical use of the word 'pay' is confusing as it also occurs in expressions as 'pay out' or 'pay down', meaning to uncoil or let out and to coil up or, as seamen would have it, to coil down.

On square-rigged ships the sails were carried by spars known as yards and these were swayed (hoisted) or struck (lowered) by halliards (haul yards) working with a block and tackle known as jeers. On 18 December the Harbour Journal refers to crossing the crossjack which means hoisting the yard without a sail. The yards were kept level by lifts, that is to say, ropes from the mast attached to either end of the yard which were hauled up so as to keep the yard level. The sails were bent (tied) onto the yard with robins (rope bands), being small pieces of cord attached to the head of the sail, one longer and one shorter, so that they could be knotted round the yard. One end might be pointed, that is to say, thinned to go through an eyelet. There is a reference to this on 7 January 1787.

The middle part of the yard was known as the sling and the ends as the yard-arms. A word with grim overtones as the yard-arm was used as a gibbet for capital offences at sea. The ropes hanging below the yard which gave sailors a foothold when working on the sail were called 'horses'. The weather edge of the sail was held to the wind by sheets at the yard-arm, braces at the foot and bowlines or bridles in between. The bowline fanned out into bridles so as to hold the edge of the sail at several places. A seaman had to know where each rope was secured and for the most part they were secured to bitts, which were small posts in pairs forming a cleat and secured to the deck. The bitter end was the last piece towards the end of a rope which would hold on the bitts without pulling free. A rope paid out to the bitter end is extended as far as it will go.

The masts were known as the foremast, the mainmast and the mizzen. The mizzen also carried a crossjack, pronounced 'crojek' which was a small yard for use as the lowest sail; in fact, the sail was rarely bent on and one assumes that it was reserved for severe storms. Anchors had a hierarchy of their own, the sheet anchor being the big daddy of them all and the word has passed into every day use as synonymous with the last resource; it was traditionally stowed aft of the forward rigging. Next in order of size came the bower anchors and as the word implies they rested on the bows ready to be cast, and these were in normal use. Smaller anchors were called stream anchors and were capable of holding the ship against the stream in inland waters, the ebb tide being stronger than the flood as it carried with it the water draining off the land whereas the flood tide was holding it back.

Finally, there were kedge anchors to be used in conjunction with another anchor where, for instance, the turn of the tide may carry a ship over its anchor and cause the anchor to drag: the use of the kedge as an additional anchor would prevent this. The anchor itself had several members consisting of a shank with two arms terminating in flukes which hold on to the sea bed and at the other end was the shoulder carrying the stock set at right angles to the arms with a ring above it on which the cable was bent.

Each anchor was attached to a cable strong enough for the duty the anchor had to perform and some of these cables were extremely thick; for instance, a nine-inch cable was nearly three inches thick, which meant that it would not bite onto a capstan. A thinner piece of rope had to be used to get a hold on the capstan called a 'messenger' and this was bound onto the cable with a small rope called a 'nipper'. The Journal refers to a messenger being brought on board on 4 January 1787.

The ship on this voyage acted as a transport taking a Company of Hanoverians to India, but at 10 am on Sunday, 31 December the Hanoverians mutinied, took to their arms, cut and wounded ten of the crew, the Gunner getting his arm broken; however by 11.30 am the mutiny was quelled.

On 9 January 1787 the ship was surveyed by Mr Travers and the Hon. William Elphinstone before going to sea and 100 of the Hanoverian Infantry were replaced by 100 of the Company's recruits. On the 10th the staysails and the topgallant sails were bent and the yards ready for swaying. The crew and the soldiers had a payment in advance of their pay and the pilot came on board to take charge of the ship; the Company had its own pilots and a sixty-ton pilot cutter with a master and crew of six cruising between Gravesend and the Downs.

On the evening of the 11th the first casualty occurred. A recruit named Matthew Baker fell overboard and was drowned in spite of the attempts to search for him with the jolly boat.

The ship weighed anchor at Gravesend on 13 January and it took until the 19th to reach the Downs, anchoring each day at low water so as to get the benefit of the ebb tide to carry the ship down the river. By the 18th the ship had reached the mouth of the Thames when a moderate WSW breeze sprang up and by Friday, the 19th the ship had reached the Downs. This was a sheltered area of sea much used by the East India Company as an anchorage; it extended along the Kentish coast from Deal to South Foreland, having a depth of water of about ten fathoms and was protected by the Goodwin Sands, which were covered by only a few feet at low water and this formed a bar behind which shipping could shelter. This was the point at which most voyages started and finished and the point at which the pilot was dropped or taken on board.

The voyage to China started at 10 am on Saturday, 20 January 1787 and the weather was still foggy with the wind in the West South West, which was not a favourable wind for a journey down the Channel. At 2 pm the ship passed the South Foreland: at 3 pm the pilot was dropped and Dover Castle was sighted to the Nor' North West: at 7 pm to the Nor' West by North the light on Dungeness was seen about four or five leagues away. By midnight the wind had veered to the West and by the early morning it had dropped but sprang up again as daylight appears. Monday morning was clouded with fog and no observation could be made at noon, the sort of morning when everything was damp and dismal, but the ship was somewhere off the Sussex coast, east of the Greenwich meridian.

All the time the ship was sailing from the Downs soundings were being taken, as this was the only way a vessel could be sure of not going aground when the coast line was not visible. Soundings were taken with a lead and line, two types of lead being carried on board, a deep-sea lead and a hand lead. A hand lead was twenty fathoms in length and had a distinguishing mark at each fathom. The two-fathom mark had a small piece of leather with two ends, the three-fathom mark has three ends and the ten-fathom mark had leather with a hole through it. Five and fifteen fathoms were marked by white bunting: seven and seventeen fathoms were marked by red bunting, thirteen by blue bunting and twenty fathoms by knots. The other marks were known as deeps, these could be felt in the dark. The lead was usually hollowed out at the bottom and filled with tallow so as to bring up the bottom, that is, traces of the sea-bed. The lead was heaved from the chains so that it landed in the sea well forward of the position of the leadsman and could be pulled up tight as the leadsman came vertically above the lead. If the depth was an exact number of fathoms such as two the leadsman called out 'by the mark twain' and that is how Mark Twain gained his pseudonym. Fractions of a fathom would be called out first such as 'and a half twain'. Swinging the lead is another expression that we have got from the tongues of sailors and this arose from the practice of sailors who got tired of heaving the lead out to sea, just letting it swing and calling out some plausible depth when the boatswain's eyes were elsewhere.

On the morning of Monday, 2d January 1787 the fog had cleared and the ship was standing in with Beachy Head; at half past four in the morning Beachy Head was to the Nor North East about ten miles away lying in the latitude 50° 44' N. and longitude 0° 20' E from which point the Captain took his departure. It was from the point of departure that the ship's position was calculated in the account kept in the Log of the course stemmed by the ship, as it would now be out of sight of land, and having to fix its position by the three 'Ls': Log, Latitude and Lookout. The word 'Log' originated with just an ordinary log of wood let out on a line to determine what headway the ship was making.

By the eighteenth century the process had become more sophisticated and the log was a fan shaped piece of wood: old writers said it was shaped like a flounder. In fact it was quadrant in shape with a radius of about five or six feet and it was weighted in the middle of its circular edge, so that it floated upright with the line attached where the centre would come if the quadrant were part of a circle. There were knots at intervals of fifty-one feet rove in between the strands in the line and the line was wound onto a reel so that it could run out easily. The log was heaved over the poop and allowed to remain floating stationarily with the line running out while the ship continued on its course.

At a point in the line ten fathoms from the log there was a red rag from which point the spaces of fifty-one feet started. The equipment was complemented with a glass in which the sand ran out in half a minute, so that as the red rag left the ship the sands started to run and the navigator would count the number of knots while the sands in the glass were running. If four knots ran out the ship would be said to be doing four knots or four nautical miles per hour. A minute or sixtieth part of a degree at the equator is equivalent to a nautical mile and was said to contain 6,120 feet which divided by 120, the number of half minutes in an hour, gives a length of fifty-one feet: modern calculations would put this figure at fifty feet eight inches. The system was not free from error, as a following wind would bring home the log and a ten per cent error was usually allowed for. It was found in practice that a ship's speed was marginally greater than that given by the log and therefore the theoretical distance of fifty-one feet was slightly reduced in practice. Then again, on a hot day the sand would run more quickly than on a damp day. The log had to remain upright to give the maximum resistance to the water and remain in the same place, and the line had to be checked to see that it had not stretched or shrunk.

By noon on Sunday, 21 January the recorded distance of the log was fifty-four miles but the actual distance as the crow flies would be about thirty miles, on account of the distance lost by having to tack, and a further distance of fifteen miles was covered on the following Monday before the ship took its departure at 4.30 am from the point ten miles from Beachy Head.

The process by which a ship determined its position when no observation could be made was known as dead reckoning; the knots were recorded each hour on a log board kept on the deck, which was usually two boards or two slates laced together. Changes in the direction of the wind or in the course of the ship were also recorded, and the entries were made up in the log book.

The working days in a sea journal ran from noon on one day to noon on the next day. Some journals used signs for the days of the week, but one can see little purpose in this unless the sign related to a working day as opposed to a calendar day in which case the date related to the second half of the twenty-four hour period. Harbour journals ran from midnight to midnight to correspond with the calendar. The reason for logs being made up from noon to noon was that noon was the time that observations had to be made with a sextant to check the ship's actual position with its recorded position, and if a chronometer was on board this would be read at the same time.

The Log book would have a page or half a page for each day divided into five columns. The first column was headed H for hours with the figures 1 to 12 and again 1 to 12 printed down the margin to make up a twenty-four hour period starting with 1 pm. The next column was headed 'Courses' in which the course of the ship was recorded and each time it changed there was an entry at the appropriate hour. The next column was headed 'K' for knots with an adjacent space for half knots or feet in multiples of ten. The fourth column was headed 'Winds' to record the direction of the wind and soundings if taken and the final column was reserved for remarks, observations, accidents and punishments. The columns were not necessarily printed in that order.

At the foot of the page there was a summary to resolve the course stemmed by the ship into a difference of latitude and a difference of longitude. The way in which this was set out varied according to the different practices adopted as the technique of navigation developed. With the Log of the *Royal Admiral* the summary was made up of eight spaces: in the first was entered the course stemmed by the ship, in the second the distance travelled, in the third these entries were resolved by traverse tables, which were printed in nautical almanacs, into so many minutes North or South and into so many minutes East or West. The next space gave the overall distance covered by the passage, the fifth space was for the latitude of the ship arrived at by adding or subtracting the minutes shown in the third space to the previous day's latitude to bring it up to date. The sixth space gave the difference in longitude calculated from the departure shown in the third space (departure is a term applied to the distance which a ship has travelled either due East or due West measured in nautical miles. This will not correspond with the change of longitude, because the distance between meridians of longitude closes up as they go farther north until they meet at the North Pole; to arrive at the difference of longitude the departure has to be divided by the cosine of the latitude where the distance has been travelled) and in the seventh space this was added or subtracted to or from the previous day's longitude to give the present longitude. In the final space was entered the bearing and distance of the next landfall.

Dead reckoning was at best an imperfect science, as it relied on an accurate account of the distance travelled by the ship and of its course which varied with the wind, but eighteenth-century navigators had to rely on it as the only method available and a certain amount of intelligent guesswork usually supplemented the figures recorded, for instance, there were generally accepted rules for leeway.

> 1. If a ship be close hauled, has all her sails set, the water is smooth, and a moderate gale of wind, she is then supposed to make little or no leeway.
> 2. If it blow so fresh as to cause the small sails to be handed it is usual to allow one point.
> 3. If it blow so hard the topsails must be close reeft, then the common allowance is two points for leeway.

And there were further rules for stronger winds.

It is now intended to follow the Log on the passage to India, from Tuesday, 23 January 1787 to Tuesday, 22 May when the ship arrived at Madras.

On Tuesday, 23 January the weather was still hazy with the wind in the NNE veering round to the West. There was no land in sight and no possibility of an observation with the Quadrant: Start Point off the Devon coast was now North 61° West and at a distance of thirteen leagues: the latitude by account was 49° 50' N and the longitude 2° 56' W.

On Wednesday the weather was the same. The ship had travelled 182 miles from Beachy Head and the latitude was now 49° 24' N and the longitude was 4° 14' W with the bearing of the Scillies N 71° W, and these islands were thirty-four leagues away. On Thursday the wind sprang up and the ship was averaging 7½ knots. The sailmaker was employed in making a new driver, that is to say, a gaff sail for the mizzen mast. At 11 pm the Log recorded 'Down Topgallant Yards' and the bower anchors were stowed and also their cables were unbent, which was the normal practice as soon as the ship was out of sight of land.

Friday saw fresh gales and ugly weather: there was a steady wind from the South, which was in fact one point East of South, keeping the ship on a course of West South West and creating a high swell from the North Westward. The main topmast rigging was set up and the main topmast stayed to take the strain of the gale. On Saturday strong gales continued with a heavy cross sea and in the morning two reefs were made in the fore and mizzen topsails; and in the evening the topsails were handed, that is to say, taken down. The noon temperature was 56° Fahrenheit so it was not cold and the ship reached latitude 45° 15' and longitude 14° 44' which was due west of the Bay of Biscay but well out to sea.

The crew, whose day would have started with washing down the decks at 6.30 am, would have been fully occupied during the first week at sea, some engaged on the helm keeping the ship close enough to the wind for the sails to draw, some heaving the log which was done every hour and others on the rigging. Until Wednesday there would be a man in the chains heaving the lead to ensure that the ship did not ground.

The men worked on alternate watches so that there would be thirty-six on duty at a time. The larboard watch was under the command of the chief mate and the starboard watch under the command of the second mate. These names arose from the situation of the seamen's hammocks. The watches lasted for four-hour periods but the watch from 4 pm to 6 pm was divided into two dog watches so that the same men did not do the same duty each day. Eight bells were struck at the end of each watch, but four bells at the end of the dog watches, the bell being struck each half hour.

The ship was now in its second week at sea and the weather was squally but nevertheless the topsails were set on Sunday, 28th, but handed on Monday when the gales persisted. At last there was a sight of the midday sun which gave an opportunity to use instruments to check the ship's position. Huddart used a Hadley's quadrant, which by now had been tried and tested for some fifty years and one of its makers was John Morgan of Finch Lane, Cornhill, London where James Watt had worked as a young man before he turned his attention to steam engines, and he proved himself to be one of their best craftsmen. Huddart had one of John Arnold's chronometers which were the best the trade produced, but most sea captains had to rely on Maskelyne's lunar distance tables and Huddart used these to check his chronometer.

By dead reckoning the ship was in latitude 43° 30' N and longitude 15° 11' W and observation put the ship in latitude 43° 35' N and 14° 38' W longitude so that dead reckoning had put the ship five miles further south than it was and about half a degree further west at noon on Monday, 29th.

On Tuesday it was discovered that the ship was making two inches of water each hour amongst the transoms; the Log does not say what action was taken but presumably this was a job for the caulker to cure. The transoms were cross members which were probably leaking by the tiller.

The ship had now been at sea for ten days and Wednesday witnessed the first occasion of what to our generation was the unacceptable face of discipline at sea in the eighteenth century – the lash. At noon Thomas Clark, one of the recruits, was sentenced to one dozen lashes for insulting the chief officer and disobedience of orders, but the sentence was commuted by the Captain to six lashes. One of the gratings on the deck would be set up: the victim for punishment was stripped to the waist and strung up by his thumbs facing the grating. The punishment was administered by the boatswain with a cat o' nine tails after which a bucket of sea water was thrown over the wounds.

Discipline was as harsh in the East India Company as it was in the Royal Navy and it had to be: many of the seamen were rough types given to brutality and drunkenness, but nevertheless, steadfast in the teeth of a

gale and unflinching in battle. For the safety of the ship the authority of
the officers had to be unquestioned, and a short, sharp shock treatment
saved the problem of keeping men in irons until the ship docked. To be
overflowing with the milk of human kindness was hardly in keeping with
running a tight ship or with the spirit of the times, but kind heartedness
was very much Huddart's nature and he tended to be more lenient over
punishments than most Commanders. Humanitarianism, as has become
self evident in our time, can defeat itself by letting crime and violence get
out of hand.

At the start of Thursday, 1 February the wind was light and the main
topgallant was fidded and reefs were let out, but towards the evening a
breeze sprang up after a calm in which no headway was made; in three
days only 153 miles had been covered which was an average speed of
only two knots. Each day the Captain made a record in the Log of the
strength of the wind. The Beaufort scale had not come into existence but
the records follow the same pattern; Force 0 was Calm, Force 1 was Light
Airs Light Winds, 2 was Light Breeze or Pleasant Breeze, 3 Light Trade
or Pleasant Trade, 4 Moderate Trade or Moderate Breeze, 5 Fresh Breeze,
Steady Breeze or Favourable Trade and 6 Brisk Trade. Gales were described
Fresh, Moderate or Strong or Increasing or Decreasing.

On Saturday the Gundeck was scraped; traditionally this was done with
a soft sandstone known as holy stone, but no one is quite sure why it was
holy. One theory[1] is that the stones of the derelict church of St Helen's
at Bembridge on the Isle of Wight were found particularly suitable for the
job and accessible as Bembridge Roads was a favourite anchorage. The
larger pieces were called bibles and the smaller prayer books. Huddart
took the opportunity that day of making lunar observations to determine
his longitude, which showed dead reckoning to be more accurate than the
chronometer.

On Sunday, 4 February there was a heavy gale in the afternoon, two
reefs were taken in and the mizzen topsail handed and at 3 am a seaman,
John Pickers, was thrown from the foreyard but catching a rope from the
waist he was fortunately saved. Several other people were hurt and a main
topmast back stay chain was carried away.

The ship had now covered 866 miles and was in latitude 42° 24' and in
longitude 18° 52' W by dead reckoning but there was a discrepancy of 88'
between dead reckoning and the chronometer with the ship about 600 miles
off Madeira; the correct position of the ship would have to be verified as
soon as the next landfall was sighted.

On Wednesday the armourer repaired the damage to the stay chain; the
expression 'armourer' was a survival from a bygone age when armour was
worn: he was in fact the village blacksmith afloat.

The sight of the island Porto Sancto made it possible to check the position
of the ship. On 10 February it was about 13 or 14 leagues distant S 10° E
which indicated that the longitude logged was nearly a degree out and the
Log had to be corrected, giving the position of the ship's latitude 33° 20'
N and the longitude 16° 43' W. At noon the north point of Madeira was
S 73° W and Porto Sancto was from S 20° E to S 43° E at 6 am

At noon a conference of the officers was called to decide the course to be
taken: the ship was East of Madeira with the wind in the WNW. It was not

---

[1] E. Keble Chatterton, *The Old East Indiamen.*

possible therefore to weather the island, that is, to keep to the windward side of it and the log entry is as follows:

> Heavy swell from the Wward & Finding the Wind would not suffer us to weather Madeira; called a Consultation – officers & read the 20th paragraph of my instructions. We were unanimously of the opinion that in order to expedite the passage we ought to continue our course to the Southward tho' we should be forced within the Islands. Ordered the consultation to be entered & signed in the Log book.

Presumably the islands were the Canaries.

It was the second week of February and on Saturday, 10th Madeira was in sight at sunset West ¾ of a point South: 'The Extremes of the Deserters' was SW by W ½ W to SSE. At 7 am on Sunday the south of Madeira round the island of Dezerte was bearing N by W at a distance of 5 or 6 leagues and the ship had now passed Madeira. The chronometer required correction having gained more than allowed. The longitude of the ship was 16° 27½' W and there was a steady south western breeze giving the ship an average speed of 4 knots. On Monday the island of Palma came into sight at sunset S 26° W and on Wednesday the breeze stiffened with the ship averaging 7½ knots which continued until Sunday when the breeze became light. On Friday the mizzen topgallant was rigged.

Owing to the sickness on board, the lower deck was washed with vinegar, the Jeyes Fluid of the eighteenth century and later was burnt on the lower deck. It is doubtful whether this had any effect as sickness plagued the rest of the voyage taking its toll in the death of recruits.

During the week the cables were paid down into the hold and an old mainsail brought into use: economy in the use of gear demanded that old sails were used in light winds. The cooper was employed in shaking butts, several of which would by now be empty, giving a chance to repair them.

On Saturday for the first time the great guns were exercised but, fortunately, they never had to be used in earnest, and during the week various observations were made to establish the sun's amplitude, that is, the number of degrees the sun was distant from true East or true West to calculate the variation of the compass which had to be done at intervals during the passage.

It was now the third week of February and on Sunday, 18th Divine Service was performed for the first time. The Company's rule for having a service every Sunday at this time was more honoured in the breach than the observance but later the rules became stricter and the Log had to show that a service had been performed each Sunday or, if not, the reason for not having a service had to be entered in the Log book.

The Commander of the ship would read such prayers from the Forms of Prayer to be used at sea in the Prayer Book as he found appropriate and in addition the Company had its own prayer entitled 'A Prayer for the Honourable English Company trading into the East Indies to be used on board their Ships'.

> O Almighty and most Merciful Lord God, Thou art the Sovereign Protector of all that Trust in Thee, and the Author of all Spiritual and Temporal Blessings. Let Thy Grace, we most humbly beseech Thee, be always Present with thy Servants the English Company Trading to the East Indies. Compass them with thy Favour as a shield. Prosper them in all their Publick Undertakings, and make them Successful in all their Affairs both by Sea and Land. Grant that they may prove a common Blessing, by promoting the Holy Religion

of our Lord Jesus Christ. Be more especially at this time favourable to us, who are separated from all the world, and have our sole dependance upon Thee here in the Great Waters. Thou shewest thy wonders in the Deep, by commanding the Winds and the Seas as Thou pleaseth, and Thou alone canst bring us into the Haven where we would be. To thy Power and Mercy therefore we humbly fly for Refuge and Protection from all Dangers of this long and Perilous voyage. Guard us continually with thy good Providence in every place. Preserve our Relations and Friends whom we have left, and at length bring us home to them again in safety and with the desired Success. Grant that everyone of us, being always mindful of thy Fatherly Goodness, and Tender Compassion towards us, may glorifie thy Name by a constant Profession of the Christian Faith, and by a Sober, Just and Pious Conversation through the remaining part of our Lives. All this we beg for the sake of our Saviour Jesus Christ, to whom with Thee and the Blessed Spirit be as ascribed all Honour, Praise and Dominion both now and for evermore. Amen.

The prayer was sanctioned by the Archbishop of Canterbury and the Bishop of London who added to their signatures 'We do conceive that this prayer may be very proper to be used for the purpose expressed in the title of it'. The prayer itself did not measure up to that appointed for the Navy and it lacked the colourful metaphors of the Collects, neither was it devoid of self-seeking overtones: but, if it aroused men's faith in the same all-powerful arm protecting those far away at home and those at sea then at least there was a moment in which doubts and fears could fade and hope be just over the horizon.

Every available man would be paraded for the Service and attend in his best dress, but there was an extra demand for hands this Sunday as a good lookout had to be kept for the Bonnetta Shoal and soundings were being taken for the twelve-hour period from 7 am till 6 pm. The latitude of the ship was now 15° 33' N and the longitude 20° 46' W. There followed a week of fair weather and fair breezes during which the ship was covering about a hundred miles each day, the temperature rising as the ship moved towards the Equator.

Sickness was now becoming a problem, particularly among the recruits and on Monday, 19th there were thirty-two on the sick list. On the following day the first death occurred among the recruits, with another on the following Sunday. On the same day the recruits' clothing was examined and they were 'served with necessaries', that is, issued with kit; the word 'necessaries' survives in Army parlance to mean kit and other uniform. It seems unlikely that the clothing was being examined for lice, because although the eighteenth-century mind realised that the best cure for lice was cleanliness, it did not associate lice with typhus, which could have been the reason for so much fever on board with men sleeping practically on top of each other.

During the week there had been attention to the rigging: on Monday the bobstays were set up and the fore topmast rigging, and the following day the worst foresail was brought into use. This process was repeated on the following Friday when the main topsail was shifted for the third best and the main topgallant with the worst.

On Thursday a Dolphin Striker was rigged as a longer jibboom had been brought into use; this is a short spar fixed under the bowsprit and at right angles to it which carried the stay on the end of the bowsprit at an increased angle giving it more purchase. Dolphin strikers were unusual at this date, and this would have been made on board: the carpenter was also engaged making a spare topgallant yard.

On Tuesday, 27th there is an entry in the Log 'Find damage go quite forward in the lower part of the breadroom amongst the Bread'. Accordingly the bread had to be taken up from the breadroom to allow a bulkhead to be made in the after part of the breadroom. On the last day of February the latitude by account was 1° 51' N and by observation 1° 65': the longitude was 17° 32' W by account and 17° 58' W by the chronometer. The ship was due South of Cape Verde, the most westerly point of Africa and about 125 sea miles North of the Equator.

Sunday,4 March witnessed another punishment. On the preceding day a recruit, Thomas Clark, had jumped overboard. It was not unknown for men under the threat of punishment to jump overboard, although hundreds of miles out to sea this could spell only suicide; however, in this case, the ship hove to and picked him up in the jolly boat. The next day he was sentenced to twenty-four lashes for 'Bad Behaviour'. Captain Huddart was usually the one with whom mercy tempered justice, but not in this case, so it seems that 'Bad Behaviour' must have been an understatement of a much graver offence. Was this a quest for the golden bolt in the keelson? There was no gay liberation in Georgian England whatever may have gone on behind closed doors, and captains were very circumspect about what they put in the Log books.

It has to be remembered that Victorianism had a reign of sixty glorious years before that great queen ascended the throne and set upon it her seal of royal approval, during which time Bowdler had expunged from Shakespeare and Holy Writ the words no longer in polite use; offending street names were swept away – Codpiece Row reappeared as Coppice Row; Dr Johnson had already denied space in his dictionary for any words he considered unfit for print, and lead fig leaves were being nailed to marble statues that displayed too much of the naked nature and the living grace. In spite of his punishment Thomas Clark survived the passage to India where let us hope he mended his ways.

On 6 March we get a glimpse of what went on on board: 'Boatswain employed fitting Bonticks Splicing Eyes in the New Messengers and drawing of Yarns Armourer at Forge & Caulkers on the Boats Sailmaker on 2nd best Foresail Soldiers picking Oakum.' The identity of Bontick seems to have been lost with the passage of time, but possibly these were metal eyes spliced into the messenger, the rope that carried the cable onto the capstan, to receive the nippers which bound the cable onto the messenger. One wonders how the soldiers were occupied as this is the only reference in the Log to what they did.

The first part of March started with light breezes from the South East gathering force after a few days; with all three courses of sails set the ship was making an average speed of six knots, its course being South Southwest and about six points off the wind, which took the ship towards the Brazilian coast. On 11 March the islands of Martinvas were sighted and the island of Trinidad, or Trinidada as it appears in the Log book, was within reach. This island was 700 miles off the Brazilian coast lying in latitude 20° 30' S and longitude 29° 50' W.

On approaching Trinidad a consultation of officers was called at which it was agreed to fill up with water there and try to get some fresh food for the sick, as there had been further deaths of a recruit and a seaman in the preceding days. It was quite evident that the infection which caused

the fevers had been brought from England as the ship had had no contact
with any White Man's Grave since it left the Downs; if any man had come
on board infected with typhus it would have spread very quickly through
the ship with fatal results.

The Log for Monday, 12 March reads:

> At 4 p.m. Sent the Pinnace ahead & at 5 Anchored with the small bower in
> 21 fm. the Nine Pin E & the Extreams of Trinidada from NE to SE dist from
> Nine Pin about ¾ Mile. Out all Boats & run the Kedge with Nine Inch Hawser
> to seaward to steady her; Sent Mr. Harriman (who I appoint Beach Master)
> to examine the Watering Place who returned at 8 p.m. with a favourable
> account. At about 4 a.m. put 30 Butts Gang Casks &c. into the Boats & sent
> them to Water – but the surf had risen so much during the Night that no
> person could land. Mr. Harriman dispatched the Pinnace between 9 & 10 to
> Inform me, Made the signal to all Boats. At 11 weighed the Bower & warped
> off to the Kedge; at Noon got under way & brought too to take in our Boats.
> We saw no inhabitants to converse except two Fishing Boats with Portuguese
> that came along side after we were under way & told us that there was water
> on the E side but a fresh Trade blowing rendered it impractible to water to
> Windward, nor can this Island be depended upon as a small swell occasioning
> a Surf that will prevent taking water from that rocky shore. We got nothing
> by comming here except a few fish. Therm 78°.

The Log for Tuesday, 13 March reads:

> Found both our Bower & Hawser rubbed by laying on coarse ground, tho'
> only 19 hours at Anchor & Commodore Johnstone says this is the only good
> anchorage about the Island.

> At 6 p.m. Took our departure from Trinidada allowing it to lay Lat 20° 26' S
> Lo Chron 29.25½ W This Lo 29° was determined by the Chron corrected by
> a Mean of 15 Setts of lunar Obs. taken between 24th ult'o & 4th inst brought
> Down by the Chronr by N 36 from Eng'd 29° 24
>
> $$\begin{array}{r} 29 \quad 26 \\ \hline \end{array}$$
>
> Mean 29 25
> Latitude Obs 22° 14' S.

Commodore George Johnston (1730–87) was MP for Cockermouth in
1768 in Huddart's young days and he was elected a director of the East
India Company in 1783. He commanded a small squadron as commodore
on the Portuguese coast in 1779 and gained some successes in leading an
expedition against the French in 1781 but his delay defeated his objective
at the Cape of Good Hope.

On leaving Trinidad there was a change of course; the ship had, in fact,
taken a big tack across the Atlantic and then had to take a tack back to the
African coast. The course was set for the Cape of Good Hope which was
reckoned to be at a distance of 882 leagues. The weather was still fair but
the wind fell away and at one time there was a complete calm. This gave an
opportunity for work to be done on the sails and rigging. Before reaching
Trinidad the sailmaker was engaged on middle-stitching the second best
foresail and shifting a part which, with the say, had been rubbed through;
say was a tightly spun and closely woven woollen cloth sewn down the
middle part of a sail to prevent the sailcloth chafing against the mast.

On 20 March there was a strong gale and the topgallant masts were struck
and the stays set up, but by noon the wind had dropped and the main and
mizzen topsails were set and the main topgallant mast fidded. But there
had been some damage to the rigging as the main topsail yard had been
sprung a foot from the slings and the topsail split. The yard had to be got

down to fish it: this was done by binding pieces of wood as splints over the part that was split.

At this point the Log also records that the armourer was engaged in making a boom iron for a topgallant studding sail or stuns'l. These sails had been in existence since the end of Queen Elizabeth's reign and they were narrow sails rigged on the leech of the principal sail to give the effect of increasing its width. The extension of their use to topsail gallants was probably a recent innovation. To give the yard additional length to carry the studding sail a boom was run out through two iron rings and these were made in the form of a figure of eight, so that one part of the iron fitted round the yard and the other part carried the stuns'l boom.

By Sunday, 25 March the ship was approaching the island of Tristan da Cunha. There was no divine service this Sunday but a service had been held on the 18th, the previous Sunday. At 10.30 am on Tuesday the fog cleared and the island of Tristan da Cunha came into view. To quote the Log for the 26th:

> At 10 Clearing up at ½ past saw the Island of Tristan da Cunha about S ¾ E dist 12 Leagues At noon the Peak bore S 2 W dist about 10 Leagues. On 12th Oct'r 1780 pass'd to the S'ward of those Is. made the height of this Peak above the Sea Level Yds 2396
> This day 2506
>
> Mean Yds 2451
>
> The difference may arise E'r in Lat: 37° 10'
> Latit: Obs'd 36.37 S
> Lo. Chr 12.   17 W Therm 68°.

The Log for the 27th reads:

> At 4 P.M. the High Peak of the Island Tristan da Cunha S 55° W dist about 11 Leagues from which I take my departure Allowing it to Lay in Latt 37° 10' Lo 12° 14' W by Chron corrected by means of 15) Obs.

In October 1780 Huddart was on his passage to India where he joined Admiral Sir Edward Hughes. As the Island was discovered by the Portuguese Admiral Tristao da Cunha one must assume, though the island was at this date uninhabited, that it was claimed as a Portuguese possession. It was not until 1816, at the time of Napoleon's exile to St Helena, that the British put a garrison there.

On taking departure from Tristan da Cunha the ship changed course which by 10 am was due East and by noon the following day the course was North 86° East and heading for the Cape. This course is held for the rest of the month with the ship averaging 5½ knots.

29 March bears another entry of a punishment.

> P.M. Punished Adam Johnston Seaman by sentence of the Commander & Officers with two Doz. Lashes for Quarrelling with the Military, Mutinous behaviour insulting Midshipmen & insolence to Mr. Moore Ch'f Officer, he was excused with one doz. but Johnston insisted on having the other doz. which he was favoured with.

There was a strong gale on the evening of Friday, 30th which split the fore topsail; as a result the main topsail was handed and a reef taken in, but in the morning the topsails were all set with the reefs out, the second best main topsail being used. The following day the ship crossed the Greenwich meridian in latitude 34° 40' S on a course which was due East for the Cape reckoned then to be at a distance of 293 leagues.

The ship had so far been making her passage in the Atlantic but during the month of April she rounded the Cape and set course across the Indian Ocean for Madras. After leaving Trinidad the ship crossed the Tropic of Capricorn going southward and by the end of April she crossed it again travelling northward for Ceylon and Madras.

At the beginning of April the ship was 800 nautical miles east of the Cape in latitude 34° 36′ S: the most southern point of the Cape Province was about 34° 49′ South and with a fair wind, mostly from the South West, it was possible to stem an eastward course veering further South to round the Cape. At one point the wind was strong enough to necessitate reefs and for a topsail brace, one of the ropes that trim the sail, to be carried away, but as the ship neared the Cape the wind veered to the North. After the first week of April the ship was logged on a course for Ceylon.

By 6 April the ship was due South of the Cape in latitude 37° 42′ S on an East Northeast course, which took the ship within 127 nautical miles of the Cape. By 10 April the course had to be changed to the South, to avoid the Agulhas currents and counter-currents.

For the last ten days of April an average speed of 5⅔ knots was maintained from the strong winds in the Indian Ocean. On the 27th there was a gale carrying away the crossjack and a topsail yard had to be rigged as the crossjack yard. The gales continued through the following day and the fore topsail was furled and two reefs made in the main topsail – the topsail gallant yards were sent down. By the following day the gale had subsided and reefs were out, the mizzen topsail set and the topsail gallant yards were up.

By 1 May the Tropic of Capricorn had been crossed and the distance to Ceylon was now 1,634 sea miles which lay on a bearing NNE by North. From a health point of view it has been a disastrous month: the sailmaker, a seaman and another four recruits had died, and another recruit drowned by jumping overboard in the darkness. Going back to 5 April there was an entry in the Log: 'This day began serving Wheat in which was put three gal. Spirits & sweetened with sugar.' What merit there was thought to be in this strange concoction one cannot say, but certainly by this time much of the illness on board ship was thought to be caused by lack of fresh food. People died unaccountably in the eighteenth century and the words of the burial service, 'in the midst of life we are in death', did not sound strange to their ears, but the mortality among the recruits must have been far above normal.

Out of a hundred recruits only eighty reached Madras, one having been discharged and yet they were exposed to no infection except what they brought with them and were only four months at sea. One assumes that the recruits were young men in the prime of life, but were probably undernourished and in a poor state of health when they came on board, and liable to succumb to any form of infection. The fever which spread through the lower deck was probably typhus, not uncommon in ships and spread, among other things, by lice which were common among the great unwashed of the eighteenth century.

At the beginning of May the ship was nearing the end of its passage. It was due South of Mysore and just North of the Tropic of Capricorn. The weather was squally and the ship's course would now be North by East with 2,000 miles to go and the wind in the East. Soundings had to be made on 7 May as the ship was nearing the Chagos Archipelago, but there was no ground. By the 8th the wind that had enabled a speed of seven knots to be maintained died away. But there were fresh gales on the 9th necessitating reefs, with the ship nearing the Maldive Islands by the 11th. Bombay was within 163 miles. The bower anchors were unstowed.

The following day the wind freshened and sails had to be shortened. The Log reads:

> At 7 A.M. made the Is of Ceylon bearing NW by N about 10 or 12 Leagues At noon the Extreams from W by N to the Elephaunt NE by N 9 Leags. dist. from the Nearest Low Land with a sandy beach Bear'g from NW to N about 3 or 4 Leagues.

On 13 May at 3.30 pm the Elephaunt bore North about five leagues away.

The ship was being guided by what was called oblique sailing, that is, fixing its course by taking bearing onto the shore. On Monday, 14th there was only a light wind from the North and soundings were being taken but no ground reached. The Log records:

> At sunset the Extremes of the Land is SW to NW Adams Peak W ½ S off shore and at Sunrise the Extremes of the Land S 15° W to N 58° W. The High Peak WW 20° South dist off shore about 40 Leagues.

Adams Peak was on the East of Ceylon: 'At noon Extremes from S 40° W to NE 70° W The Fryers Hood N 79° W dist off shore about 4 Leagues.' Friar's Hood was also on the coast of Ceylon.

The Log for Tuesday, 15th records: 'Spoke a Grab ship Capt'n Dane bound to Madras left Bombay the 20th ulto No news.' The Grabship was the *Dolphin*, a two-masted coasting vessel with a prow peculiar to the East.

> At Noon Fryers Hood bore S 30°. 5 W Dist 6 Leags. from which I take my departure allowing it to lay in Latt per Nicholson 8° 16' N Lo per Chron 81.48 E.

The weather has been threatening since Tuesday and now on Saturday 19th the Log reads:

> A heavy loaded Sky threatening much No Sun all day at 6 P.M. saw the high land & two ships in Pondicherry Road bear'g W ¼ N dist about 5 Leag's. From 6 till midnight heavy squally variable but Principaly from the Northward. At 1 A.M. clear'd a little but at 6 came on heavy with a Cross confused Sea Principaly from the ENEward which makes the ship Laboursome & Strikes heavy abaft.
> At noon brought too head per NEward   No Observation.

This was followed by a day where the ship was obviously at the centre of a violent storm, with the wind changing as the eye of the storm moved northwards; a hard gale was logged and little progress was made. By Monday, 20th the storm had abated but at midnight there was a squall and the mainsail was split, and then a footrope was carried away.

On 21 May at Sunrise land was sighted W by N and at noon Kettle Bottom was S 72° W four leagues off shore; then at 6 pm the the Pulicat Flagstaff was WSW at a distance of three leagues. On Tuesday, 22nd Fort St George came into view at sunrise and by 2 pm the ship was anchoring in Madras Roads: the flagstaff was now NW by W.

The Fort was saluted with nine guns which it returned. The Packet was sent ashore with the Purser; the Purser, it appears, was the first to go ashore when a destination was reached and the last to come on board when the ship sailed. Another recruit died shortly after anchoring. The Sea Log continued until midnight at which time the Harbour Journal commenced so as to coincide with the days in the calendar.

The ship had made its passage to Madras in 120 days with no hazards, no unnecessary delays and with no damage to be repaired. At Madras ships had to ride at anchor out to sea, with no relief from the relentless motion of the waves.

CHAPTER IV

Whampoa

MADRAS CENTRED round Fort George which was built by the British in 1639. Its position had no real topographical significance and there was no harbour apart from Coum River for small vessels. Until the end of the eighteenth century the only harbours were natural harbours. The Company's ships lay at anchor in Madras Roads, being joined by the *Royal Admiral* on Tuesday, 22 May at 2 pm. The customary salute of nine guns was given by the ship and returned by the Fort and the next day at noon the Captain went ashore and was saluted by the Fort with nine guns, which was returned by the ship. The recruits were also sent ashore.

Strong southern breezes set up a swell making it an uncomfortable anchorage. On Thursday and Friday the Company of Hanoverians and their baggage were disembarked, glad no doubt to be on terra firma after four months at sea. Owing to sickness among the crew, sixteen of them were sent ashore to hospital, while eighteen Lascars were brought on board to replace them. Two midshipmen and two of the tradesmen had died: Thomas Temple, one of the midshipmen, had signed on as a seaman and possibly had to wait to reach the age of fourteen before becoming a midshipman.

The first three weeks after reaching Madras were spent in getting the cargo ashore, including a quantity of coal required, no doubt, for forges. Loading and unloading ships was a slow business as it had to be done with the aid of lighters. There were frequent entries in the Log of 'Clearing the Hawse'. The 'hawse' was the distance of the ship from a point on the water immediately above the anchor and it was necessary to ensure that there was nothing fouling the anchor. Two anchors would have been used to moor a ship and changes of wind and tide could have resulted in the cable of one anchor catching on flukes of the other anchor and causing it to drag.

From 12 June to 9 July, when the ship took its departure from Madras, fresh cargo was taken on board to get the ship ready for its passage to China. China in the eighteenth century was not a market for European imports – according to the Emperor Chien Lung, China had everything it needed. This was a short-sighted boast, because technical advancement in the West was far ahead of anything in the East in spite of the skill and ingenuity of their craftsmen.

It appears that cotton was a commodity which found a market in China and seventy-eight bales were loaded on board and an unspecified number later. The amount of cotton in a bale varied from place to place. Most of the cotton for Britain was shipped from the Antilles in three-hundredweight bales and probably bales from the Coromandel Coast weighed about the same, which gives some idea of the tonnage involved.

The journal mentions 'People stowing the Lazaretta'. This was not a sick-bay as might be expected but a space between decks in merchant ships used in this case for stowing bales of cotton.

Taking water on board was left until the last few days before the ship sailed, when sixteen leagers and eight butts were taken on board. A leager contained 159 gallons and a butt 108 gallons, so that the total amount of water taken on board was over three thousand gallons, which was sufficient for three pints a day for each of the ship's complement. Rice was evidently intended as a daily ration, and cooking it would in itself require a considerable amount of water.

A week before the ship sailed the effects of the deceased midshipmen and seamen were sold at the mast: in a more sentimental age parents of young mariners would have liked their few possessions as mementoes rather than a trifling sum of cash their sale might raise.

On Monday, 9 July the Purser was the last to come aboard, waiting for any last minute mail or orders, and at 10 am the ship weighed anchor, saluted the Fort with nine guns and took her departure from Fort St George (Latitude 13° 47' and Longitude 80° 21¾' E) for the Prince of Wales Island, otherwise Penang, an island off the Malay coast at the northern end of the Malacca Straits. This island constituted one of the settlements of the East India Company and was dominated by Fort Cornwallis. The Company had already started to develop what became British policy in the nineteenth century of having ports of call round the world, which became coaling stations in the age of steam. Thus Britannia ruled the waves. The East India Company was concerned only with ports of call on its own trade routes.

The ship's course was set for the Islands of Nicobar, a distance of 763 miles which took a week to reach. Monday was a stormy night and about midnight we have an eyewitness account of a phenomenon that is inclined to be regarded as fictional rather than real – St Elmo's fire: 'A Corposant or ball of fire as large as a plannet was visible on the truck of the Main Top Gallant Masthead about 4 Hours in the first and middle Watch.' The first watch was 8 pm until midnight and the middle watch was midnight to 4 am.

Huddart was an accurate observer of scientific phenomenon and, of course, electro-static discharges of this nature are not unknown, but one rarely comes across such a positive account. To sailors of that period it was a favourable omen and medieval sailors attributed it to their patron saint Erasmus, martyred in 304 AD, whose name became corrupted to Elmo: it was regarded as an outward and visible sign of the saint's special protection. 'Corposant' was borrowed from the Portuguese word 'corpo santo'.

A southerly wind enabled the ship to stem an East Southeastern course across the Bay of Bengal at an average speed of 5½ knots and after six days at sea the islands of Nicobar came into view at 1 pm on 15 July.

At 6 pm on Sunday, 15th there appeared on the horizon 'the extreams of the Nicobars from SE by S to S by E ¾ E Katchowel N ¾ E to N ¾ W (Katchall) Mirrow SE by E ½ E dis't about 2 Leagues'. Then there was a further entry 'At Sunrise the Extreams of the Great Nicobar at S 55° W to S 67° W dis't about 12 or 13 Leagues'. A fair breeze continued throughout Monday but after midnight it died away. On the 17th the Log records:

Strong ripplings which extends in a right line from SW to NE as far as the eye can reach. In succession they pass us, & proceed in a progression motion to N.W'ward at intervals of a few Hours; with a velocity of from 5' to 12' per hour.

The ripplings continue until:

This morning the 19th ripplings have changed. The Line extends from East to West & pass with near the same velocity to the E'ward. They are more in number than yesterday. Sometimes can view three lines at the same time & pass the Ship more frequently. The Sea quite Glossy between the ripplings.

On the morning of 20 July, quoting again from the Log:

Saw the High Land of Junk Ceylon the top of the Highest Mountain N 60½° E – dis't about 17 Leagues.

Junk Ceylon is an island off the extreme south of Siam known as Ko Phuket. The wind had died away now and the speed of the ship was about one knot, but a moderate breeze sprang up again on the 21st when there were further sightings of land as the ship reached the North of Sumatra.

At this stage there was an incident on board in which a seaman, Matthew Denton, threatened to stab another, Elias Corbly, and cut the driver. Denton seems to have gone berserk and he died on 10 September, but in the meantime there was no sympathy for psychiatric cases: he got a dozen lashes.

The wind soon died away again as the ship got under the lee of Sumatra. At 5 pm the highest mountain of the Boutan Islands was seen South East of the ship about 9 leagues away and by noon of the following day the extreme of the island was South South East. At this point soundings were taken; in fact there was a man in the chains throughout the Malacca Straits.

On Monday, 23rd light airs and calm is the weather report and the ship barely averaged one knot. To quote from the Log: 'at 5 p.m. the Ex's of Pt Boutain @ 38° 45' to S 53° 50'' on the 24th 'At Sun Sett Boutan Is from N 62° E to S 86. 30 E dis't from nearest Land about 5 miles'. The ship was travelling southwards along the Malay Coast to Penang, which came into view on the 25th East South East of the ship and the depth of water was 30 to 40 fathoms. At sunset the extremes of Penang were from S 22° 30' to S 51° 30' E and its distance is about six leagues. The depth of water was only 18 fathoms and the ship anchored till daylight.

The Log records: 'Came too with best Bower in 16 Fath. veer'd to ½ cable – Quedah Peak E by N Nothern Extreme of Puli Penang SE'. Half a cable was the length of the mooring and that was 300 feet. At daylight the ship weighed anchor and twelve hours later came to anchor again in the Penang Roads. The Log for the 27th reads:

Moderate breezes & fair – At 5 P.M. out Pinnace & set her ahead; at 6 Anchored with small Bower in 3¼ Fm. Prince of Wales Island from 51° 10 W to S 53° E Quedah Peak N 35. 10 E – At 5 A.M. weighed Wind ESE to work into the Harbour, but finding only 4¼ Fm & a heavy swell from the NW'ward stood off again & Anchored with best Bower in 6 Fm. at 8 A.M. sent the Pinnace on shore with the Purser & Letters. The Lascelles came out of the Harbour & Anchored at 11 A.M. about a mile within us, the Wind faltring under the Lee of the Island. Lat Obs 5° 32' 20" at 4 P.M. sighted the Anchor & found it foul. Let go the small Bower.

N.B. This Log consists of 36 hours to begin a Harbour Journal.

An impression of Prince of Wales Island, as Penang was then known, can be gained from a watercolour painted a generation later, which shows the sea in the foreground and the fortifications of Fort Cornwallis stretching along the sea shore with the Union Jack flying from a tall flagstaff to identify the British presence. A scattering of other buildings extend along the shore with the vegetation of the jungle behind of that intensive green which makes England's green fields appear brown to the returning traveller. Forming the background are the bare mountains of Malay with their hillsides not yet covered with rubber plantations. When the ship left England it was cold and clammy: here it would be hot and clammy with temperatures in the eighties Fahrenheit, though one might expect much higher temperatures in an equitorial region were it not for the excessive humidity.

It took from 6 August to the 25th to get through the Straits of Singapore during which time no account was kept of dead reckoning: the ship's position could be determined by what was called oblique sailing, that is to say, by taking bearings off the shore. At the same time, continual soundings were made as the depth of the Straits was thirty to forty fathoms, shelving off to no depth at all near the coast line. The last sight of Penang was at noon on the 8th when the highest part was recorded as 20 leagues away bearing N 26° E.

On the 9th Pulo Jarra was recorded as S 45° E, on the 10th it was South South East 6 or 7 leagues away, on the 11th its bearing was SE ½° S about 4 leagues away. On the 12th Pulo Jarra was 3 leagues due South and by the 13th it was South West by South and at noon the ship passed within 3 leagues of the place. Although the ship was averaging about 1½ knots it had made very little progress through having to tack. On the 16th the *King George* bound for China was encountered and this ship would be one of the ships at Whampoa, sailing for England two weeks before the *Royal Admiral*.

The ship was now leaving the Straits of Malacca for Singapore and was still meeting up with the *King George*; Pariclar Hill on the larboard or port side was due East at 10 am on the 16th and thus the ship made slow progress round the Malay Peninsula to Singapore. The Log records on the 18th: 'At Noon the Ext. from the Water Islands N 34° W to S 82° E Mount Formossa S 85° E off shore about 3 or 4 Leagues – *King George* hull down ahead'. Each night the ship anchored during the hours of darkness.

At 5 pm on the 19th the pinnace was sent to reconnoitre, keeping along the northern shore in not less than six fathoms. A pinnace was an open boat about thirty feet long manned with oars rigged as a barque or a schooner and used for scouting. So long as it kept a course with a depth of six fathoms the ship could follow without any fear of grounding. Actually the minimum depth recorded by soundings was four and a half fathoms.

At sunrise on Monday, 20 August 'The Great Carriman (Karimoen) E Hum'k S 30° E – Po Pissang (Pisang) N 69° E. Mount Formossa N 38° W.' The ship weighed anchor while the pinnace was off again to reconnoitre. The Log continues:

> 7 P.M. Anchored off Barn Island but finding the Ground Coarse &c. too near the shore at 8 Weigh'd & at 10 Anchored again in 18 Fm. soft Ground – The Ext'mes of Barn Island from E to NE by N the Coney E by S½S dist. from

the Island about ¾ mile. At daylight out Pinnace & Jolly boat & sent all the empty Cask on shore. Sailmaker repairing M. Topsail & Driver.

On the 21st the ship remained at anchor and the Log records:

> Light Airs variable and cloudy weather with some rain. P.M. Received on board Fifteen Butts and ten Gang Casks of water. At 1 P.M. departed this Life Dennis Macdonald Ship's Cook. Sent the Corps ashore to be interr'd. Having little wind sent the Carpenter on shore awooding – Received on board two boatloads of Wood – In Boats – Anchored here the Soloman Grab Ship from Pulo Pinang.

> At 10 A.M. a small breeze from the SW Weigh'd and made sail but a Squall comming from the SE'ward. Anchored again with best Bower at Noon. The Ext's of Barn Island from the N 50° to N 79° E in 12 Fm about 2 miles from Barn Island.

The Log for the remainder of Thursday the 23rd records:

> The first part much rain & heavy looking Weather, at 6 A.M. Weigh'd fresh breezes from the W'ward.

> At 7 Rounded the Rabit & Coney at the distance of about ¾ of a mile – at 8½ A.M. Part the Is'd of St. Johns S 77° W about mid Channel.

At 9 pm the ship anchored with the small bower and at 5 am the following morning weighed anchor again with a fresh gale from the North West by West and it was squally; at 8 Pedro Bianco was seen S 11° E and at noon Barbucett Hill was bearing S 70° 30' W Bintang S 14° W the ship's distance from land being 4 or 5 leagues.

On the 25th the ship emerged from the confined waters of the straits to the South China Seas; on Sunday, 26th with light winds and a smooth sea at 6 am the Anambas Archipelago had been passed in the night and lay ten or twelve leagues to the South.

From the Straits of Singapore the course was set for the Island of Sapatu a hundred miles off the coast of Vietnam. On the 25th the Extremes of Anambas were bearing N 86° 50' E to S 67° 5' E to starboard and the western hummock of Po Timoan (Tioman) was S 69° W; soundings were still being taken until Latitude 4° N is reached when the depth was 40 to 50 fathoms. The winds were light in the South China Sea and it being Sunday, 2 September a Divine Service was held.

At 9 am on Monday, 3rd Sapatu was sighted from the masthead and at noon the Captain took his departure from Sapatu latitude 10° N and longitude 109° 7' E. The destination was now Macao. On the 9th the ship reached the Macclesfield Shoal and soundings had to be taken again. The name Macclesfield sounds out of place in the South China Sea, but it must be derived from the Macclesfield which was the first ship to start the trade with Canton and which arrived back in England in the year 1700 laden with a rich cargo of silks, pepper, tea, etc.

It was now 10 September and the ship was on course for Macao which it took five days to reach. A ship which had already been sighted now proved to be the *Surprize of Bengal* and at 1 pm a boat came from the ship and brought the disagreeable news of the death of William Huddart. He was Joseph Huddart's eldest son and the commander of the *York*, then at Macao.

William Huddart had died on 30 March 1787, nearly six months earlier, and since then Joseph Huddart had been at sea apart from stopping at Bombay. William Huddart was a promising young man, who had started as an apprentice in his father's brig *Patience,* and served with his father as a midshipman in 1777 on her voyage to Bombay and then again in 1779 as fifth mate. At this point, his father could not promote him further in the *Royal Admiral* as it would have meant advancing him over his other officers, but he managed to get him appointed as second officer with Captain Frazer in the *Mansfield,* which returned to England in 1785. At this time the *York* was being chartered for an extra voyage to St Helena and China and Sir Richard Hotham offered the command to William although he was only twenty-two years old.

Though William was a young man, he had already had trouble with his health and should have declined the offer, but the opportunity was too good to miss. However, the strain and fatigue of the command hastened his declining health and he died in China. During his time at Canton he formed a friendship with John Henry Cox, who had come to Canton in 1781 and established himself as a successful trader, and who is said to have fathered the well-known firm of Jardine Matheson & Co. He was the son of a clockmaker and goldsmith in Shoe Lane, London, who made time pieces and automata for the Chinese market, but finished up bankrupt and his son had to pay off his debts. His letter of condolence to Mr Mills, the Purser of the *York,* reads as follows:

Canton 4th April 1787

Dear Sir,

I have just received yours of the 31st March last from on board the York in Macao Roads, confirming the melancholy intelligence of the death of Captain William Huddart; I do assure you that none of his friends can more sincerely deplore this unfortunate and untimely event than myself, having, during the little time I enjoyed the pleasure of his acquaintance, conceived a very great regard and friendship for him; this, together with the respect I bear to his father, had determined me before the receipt of your letter to pay all possible honor to his memory, and to have a handsome marble tablet placed over his grave, with a short and suitable inscription. I expect to set off for Macao this afternoon and will immediately upon my arrival give the necessary orders for this purpose; should his friends in England be desirous of having any particular inscription placed over his tomb, they may be assured of their wishes on this head being most punctually attended to. With respect to any expenses that may be incurred in carrying these intentions into execution I shall insist upon being permitted to bear them myself accepting with a melancholy satisfaction the opportunity of testifying my regard and attachment to so aimable and valuable a character as was that of your friend.

I remain, dear Sir,
Your obedient Servant,
JOHN HENRY COX

Joseph Huddart's motto had been 'Fear God' but on the death of his son he admitted that his faith had deserted him; we are told 'that it was the first and only time in his life of hardships and vicissitudes he had repined the dispensations of Providence, but he hoped the Almighty in his infinite mercy would forgive him'.

Unfortunately, William Huddart's success at sea was not matched in his private trade; when the *York* arrived back in England there was a loss of £700. Although his father could ill afford to make good the loss, out of respect for his son he discharged it rather than allow the creditors to suffer the loss.

The passage to China was nearly completed. At noon on the 16th the

Asses Ears came into view on a North West bearing about 7 or 8 leagues away and at 2 pm on the following day a pilot came on board from Macao to take the ship into the Macao Roads where she anchored at 10 pm. The Harbour Journal commenced on 18 September on a fine warm day. Huddart must have had a feeling of relief that the voyage had concluded without any mishap but tinged with grief at the loss of his eldest son, who had shown such promise in the Honourable Company's service.

The ship was lying about twelve miles out to sea with Macao West North West by West, situated as it is on the starboard entrance of the harbour that is to say the west side of the harbour. Macao was a Portuguese settlement founded as far back as 1557 and from paintings of George Chinnery done some forty years later, one gets the impression of a quite extensive town rising up from the Praya Grande, the water front, with Portuguese style architecture dominated by a church and convent on the skyline.

There were two bars at the entrance of the harbour to be crossed at high tide, but while the tide was still flooding. When the ship anchored the wind was coming off the land but by 10 pm when the flood tide began there was a breeze from the South. Even so the ship refused to steer and had to anchor. Eventually, on the following day, she was able to reach the Bocca Tigris – the entrance to the harbour. Chinese paintings show the Anunghoy forts on the right and those of the Wantong Island on the left lying below the hills on either coast, with the harbour entrance in between.

At this point a Mandarin came on board and the ship ran up to the second bar and anchored: it took two days to cross this bar even with the help of boats from other ships. After three hours warping, that is to say, taking an anchor out in the longboat and winching up to where it was cast and then repeating the process, the ship eventually reached the first bar. On the following day, Friday, 21st, she weighed anchor at 6 pm and after four hours with the aid of boats reached Whampoa about the point of Danes Island, where she remained at anchor until 7 February 1788.

Whampoa (Huangbu) was a reach of the Canton River ten miles below Canton adjacent to Whampoa Island and this was as far as ships could go up the river. Contemporary paintings show a crowded anchorage, which is borne out by the number of ships referred to in the Harbour Journal. The anchorage offered a good depth of water – about forty fathoms is recorded in the Journal.

The island was dominated by a pagoda and was also the situation of a customs' house. It is noted from the Journal that on 1 October the Hoppo came on board and measured the ship; he was the customs official. There was another death on board of a midshipman, James Emmerson, who must have signed on as a seaman and been made up when a vacancy occurred.

William Hickey, who was on board the *Plassey* in 1769 and left several records about the China trade, gives the following description:

> Whampoa is pleasantly situated having two islands close to the ships, one is called Danes Island, upon which each ship erects what is called a Bankshall (or Banks Hall as some would state) being a lightly constructed wooden building from sixty to a hundred feet in length into which, yards, spars, sails, rigging and stores are deposited and all are repaired and put in order. The other is called French Island.

Danes Island was appointed by the Chinese government for English seamen to stretch their legs on and French Island for the French. There were strict orders that the English seamen should not enter onto the

French Island in case of quarrels.

A picture of the Canton river front at this date can be gleaned from a Chinese scroll painted on silk, now in possession of the British Museum, made about a decade earlier, which gives a panoramic view of Canton. The River from the North of Whampoa Island sweeps round in a curve to the West.

Whampoa Island appears as if it is dominated by a mount capped with a nine-storey pagoda and it tails off to the westward in a low bank; then travelling North westward is Napier Island, a low narrow stretch with a village beyond and going further westward we come to the outskirts of Canton with the end of its suburbs and the Customs House. There is a French folly fort in the river in the foreground. From this point the river is bordered with godowns crowded with junks, behind which can be seen the castellated wall of the city. Travelling further westward again a Mohammedan Mosque and the Flower Pagoda come into view and the watch tower, which is a five-storey pagoda built on the city wall. There are more godowns along the water's edge.

From this point there are extensive suburbs with a Dutch folly fort in the river until we reach the Hongs. These are market halls where each trading nation purchased their wares and sent them down the river in junks or chop-boats, which were licensed lighters, to the ships at Whampoa. The Hongs had a courtyard in front of them leading down to a quay or jetty where the junks could moor. Apart from the Chinese Hong there was a Danish Hong, a French Hong, an Imperial Austrian Hong, a Swedish Hong, a British Hong and a Dutch Hong.

William Hickey, writing in August 1769, describes Canton as follows:

> About half a mile above the city suburbs in going from Whampoa, is a wharf, or embankment, regularly built of brick and mortar, extending more than half a mile in length, upon which wharf stands the different factories or places of residence of the Supra-cargoes, each factory having the flag of its nation on a lofty staff before it. At the time I was in China they stood in the following order; First the Dutch, then the French, the English, the Swedes, and last the Danes. Each of these factories besides admirable banquetting or public rooms for eating, etc, has attached to them sets of chambers, varying in size according to the establishment. The English being far more numerous than any other nation trading with China their range of buildings is much the most extensive. Each Supra-cargo has four handsome rooms; the public apartments are in front, looking to the river, the others go inland to the depth of two or three hundred feet in broad courts having the sets of rooms on each side, every set having a distinct and separate entrance with a small garden, and every sort of convenience. Besides the factories which belong to the East India Companies there are also others, the property of the Chinese, who let them to European and country captains of ships, merchants and strangers, whom business brings to Canton . . .

The Supracargoes were the merchants who dealt with the Chinese, their opposite numbers being the Cohongs, who were Chinese merchants that had purchased the exclusive right to trade with the British or other foreigners. The Supracargoes also fulfilled the office of the Resident or Consul in the port. Officers from the ships had to appear before a Select Committee of Supracargoes in full uniform. There were twelve employed by the East India Company in the second half of the eighteenth century and they lived luxuriously within the confines of the Hong and entertained generously.

The Supracargoes acted as the local agents for the East India Company purchasing merchandise and making it up into cargoes for the Company's ships sent to China. Their local buying was governed by the demand in England for the various Chinese goods, as apparent from the sales made by the Company in London. They were the British presence in Canton and, therefore, responsible for law and order among the British, settling disputes and maintaining good relations with the Chinese.

The principal export was tea, but chinaware was also shipped to England in large quantities particularly in the earlier part of the eighteenth century. It is surprising that such a large consignment left Canton in 1788 because trade in chinaware in London was by then poor. In Octobter 1788 William Duesbury's manager at the Derby Porcelain Works reported to him:

> At the India House sale this week I am informed out of more than eighteen hundred lots there were not more than five hundred sold and trade was 'very dead'.

Perhaps much of the consignment remained unsold. The drop in trade prompted a cutback in purchases in China and on 21 January 1779 the Council of Supracargoes wrote from Canton to the Court of the Honourable Company:

> As the orders this year from the Honourable Court give us reason to suppose that China ware is not now an article so high in demand as some seasons past we have come to the resolution not to make any contract for the ensuing year as the quantity we have remaining will be sufficient to load eight ships and in case we should want a small quantity it will be much better to purchase a few chests than be encumbered with a large quantity by engaging beforehand for it . . .

The trade in which the East India Company had a monopoly started about the time of the Restoration of Charles II and in China with the Emperor Khang H'si, the first of the Ching Dynasty. The Dutch were more active originally than the British, their East India Company being centred in Batavia, or Jakarta as it was originally known, and is now known today. This was the blue-and-white period which it may be said continued for the period of Khang H'si – 1662 until 1722. Yung Chen succeeded Khang H'si and during his reign colours other than blue started to be introduced and coloured porcelain reached its height of excellence under Chien Lung, 1736 to 1795. During the eighteenth century, tons of chinaware came to England every year from Canton and the designs such as *Famille Rose* and *Famille Verte* developed instead of the blue-and-white of the previous century.

The Emperor Chien Lung was himself a patron of the manufacture of Chinese porcelain and during his reign vast numbers of armorial dinner services were ordered by the British through the East India Company, which are now often known as 'export ware'.

The Chinese copied European designs and European tastes, they boasted that there was no design that they could not reproduce in china ware. But the Chinese were very jealous of their secrets and this meant that everything had to be done through factors; there was no question of the British visiting the kilns and explaining first hand what they required, although William Hickey did have the opportunity of seeing the finishing processes. It was not surprising, therefore, that the Chinese fell down on some of their designs.

It was traditional for the Chinese to eat out of bowls and to drink their tea out of bowls and these were elegant and well proportioned. But when it came to supplying coffee cups for armorial dinner services the same thimble shape was reproduced over and over again with clumsy handles and the cups were heavy, weighing one and a half times the weight of their European counterparts and twice the weight of tea bowls of the same capacity: cups usually shared with the tea bowls the same saucer, which did not quite seem to belong to either. In the same way the mugs had the appearance of brush pots with the addition of a teapot handle.

Their attempts to reproduce metal objects such as loving cups made quaint and not unattractive ornaments, but could serve no practical purpose. There was a lot of repetitive designing such as cartouches of blue mantling which reappeared with a number of different monograms and crests. In short, Europe had been flooded with Chinese porcelain by the last quarter of the eighteenth century and customers were beginning to look to Europe for new and more attractive designs which were more in tune with European tastes.

Meissen was the earliest attempt at European porcelain, which was first sold at the Leipsig Easter Fair in 1713, but this factory throughout the eighteenth century concentrated on decorative ware rather than tableware. Porcelain-making in England was started much later by William Cookworthy in Plymouth, but he had only a handful of workmen making decorative ware; no one in Europe could yet rival the Chinese for mass production.

The English country houses required dinner services on a massive scale; an eighteen-foot dinner table would accommodate twenty-four people which involved that number of plates six times over so as to have soup plates, pudding plates, small plates and six dozen ordinary dinner plates to cater for the different courses. Added to this there would be tureens, dessert bowls, sauce boats, punch bowls, and a dozen meat dishes of various sizes, making at least two hundred pieces. Captain Easterbrook's service, which was sold by Christies in 1951, consisted of 265 pieces.

Once Europe was able to compete in this market Chinese dinner services were priced out of the market by a duty of nearly fifty per cent, which rose in 1799 to over a hundred per cent. Chinaware was usually packed for shipment in half chests thought to be 3 ft 4 ins by 2 ft 4 ins in superficial measurement and about 18 ins deep.

Before taking cargo on board the *Royal Admiral* the month of November was spent in preparing the ship for the return voyage; already in October the caulker had been at work on the bends, that is, the timbers above the water line, and the bowsprit had been gammoned. The work was then below the water line: first the longboat was hogged, in other words the bottom was cleaned with a stiff brush; then the bottom of the ship itself was breamed which was done by singeing it with burning brushwood to get rid of the barnacles, and after this it was payed with pitch. On one day the starboard side was hoved out of the water to be worked upon and the following day the larboard side was worked upon.

At the end of November after twelve tons of stone ballast had been loaded the cargo started to be brought on board with eighty-nine chests of chinaware on one day and a further consignment later. These were stowed at the bottom of the hold where their weight was needed for ballast and where they would protect the tea from any bilge water that may penetrate the hold in rough weather. Finally, the tea was loaded and there were further loads of ballast from the bankshall. Even space in the great cabin had to be used to accommodate the cargo.

The total cargo of tea taken on board was as follows:

3260 Chests of Congo
200 Twankeys
30 Chests of Souchong
5 Boats of Tea
3 Boats of Small Teas
1200 Chests of Singlos
70 Chests of Hyson

According to a well-known firm of London Tea Merchants established in the eighteenth century:

There were two main types, Black and Green. Black teas included: Flowery pekoe, orange pekoe, pekoe souchong, souchong congou and bohea. Green teas: Gunpowder, imperial hyson, singlo, bing and capter.

Pekoe – pak-ho (white hairs) showing the fine downy tips of the young buds; Souchong – siauchung, meaning little plant or sort; Congou – kung-fuo, i.e. labour (in preparation of Congou the leaves were hand rolled); Bohea – wu-i from the mountains in Fu-kien, the centre of the black tea country, Hyson – yu-tsien, meaning before the rains, or tu-chun, i.e. flourishing spring; Singlo or Twankay was the hyson shrub improved by cultivation, it came from Singlo mountain in Kiang Nan. Tea was grown for consumption all over China, except in the far north, but the provinces that grew the tea for export were in the south-east, Kwang-tung, Fu-kien, Keange-se, Che-keange, Keange-su and Ganhwuy. Black and Green teas were made from the same plant, the difference being the method of manufacture; green tea was not allowed to ferment and in order to retain its colour, it was faced or glazed with a powdered mixture of gypsum and prussian blue.

Packages were described as: chests, boxes, tubbs or potts. The Chinese packed some tea in tins which were either called chests or tubbs, though from examination the tubbs generally held smaller quantities than the chests. Tubbs varied from 17 lb. to 73 lb. Potts contained 56, 60 or 64 lb. These were made of earthenware with narrow mouths for the common tea, the better qualities were packed in porcelain pots or vessels.[1]

The price of tea in the shops ranged from sixteen shillings a pound to six shillings a pound at that time, and following the reduction of the tax in 1784 the consumption of tea doubled from what it had been in 1768. By 3 February the ship was fully laden and on the 7th the pilot came aboard and the ship was ready to take its departure.

During her time in port the *Royal Admiral* had not been free from disciplinary problems; one seaman, Richard Wilson, had been put in irons for theft and later flogged, another, John Collins, had been given a dozen lashes for disobedience of orders and threatening to heave the third officer overboard, and two men had 'Run from the Longboat', in other words, deserted. But these delinquencies were completely overshadowed by the mutiny on the *Belvedere* anchored at Whampoa, which broke out on Sunday, 2 December following a seaman being put in irons.

According to the *Calcutta Gazette* published a month later, 'every officer down to the midshipmen was thrown overboard but none drowned'. After considerable resistance the ringleaders were secured and confined on board the *Earl Fitzwilliam*, Captain James Dundas, the senior Commander, being in command of the ship.

On 15 December a court of sixteen commanders was formed, of which

[1] This information is given with the courtesy of Mr S. H. G. Twining, a Director of R. Twining and Company Limited.

no doubt Huddart was one and the following judgment pronounced and approved by the Select Committee of the Supracargoes at Canton.

> It has not appeared (say the Captains) that there has been the least cause for murmur among the ship's Company either for ill usage from the commander or any one officer or petty officer in the ship. This daring mutiny has arisen from a spirit that prevailed that they were on board of a merchantman where according to their own expression they would not meet with due punishment. It also appears that on the second day of the meeting the prisoners were all sober and deliberate but one man, Kelly, who pleaded drunkenness, the others never attempting any defence of that sort or saying anything in their own vindication. We are therefore of opinion that this daring mutiny, had it not been immediately suppressed by about eighteen boats manned and armed from the Company's ships, the consequences would have been dreadful not only to that ship, but (through) this spirit spreading to the fleet in general where there are above three thousand of His Majesty's subjects.

On 24 December the Log of the *Belvedere* relates:

> At seven A.M. having unrigged the longboat made a stage on her and sent her on board the commodore for to have Berry and Lilley flogged round the fleet, which has done accordingly – round eighteen ships. At noon the captain (Greer) brought Lieff, Ladson, Jackson, Skinner, Langford, Connor and Hastings on board from the Earl Fitzwilliam to receive their punishment: when Kieff and Ladson had five dozen lashes each, Connor, Jackson, and Skinner four dozen, and Langford and Hastings two dozen.

The events so far as the *Royal Admiral* was concerned were that the ship received a signal at 3 pm on Sunday, 2 December from the Commodore for all Commanders, when orders were given for each ship to man and arm a boat to quell the mutiny. The third officer, Thomas Hemmings, was sent in the pinnace with a boarding party to assist and the mutiny was quelled. On the 10th three of the mutineers were taken on board the *Royal Admiral* so as to separate the mutinous crew and on the 24th the following record appears in the Log.

> At 10 A.M. Punish'd . . . Lilly Seaman with 8 Lashes being part of his sentence inforced by an Order of the Council of SupraCargoes for Mutiny on board the Belvedere on Sunday 2nd December 1787 in which he was the Ring Leader.

It is apparent that the Supracargoes and not the Commodore were the supreme authority over the shipping at Whampoa: it was they, after all, who had to maintain good relations with the Chinese on whom the whole Far East trade depended and the Chinese reactions could be unpredictable. During the whole time the ship lay at anchor the seamen would probably go no further than Danes Island except in expeditions in the longboat to fetch water and stores as there was no water fit to drink at Whampoa. No doubt the officers were entertained on shore in the Hong.

On 10 February 1788 the *Royal Admiral* took her departure from the Grand Landrome at 5 pm and a week later the island of Sapatu was sighted and on the 23rd the ship crossed the Equator.

> The sail seen Last Night proves to be the Company's Ship Hawke. At Noon Capt'n Pennell came on board determined to keep Compan'y Thro' the Straits of Gasker.

On the 25th: 'At Noon the Extremes of Banka from the Mast Head from S 44.30 W to S 82.50 W.' The *Hawke* remained in their company until the ships had passed through the Sunda Strait on the 29th.

29th February at 11 A.M. a gentleman came on board with a letter from the Governor and Council of Bombay dated 20th Nov & drafted to the Commanders of the Company's ships informing us of the critical situation of National Affairs of Europe in order to put upon our Guard on speaking with a Ship or touching any foreign Port.

It is not clear what event prompted this letter; undoubtedly France was bankrupt and becoming ungovernable and Paris was *regorgé de brochures*. Thomas Carlyle said in the spring of 1788:

By no path can the King's Government find passage for itself, but is shamefully flung back. Beleaguered by Twelve rebellious Parlements, which are grown to be the organs of an angry Nation, it can advance nowhither; can accomplish nothing, not so much as money to subsist on; but must sit there, seemingly to be eaten up of Deficit.

This was the calm before the storm, but the storm did not break for another year.

The ship had now passed Krakatoa and was on course for the Cape. On 13 April the Cape was reached and the course changed for St Helena. This island, like Penang, was an East India Company settlement where ships could replenish their stocks of fresh food and water and pick up despatches and the latest news. It had been held by the East India Company since 1659 when they seized it from the Portuguese.

On Friday, 2 May the ship reaches St Helena. At 3.30 am the pinnace was sent ashore and at half past nine the ship anchored and saluted the fort with nine guns which was returned. Jamestown the port, where the ships rode at anchor, was a small town squeezed between the surrounding volcanic mountains which dwarfed and overwhelmed it. A few buildings occupied the waterfront with other houses behind. The longboat was sent ashore with empty casks and returned with water; the following day twenty butts of water and two barrels of tar were taken on board and on Monday, 5th twenty-one butts of water followed by twelve hogshead the next day and eleven casks of bread. A barrel of gunpowder was sent ashore for the garrison, this was much in demand for salutes if not required for defence.

On Wednesday, 7 May at 9 am Mr Wrangham came on board to muster the ship's company and was saluted with nine guns. Later the signal was made for sailing, the sails were bent on and the longboat hoisted on board. The following morning there were moderate breezes and fair weather and at 6 am the Purser came on board with the packet; at 8 am the ship weighed anchor, saluted the fort with nine guns and made sail.

After nine weeks at sea Portland Bill was the first part of the English coast to come into view at 4 pm on 1 July and at 7 pm on the following day the ship anchored in the Downs.

A Harbour Journal continued for a month while porters came on board to work the ship and unloading started. The first thing to be landed was the gunpowder: this always had to be taken off the ship before she entered port. On 15 July the ship was anchored at Deptford, unrigged and the rigging taken ashore. On 8 August an Inspector came on board to clear the ship.

The Commander would have been supplied with charts from the Company's India House and these had to be returned at the end of the voyage with the Commander's Journal and track charts.

Huddart had concluded his last voyage with no loss of cargo, no damage to the ship and no accidents to the crew. A few of the crew had deserted and some had died which was to be expected in the eighteenth century particularly with an epidemic of fever on the outward passage. Huddart had been an exemplary commander, but undoubtedly owed a debt of gratitude to Sir Richard Hotham for singling him out for the command of the *Royal Admiral*: the command of an Indiaman would not have come to him otherwise.

Now Sir Richard was to exact his price, he wanted to retire from shipping and to realise his assets. The captain of an Indiaman was like a sitting tenant in a controlled house and had to be bought out if the vessel was to realise its true value. Sir Richard offered a thousand pounds compensation for the command which Huddart reluctantly took: he was in no mood to bargain with one who had shown him such kindness in the past, although he must have felt that he was being seen off. When Sir Richard sold the ship he got £8,000 for the command alone, but it has to be remembered that Huddart paid nothing for the first vacancy when he took up the command.

Today's technology gives a command over the elements undreamt of in the eighteenth century, when no mariner could claim to be the master of his fate, seeing that his course and his speed were dictated by the wind, and it is a tribute to the skill of the mariners of the days of sail that they achieved so much in the development of the shipping trade when surrounded by so many difficulties.

To make a successful voyage a captain had to run a tight ship with a large crew, be able to determine his position at sea and make the best use of his only motive power, the wind, which might preclude the very course the ship sought to take. There is no doubt that in the four voyages he made in command of the *Royal Admiral* Huddart proved himself to be a first-rate nagivator with an unchallengeable command of his officers and crew.

There was no fame or glory for those on board Indiamen, the purpose of the John Company was trade and personal profit, of which Huddart hardly had his share though admittedly he had no entrepreneurial gifts. In his first voyage in the *Royal Admiral* he was standing in for a dead captain whose estate was entitled to the profit due to the captain; in his second his ship was seconded to the Navy and it was only in his third and fourth voyages in the Company's service that he reaped the reward of his command.

Huddart was now forty-seven and not too old to take command of another voyage so that it must have been a great disappointment to him that Sir Richard wanted to sell up and bring his career to an end, particularly as he had no family to join except his old mother living at Allonby and now in her eighties: his wife had died and his sons were abroad.

CHAPTER V

Trinity House

HUDDART'S ACTIVITIES after his retirement from the sea kept him engaged in London and although he still had his house at Allonby he needed a London house, so on 2 October 1792 he purchased from a Mrs Agnes Gray of Smithfield the leasehold of No. 12 Highbury Terrace in the parish of St Mary Islington, for which he paid £1,265. The lease ran for seventy-one years from 24 June 1789, when presumably the house was built, subject to an annual ground rent of five guineas. It was a moderately sized house, built in a terrace, having a frontage of 21 feet, and, together with a garden, it ran back 200 feet. This gave him space to build an observatory, workshop and forge and a coachhouse at the rear of the house.

Evidently indoor sanitation was beginning to emerge at this period as the house was connected to a common sewer. The innovation of modern conveniences was made possible by the invention by Joseph Bramah of his patent water closet in 1778. This was the valve type of closet, which has long since been replaced by a siphon.

Astronomy and making mathematical instruments had now become Huddart's hobby. On the sale of his effects in 1817 after his death, Sir James South, the astronomer, purchased the Equatorial Instrument which Huddart had made with his own hands. It cost Sir James only £600 and he considered it to be superior to one constructed on the Continent and costing ten times as much. Astronomers and instrument makers were anxious to examine the construction and framing of the tube of the instrument to ascertain how Huddart succeeded in preventing any vibration, but Sir James would not permit any examination for fear of deranging any of the parts.

While still at Allonby after his retirement from the East India Company Huddart spent some time on his favourite pursuit of carrying out experiments to determine the lines which would give a ship the greatest velocity, taking into account stability and the capacity of a ship for stowage. He laid down an experimental vessel at Maryport, presumably at William Wood's Yard, which was fitted with different types of bows including a conical bow. By towing the vessel under differing conditions he endeavoured to ascertain the resistance resulting from the division of fluid, and from the cohesion of water to the surface. The after lines of the vessel were very fine and were carried out to the rudder which had a fine edge. He was anxious to establish the proportion of the power required to move a body through the water which was expended in overcoming the friction of the fluid against the sides. To arrive at this he towed a plane having the same surface as the immersed part of the vessel at the same velocity as he towed the vessel itself. Planes of wood, of painted sail cloth, of metal and other substances were also used. The experiment proved that surface friction was a considerable element in resistance; in this connection Huddart was attracted by the speed and little effort with which fish dart past a sailing ship due to the little friction set up by their oily skin and scales. From the facts he had elicited he made drawings and calculations to show the lines which offered the least resistance.

At a later stage Huddart had a plane of mahogany which he could adjust by screws to a variety of curves: this was about twelve feet long and thirty inches broad and was suspended in the river, so as to be nearly immersed, being held by a steel yard against the stream to show its resistance to the current. To the interior surface of the plane at short distances from each other perpendicular tubes were attached; a continuous hole was pierced through each tube and the plane, the hole from one tube being opposed to the current and that from the next being in the direction of it. Each tube contained a float rising to the top of the tube which showed by its rise or fall the altered resistance to the water as the plane was adjusted to different curves.

In order to suspend the plane in the river, two rafts were joined at each end above the water level with the plane hanging in between. The raft was moored under one of the bridges of the Thames so that Huddart could observe the effect of the current protected by a wooden hut fixed onto the raft.

In 1797, as an experiment, Huddart built a twenty-five ton vessel at William Wood's Yard at Maryport, based on the drawings and calculations he had made. This was brought to London in 1802. The lines of this experimental craft were regarded as peculiar at the time, but later they were found to be worth copying. The maximum width of the craft was mid-way between bow and stern with the bowlines and the afterlines being nearly similar.

When, after his death, the *Saucy Jack*, an American privateer, which outsailed other craft, was captured and the lines taken off her they turned out to be very similar to those determined by Huddart's experiment. Huddart wanted to try this craft with a coppered bottom to reduce friction and after his death she was bought for a droger and coppered. His suggestion was proved correct on a voyage to Madeira where unfortunately the craft was lost.

Huddart also gave his attention to the construction of ships and submitted plans to the Admiralty for strengthening a large man o' war by the use of trussed bulkheads, but his suggestion was never adopted. Later he built another vessel at the shipyard of his friend Sir Robert Wigram. The detailed drawings were prepared by Huddart himself and every part was completed under his inspection. The craft drew exactly the amount of water he had calculated and her increased deepening was in exact conformity with his calculations and, in fact, she performed in accordance with his best hopes.

His son kept all his papers and drawings, but they were too technical to be sufficiently within his grasp to give a detailed account of his father's observations. Over the lapse of nearly two centuries all these records have been dispersed so that it is not possible today to provide more than an outline of these experiments.

Aware of Huddart's abilities as a hydrographer Trinity House engaged him in 1790 to carry out a survey of the shoals at Hasborough Gatt and Newarp on the Norfolk coast with a view to establishing a floating light to warn shipping. Huddart carried out an accurate survey and provided a chart with sailing directions, which was available to Northern coasters on payment of their light dues. At the same time, he established the longitude of Great Yarmouth Church, which was hitherto unknown.

Reporting in 1818 Captain Joseph Cotton, FRS, the Deputy Master of Trinity House at that time, says:

HAPPISBURGH or HAZEBORO LIGHTS

. . . After careful surveys of the shore and sands, The Corporation built two lighthouses on the cliff at Happisburgh, and placed a floating light close to Newarp Sand in the Gatway; and thus rendered the navigation thereof safe by night as by day, and danger of that kind no longer exists.

i.e. the collision of two fleets.

On 15 September 1791 the Corporation of Trinity House, realising the value of the services that Captain Huddart could render to navigation, elected him as an Elder Brother to fill a vacancy that had occurred. Some explanation is due of the history and function of this unique body. It was founded by Charter in 1514 as the 'Brotherhood of the Most Glorious and Undivided Trinity' to constitute a mariners' charity. All charities in pre-Reformation England came under the auspices of the Church and hence the body started with a sort of monastic framework though not belonging to any particular order.

The original function was to provide for the pilotage of the Thames and also to provide almshouses for poor and aged seamen; it was under the organisation of a Master, four Wardens and eight Assistants. During the suppression of all religious houses Henry VIII spared the Brotherhood, because of the valuable services they were rendering in connection with shipping; in 1547 Edward VI confirmed their charter. The full title varied slightly then from that later adopted which is 'The Master, Wardens and Assistants of the Guild, Fraternity or Brotherhood of the most glorious and undivided Trinity and of St. Clement[1] in the Parish of Deptford Strond in the County of Kent'.

In 1573 the Corporation was granted a coat of arms and the achievement is quaintly described as follows:

Argent, a plain cros geules, between four ships sable, the fore and top-sayles up. Underneath on a wreath of theyr colors a demilion rampant, gardat, and crouned with a croune imperial or, in his right pawe an armying swoord argent, hylt and pomell or, langued and armed azure, mantled argent, doubled geules.

These were the armorials engraved on the gilt coat buttons worn by Captain Huddart which appear in the portrait of him painted by John Hoppner. In fact, some of the buttons are still in existence.

On the restoration of the Monarchy in 1660 the Corporation moved its headquarters to Water Lane in the City of London. On 2 January 1661 Samuel Pepys writes:

---

[1] St Clement is traditionally regarded as the Clement referred to in the fourth Chapter of the Epistle to the Philippians.

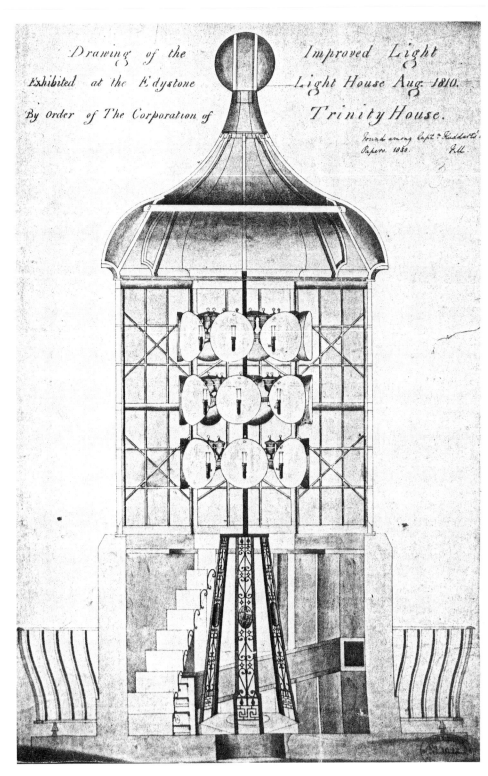

Illustration of the arrangement of Argand Lanterns in Smeaton's
Eddystone Lighthouse. (Drawing taken from Huddart's own papers.)

This day I lent Sir W. Batten and Captn. Rider my chine of beef for to serve at dinner tomorrow at Trinity House, The Duke of Albemarle being there and all the rest of the Brethren, it being a great day for the reading over of their new Charter, which the King hath newly given them.

Pepys himself in due course became the Master. By this time the Master had ceased to take an active rôle in conducting the affairs of the Corporation: these duties were delegated to the Deputy Master.

The Headquarters of Trinity House occupied various sites and eventually the present building was erected between 1794 and 1796, designed by the Corporation's architect Samuel Wyatt, the brother of the famous James Wyatt, who was also responsible for the design of many of the lighthouses.

To commemorate the event the large painting which occupies the quarterdeck of Trinity House was executed in 1794 by Gainsborough Dupont depicting a group of life-size portraits of the members of the Court of Trinity House at that time. Huddart is shown on the extreme right and the painting of him was stitched to the rest of the canvas as, at the time the canvas was executed, he was away surveying for his chart of the Western coast of Scotland. In fact, it is said that longshoremen stood in for all the Elder Brethren in their clothes once a portrait had been done of their faces.

Attention is often drawn to the fact that Huddart appears without a wig and in this respect he is the odd man out. One can only say that by the end of the eighteenth century wigs were no longer in fashion. The fall of the Bastille introduced a less extravagant taste in dress to avoid the sort of ostentatious provocation that had brought about the revolution in France.

Huddart became one of the most active members of the Corporation for twenty-five years until his death in 1816, during which time he carried out a number of surveys for light vessels, including one at the Owers Shoal off the Isle of Wight to guide vessels using the Channel or Spithead. According to Cotton:

The situation of this shoal . . . had been cause of loss in numberless instances and the attempt to exhibit a light near or on it looked visionary. Mr. Smeaton was consulted on the idea of building a lighthouse upon the rock at the east end of it, called the Shoal of the Lead. A proposition was also made to Trinity House to erect an iron lighthouse there, and these, with the plan of a floating light, severally occupied the minds of the Brethren. The latter, as the soonest accomplished and the most feasible, was adopted: but the vessel broke adrift many times getting into St. Vallery once; and the repetition of sad events occasioned great doubts of the realisation, and were only prevented in future by perseverance of the Brethren, who, in their renewed exertions, at length accomplished the undertaking. The great utility it has been of to vessels passing these rocks, bound to Portsmouth from eastwards especially, is very well understood by all seamen.

Ships on a course from the coast South of the Isle of Wight would probably be too far out in the Channel to encounter the Owers. St Valery is on the coast of Normandy.

In 1794 and the year following, Huddart carried out a survey for a floating light off the North Head of the Goodwins, together with charts and sailing directions. Again in 1802 he surveyed the channels at the mouth of the Thames for the establishment of a light on the Sunk sandbank in the North Channel. A light vessel was established in 1795 at the Goodwins at a cost of £5,000.

Placed on the North East of the Goodwin Sand (upon which numberless vessels, British and foreign, chiefly the latter were wrecked) was provided on the representation of the trade, and exhibits a distinct and good light in a triangle: it has rode there, though exposed to the whole force of the German Ocean, with a very few instances of change of situation, and hence useful to all vessels navigating at the back of the Sands.

Of corresponding utility with the preceding [the Sunk Floating Light], lays at the extremity of the sand of that name, and being at the entrance of the North Channel into the Thames, constitutes such a guide to ships entering or sailing out, as has preserved numbers which otherwise would have been lost. It is equally useful to vessels crossing from the North Foreland to Orfordness, and vice versa.

The exhibition has been highly satisfactory to the trade: and although the vessel is equally exposed to the gales from the German Ocean she has seldom drifted from her station.[1]

The Sunk light vessel was positioned in 1797 at a cost of £5,000.

During the eighteenth century considerable development had been achieved in the construction of lighthouses. Lighthouses on the mainland coast had existed since Roman times, in fact, they had lights to mark the crossing between Dover and Boulogne, but these were merely beacons elevated on towers. At the beginning of the eighteenth century an attempt was being made to light rocks at sea. The most notable is the Eddystone fourteen miles South West of Plymouth, which was first attempted by Henry Winstanley. His lighthouse was more of a fantastic folly than a building capable of beating back the envious seige of watery Neptune, but it did withstand the storms for five years.

The next attempt was a good deal more successful, being based on ship's carpentry, but eventually it caught fire. The final breakthrough came with John Smeaton, who based his design on a tree, which spreads out at the bottom sinking its roots into the ground. Smeaton built his tower of granite blocks dovetailed together and dovetailed into the rock which made its foundation, the lower courses of stonework being solid right through the diameter of the tower. This was completed in 1759 and became the pattern for all offshore lighthouses; but when completed it was lit only with candles on a suspended iron hoop like votive candles in a Roman Catholic church. It was not until the Argand lamp was invented that the modern lighthouse really came into being. In 1810 the candles were replaced with twenty-four Argand lamps with reflectors at a cost of £3,000: these lamps burnt whale oil, as mineral oils had not yet been discovered. In each lamp the cylindrical wick was contained between two concentric metal tubes: the inner one open at the bottom to provide an air current, but sealed to the outer one to make an oil container fed from the receptacle behind the reflector.

The headland of Land's End is encircled with rocks and was the scene of many shipping disasters in the eighteenth century and earlier. As with all parts of the Cornish coast it was said that the inhabitants lived off plunder from the wrecks.

On 30 June 1791 the Corporation obtained a patent for the erection of a lighthouse and granted a lease to Lieutenant Merry Smith at a rental of £100 for a term of fifty years to erect a lighthouse and collect the dues. The Tower was then built on Carn Braes, the largest of the Longships Rocks to

[1] Report of Captain J. Cotton FRS August 1818.

the design of the Trinity House architect Samuel Wyatt.

The construction followed the Smeaton pattern of a circular tower which rose 40 feet above high tides, giving a space for stores and a water tank on the bottom floor, a living room on the next floor and a bedroom on the top storey under the wood and copper lantern. The lantern stood 70 feet above the sea and held eighteen parabolic metal reflectors with Argand lamps arranged in two tiers. Metal sheets cut off the light towards the land. A crew of four manned the light, two being on duty at any one time. They received £30 a year and free food at the lighthouse. Huddart carried out a survey and prepared sailing directions for the use of mariners.

In 1818 Cotton commented as follows:

> This light, at the extremity of Land's End, upon a rock of great height, and steep as a ship's side, was intended to facilitate the passage from St. George's into the Bristol Channel, or the reverse, for the benefit of vessels that had been driven by stress of weather or mistake into the Bristol Channel: and for coasters particularly.
>
> A lease was granted to Lieutenant Smith of the Navy, as a reward for the suggestion: but after erecting it, he became incapable of conducting the concern: and it is now under the management of the Corporation, for the benefit of his family, for the remaining term.
>
> It is a work of great solidity, built of granite, and from what has been stated, may be supposed highly useful to many descriptions of vessels. The Wolf and Rendle Stone, two dangerous rocks in the neighbourhood, are thereby rendered less formidable, although the beacons that were fixed upon them could not be retained.

In 1806 Huddart was engaged on a survey in connection with Flamborough Lighthouse on the Yorkshire coast. Any association of the name with a flame seems unlikely: the Domesday Book refers to the headland as 'Flaneberg' which may be derived from the Saxon word 'Flaen' meaning a dart, which is the shape suggested by the headland.

A lighthouse had been established at this place by Sir John Clayton in 1669 but never kindled. The present lighthouse was designed by the Corporation architect Samuel Wyatt and built by John Matson of Bridlington at a cost of £8,000 and first lit on 1 December 1806. The original lighting apparatus was designed by George Robinson and consisted of a rotating vertical shaft mounted with twenty-one parabolic reflectors, with seven on each of three sides with red glass covering the reflectors on one side, giving, for the first time, two white flashes followed by one red flash.

Huddart is regarded as the actual inventor of the use of coloured glass in lighthouses, which was subsequently adopted in the Bell Rock lighthouse designed by John Rennie. The light was provided by oil-burning Argand lamps giving an equivalent candle power of 13,860. The height of the tower was 89 feet and the height above mean high water 214 feet.

On the subject of the use of coloured glass, John Rennie wrote to Matthew Boulton of the well-known Birmingham engineering firm on 12 March 1814 as follows:

> When the Bell Rock Lighthouse was erected, Stevenson was employed to superintend the whole. A regular head mason and carpenter were employed under him. The original plans were made by me, and the work was visited by me from time to time during its progress. When the work was completed, Stevenson considered that he had acquired sufficient knowledge to start as a civil engineer, and in that line he has been most indefatigable in looking

after employment, by writing and applying wherever he thought there was a chance of success.

He has assumed the merit of applying coloured glass to lighthouses, of which Huddart was the actual inventor, and I have no doubt that he will also assume the whole merit of planning and erecting the Bell Rock Lighthouse, if he has not already done so. I am told that few weeks pass without a puff or two in his favour in the Edinburgh papers.

Cotton reporting in 1818 says:

The site of Flamborough Head was of all others the most calculated for a lighthouse, either for coasters or for vessels from the Baltic and North Sea, but it was not concurred in by the trade until lately, when its utility having been admitted, the present lighthouse was erected, and the light exhibited upon the principle of the Scilly light, but with red glass in front of the burners, by which it is distinguished from Cromer.

The erection of the South Stack lighthouse in 1809 is discussed in the next Chapter in connection with the crossing from Holyhead to Dublin.

In 1812 Huddart undertook to superintend of the building of an additional light at Hurst Point, which is on the mainland side of the entrance to the Solent opposite the Needles and near Hurst Castle, a defence built against invasion by Henry VIII. To carry out his work Huddart had a small cabin attached to the old lighthouse so that when necessary he could live on the site. The positioning of the tower had to be exact to form a leading mark. Hurst Point had been the site of a lighthouse since 1733. As the result of a petition in 1781 by ship masters and merchants, Letters Patent were obtained in January 1782 which stated that:

. . . ships and vessels have been lost . . . and the lives, ships and goods of His Majesty's subjects as well as the King's Royal Navy continue to be exposed to the like calamities more especially in the night time and in hard southerly gales.

The patent directed that the lights should be:

. . . kept burning in the night season whereby seafaring men and mariners might take notice of and avoid dangers . . . and ships and other vessels of war might safely cruise during the night season in the British Channel.

In 1781 there were negotiations with William Tatnall, a merchant of Ironmonger Lane, London to erect lights with necessary buildings and approach roads at the Needles and at St Catherine's Point on the Isle of Wight and Hurst Point at sites chosen by Trinity House or its surveyor. These negotiations fell through and Trinity House undertook the erection of these lights to the designs of R. Jupp. Hurst Tower was first lit on 29 September 1786, but this light was obscured from some directions and a further higher light had to be erected in 1812 both to remedy this defect and to give a guiding line to vessels. The towers were known respectively as Hurst front and Hurst rear, the height of Hurst front being 52 feet and the height of the rear tower being 85 feet with their heights above mean high water being respectively 50 feet and 75 feet. Much of the coast between Hurst Point and Lymington is below the high water mark.

J. Cotton reported in 1818:

This light upon the Needles Point, and that upon Hurst Beach, were erected to give facility to ships coming up or going down the Channel, (when caught by a contrary wind or storm) to enter that intricate passage to an anchorage, by day or night: and owing to the narrowness, the danger from the Needles Rock, Shambles on the one side and Warden Ledge on the other, they became expedient and useful.

Great attention was requisite to regulate a vessel's course by the old masked light of Hurst; this being found by experience insufficient, an additional lighthouse has been built, which, when in line with the former, marks the direct track of safe navigation, and fully effects the proposed object.

Before leaving the subject of Trinity House, it should be mentioned that on a number of occasions the Corporation was called upon by the Admiralty to assist in the defence of the Thames providing a passive rôle so far as possible. What one might call a 'Dads' Navy' and one such occasion was at the time of Napoleon's threatened invasion in 1803.

On 26 May 1803 in connection with the defence of the Rivers Thames and Medway, two Elder Brethren were detailed to attend on Lord Keith, Commander-in-Chief at Sheerness, to advise any alterations, etc.

So far the Trinity Brethren had only taken passive defence measures, but in the next emergency they filled a far more warlike rôle and were ready to fight. The previous scares had each lasted only a matter of days, but the Napoleonic bogey of 1803 was not laid for two or three years. On this occasion Trinity House offered to equip ten frigates and moor them across the Thames as a sort of barrier of floating forts. The place chosen was the Lower Hope where the river is almost exactly a mile wide. In the accounts of the proceedings, the place is sometimes given as the 'Hope' but this must be merely an abbreviation for there is actually no part of the river so named other than the Lower Hope.

A letter dated 13 October 1803 states that the *Solebay*, *Unité*, *Daedalus* and *Vestal* had proceeded the day before and that the Deputy-Master was there, mooring them in the Hope according to the disposition acquiesced in by Sir Harry Neale and Captain Grey. The *Heroine*, *Iris*, *Modeste* and *Quebec* were expected to move the next day, but the Brethren had bitterly complained that the sailings were seriously delayed owing to the failure of the responsible pursers to issue provisions, so that some of the men had already deserted in consequence. Having accepted the Corporation's somewhat altruistic offer to help in the defence of the Thames, it was a bit hard on the part of the Admiralty and the Navy Board not to do their share in facilitating the project. On 3 December 1803 Captain Joseph Cotton wrote to the Admiralty that he could no longer resist the painful task of mentioning that the Purser of the *Modeste* was not at his duty, and the inconvenience that the ship was subject to from his absence. In the *Solebay* the gunner was under notice and was to be exchanged for a more competent man.

The Corporation also raised a body of volunteers or fencibles known as the Royal Trinity House Volunteer Artillery, and 600 men of the corps were on board the first part of the squadron, and the ships were flying the Trinity House ensign. Eventually there were ten frigates mounting a total of 200 guns, stretching in an arc right across the Thames. The RTHVA seems to have achieved a certain distinction and reputation as Pitt was its Colonel, in his capacity of Master of Trinity House, and Captain Joseph Cotton, the Deputy-Master, was the Lieutenant-Colonel.

Frigates under the command of the Elder Brethren of Trinity House. From an aquatint of 1804 showing from left to right *Daedalus*, *Vestal*, *Retribution*, *Iris* (Captains Huddart and Easterby),

Generally speaking, the Elder Brethren acted as Captains in the corps, and the Younger Brethren as Lieutenants. The total strength of the force was 1,200 men. Cotton states that the whole organisation cost the Corporation at least £10,000.

The illustration shows the frigates riding at anchor to the ebb tide and from left to right they are *Daedalus* under the command of Captains Sir Robert Preston and Chapman, *Vestal* (Captains Reed and King), *Retribution* (Captains Pelly and Deffell), *Iris* (Captains HUDDART and Easterby), *Heroine* (Lieut.-Colonel Cotton), *L'Unité* (Captain Woolmore), *Modeste* (Captains Barton and Fraser), *Quebec* (Captains Calvert and Laurens), *Solebay* (Major Travers and Captain Curtis), *Resource* (Captains Brown and Sealy) and the *Trinity Yacht*. The *Modeste* was anchored upstream to allow the passage of trading vessels with the two King's Yachts under the command of Sir Harry Burnard Neale and Captain Grey to starboard of her.

After Captain Huddart's death in 1816 his son made enquiries for information on his father's work as a hydrographer from the leading cartographer Mr Laurie, who referred the matter to his geographer, John Purdy. The following is Purdy's reply:

London, 16th April, 1818.

Sir,

Mr. Laurie has been pleased to refer to me the expression of your wishes relative to the hydrographic works of your honoured parent, the late Captain Huddart, and I sit down most willingly to fulfil them, – not, indeed, with entire satisfaction, because inadequately qualified; but with an earnest wish to do justice to a subject affecting the reputation of a gentleman whose character I have, for many years, held in the highest respect.

I have read, with great pleasure, the biographic notices of Captain Huddart which have appeared in several periodic publications; particularly the memoir given in the 'Gentleman's Magazine', wherein the large Chart of St. George's Channel is particularly mentioned, as one of Captain Huddart's first efforts in the improvement of hydrography. This work, originally dated on board the Royal Admiral, 31st March, 1778, still maintains its well established reputation; and, perhaps, requires no further comment. It is pleasant to find that, as the *original survey*, with requisite additions, it is yet prefered to all the imitations of it that have since been published.

The same remarks apply, with at least equal force, to the Chart of the western coasts and islands of Scotland, which first appeared, and was dedicated to the Society for the encouragement of the Fisheries, between the years 1787 and 1794. This Chart, in three sheets, comprises all the Coasts and Channels between the Mull of Cantire and Cape Wrath, and is therefore to be considered as a continuation of the preceding one of the Irish Sea. It possesses, exclusively, the merit of rectifying the geography of this part of the British Empire in all succeeding works, particularly the large Maps of Scotland, &c. Without its limits, and immediately without them, error has still been found to commence. Mr. Colin Lamont, a respectable mathematician of Greenock, has furnished me with his esteemed testimony in its favour. This gentleman has employed himself occasionally, for many years past, in prosecuting an extensive survey of the West of Scotland, and he has particularly examined the points settled by Captain Huddart. It is expressed on the face of the Chart that, 'the survey was carried on from observations made at Campbelltown, Tobermory, Cana, Ullapool, Laxford, Stornaway, Glash, Namaddy, and Barra, to determine the latitude and longitude by astronomical instruments and chronometers, from which a series of triangles, determined from the true meridian, was carried on, to find the situation of the intermediate places, &c.' Upon this Mr. Lamont has said, 'As to the consistency of Captain Huddart's results in latitude, and my humble attempts, nothing ever afforded me more genuine satisfaction than the almost incredible coincidence of two observers, at distant periods, total strangers to each other; insomuch that, of the ten or eleven different positions which he settled in Scotland, and which are included in very nearly five hundred that I have observed, none differ equal to the breadth of the lines usually drawn on Maps or Charts.'

The Survey of the River Tigris, from Canton to the island of Sankeet, is dated London, 10th of October, 1786, and comprises copious directions for the navigation of that river, appearances of land, &c. To these are added the important determination of the position of Canton, viz. Lat. 23° 6' 57" N. Lon. 113° 16' 15" E., as shewn in the Tables prefixed to the *Oriental Navigator*, in 1816, and therein given, (from reasonable conviction of its accuracy) in preference to many other and later results, which have appeared to the present time.

This is particularly noticed, because the mouth of the Tigris is the grand point of departure for all vessels bound from Canton to every part of the adjacent seas; and, being finally settled, it serves for the rectification of the whole.

In 1788, Captain Huddart made his sketch of the Straits of Gaspar. It was published as merely a *sketch*, yet its longitudes varied but four minutes from the longitudes since adopted, and it afforded an important rectification of the previously existing Charts, &c. of this navigation. An improved edition has been lately published.

False Bay, at the Cape of Good Hope, was surveyed by Captain Huddart in 1797. He had previously surveyed Simon's or Seamon's Bay. Of False Bay there is a new edition, with additions.

Captain Huddart also made some surveys of the Road of Bencoolen, and of a part of the Western Coasts of Sumatra, with the detail of which I am not correctly acquainted; and he, at different times, materially improved the 'Oriental Navigator,' or Directory for the East Indies, the volume to which the Tables of Positions, composed by myself, are now affixed.

The Charts above mentioned are, as I believe, all the larger Charts that the Captain published: but the honorable testimony of Major Rennell has shown that his active mind was occasionally engaged on other important objects.

In the Preface to his Memoir of a Map of Hindoostan, this gentleman writes, 'By the aid of a series of observations of latitude and longitude, taken by Captain Huddart, along the Malabar Coast, or Western Coast of India, the form of the peninsula is now brought very near to the truth.' (Pref. page iv.) And again, 'As Captain Huddart's series of longitudes commenced at Bombay, in lat. 18° 58', and were continued to Anjenga, in Lat. 8° 39', and then back again to Bombay, by which the error of his timekeeper was ascertained, and which was only as much as amounted to 2¼ minutes of longitude, we have every reason to be satisfied with this series, as far as respects general positions: and, indeed, Geography is greatly indebted to the labours of this gentleman, who has presented us with the longitudes of sixteen places on this coast, and by that means given the true general figure of it, which exhibits, to those who have been in the habit of contemplating it, a very different form from what it ever did before.' (Memoir, edition of 1788, page 18.)

To this remark of Major Rennell it may be added that the true longitude of Bombay appears to be 72° 58' E; Captain Huddart made it 72° 54': so that thus, in all this extent of coast, the approximation was to about four minutes, from the results of our best observers to the present day.

A remarkable instance of Captain Huddart's merit as an observer, occurs in Colonel Mudge's account of the Trigonometrical Survey. The Scilly Islands had previously and generally been placed twenty minutes, and more than twenty minutes, of longitude, to the west of their true meridian. In a note on this subject, Colonel Mudge says, 'In the *Requisite Tables*, published by order of the Board of Longitude, the latitude of the Scilly Lights is said to be 49° 56' 0", and longitude 6° 46' 0". The latitude, according to the survey, is 49° 53' 36" 8, and longitude 6° 19' 23" 4. An error of 2' 23" in the latitude, may not perhaps be considered extraordinary; but how, in a maritime country like our own, where chronometers are in such constant use, so great an error as 26' 37" (1^m 46½^s in time) in the longitude, should have remained undetected, excepting by one person, is surprising. J. Huddart, Esq. visited the Scilly Isles, having with him a watch made by Arnold, and obtained his time at that spot in the island of St. Mary, where the body of Sir Cloudesly Shovel is said to have been thrown ashore, by means of equal altitudes of the Sun's limb; he then found, comparing his time with that shewn by the watch, that 0^h 25^m 18^s was the difference between the meridians of Greenwich and this spot in St. Mary's. Now St. Agnes' light-house is about 2' of a degree west of the place to which Mr. Huddart alludes; therefore, 25' 18" + 8" = 25' 26" is the longitude of St. Agnes, through these means; which differs only 4^{s}5 in time, *or a little more than one minute of longitude from that found by the survey.'*

It would be superfluous for me to point out the meritious acts of Captain Huddart as an Elder Brother of the Trinity House, or I might expatiate considerably on the numerous and important services which he has rendered to the country in that capacity.

It is well known that, so long as his health permitted, he was one of the most active and useful members of that honourable and beneficial institution; and that, during this period, more improvement in our light-houses, and other sea-marks, was made than in any preceding, or than probably may be made in any succeeding period of equal length. ALL were improved, and many added, as those for the passage of the Needles, &c.

In 1790, when the new Lights of Hasborough, and that off the Newarp were established, the adjacent sea and shoals were accurately surveyed by Captain Huddart, and a Chart was delivered, on paying light-dues, to the northern Coasters, with complete directions, &c. This Chart gave the longitude of Yarmouth church, a most important position, which has been adopted for all Maps and Charts since published; for, previously, the longitude of the coast of Norfolk was unknown.

In 1794 the Light-vessel at the Owers was established for the guidance of all vessels bound up and down the English Channel, and especially those bound in to Spithead, &c.; and, in 1795, the still more useful one off the North Sand Head of the Goodwin. The description and uses of the latter were, I presume, drawn up by Captain Huddart.

In the same year was established the very useful Light-house of the Longships, near the Land's End of England, for the purpose of guiding vessels from the numerous dangers in the vicinity of the Cornish coast. This was aided by a similar description, with directions.

In 1802 a Floating Light was placed near the Sand called the Sunk, in the King's or North Channel of the Thames' mouth; a survey of the adjacent shoals and passages was made by Captain Huddart; copies of which, with directions, were distributed to the Mariners in the Coasting Trade.

The year 1806 saw the new and most useful Light-house on Flamborough Head, on the coast of Yorkshire, the environs of which were, in like manner, surveyed and described by Captain Huddart.

In the West, the Light-house on the South Stack, near Holyhead, was established in 1809.

The works of Captain Huddart, above enumerated, are the principal that I have any knowledge of. They are not numerous in proportion to their consequence, for they have, in every instance, obviated glaring deficiencies, they have filled up chasms of ignorance with useful knowledge; and they have been, invariably, the results of arduous exertion, most *skilfully applied,* in situations and circumstances of peculiar danger and difficulty; for who but he would *voluntarily* have selected the extremity of Africa, or the rugged cliffs of Western Scotland, for the display of those talents which might have been exhibited, in circumstances of comparative safety, with more benefit to himself in point of emolument, though proportionably with less advantage to others. This evidently was not his object; and his motives seem to have been as pure, as unsophisticated, as were his manners. He made no parade of science, but he possessed it, and was particularly distinguished as one of our earliest Lunarians.[1] Thousands have reason to bless his name for that safety which has been derived from his labours; and the Navigators of all nations, may consider it as synonymous with BENEFACTOR.

I have the honor to be,

Sir,

Your humble Servant,

JOHN PURDY.

---

[1] A member of the Lunar Society of Lichfield whose evening meetings were arranged to coincide with the full moon.

CHAPTER VI

The Royal Society

THE ROYAL Society, as is well known, was founded by Charles II on 22 April 1663, but it was under the Presidency of Sir Isaac Newton during the first quarter of the eighteenth century that the Society really became established on a sure footing which made its fellowship the hallmark of scientific achievement.

In 1772 Joseph Banks was elected President having been a Fellow since 1766. He was a man of wealth, good looks and wide interests but classical knowledge and the grand tour were not for him; his interests lay in natural history and botany. When the voyage of the *Endeavour* commanded by James Cook was planned, Banks petitioned the Admiralty to be allowed to join the expedition. This took him to Tahiti, New Zealand and New South Wales and resulted not only in an accumulation of charts and geographical data of the southern hemisphere by Cook but also in an outstanding collection of botanical specimens by Banks.

In 1791 Joseph Huddart was elected a Fellow. His contribution to scientific knowledge had been his charts and his observations on colour blindness contained in a letter to Joseph Priestly which was published in the Philosophical Transactions of the Society. There is also another small contribution contained in the following letter of 22 December 1784 which, incidentally, tells us the type of quadrant he was using. John Bird was an early maker of Hadley's quadrants. Usually quadrants were rather larger than a twelve-inch radius as this would allow little more than a tenth part of an inch for each degree, which would have to have six subdivisions to give a reading of minutes with the aid of a vernier. The instrument makers, who worked by hand, would have to do some very fine engraving.

D Sir

As every actual Observation adds something to the Stock of Astronomy I beg you will present to the Royal Society the following Extract which I lately received from Capt *Joseph Huddart* of the *Royal Admiral* Indiaman dated St Helena 7th July 1784

'I have diligently looked out for Eclipses of Jupiter's Satellites but have been unfortunate, the weather has been almost perpetually cloudy with much rain since we have been here, & altho' I have always attended have only been able to observe one Immersion & Emersion of the said Satellite as under

	h	m	s		h	m	s
21st June 1784							
Mean Time of Chron'r	14.	20.	22½	Emers	17.	48.	4½
Chron'r fast M.T.		27.	44½			27.	44½
Mean time of Observ'n	13.	52.	28		17.	20.	20
Equat'n		1.	31½			1.	32
	13.	51.	6½		17.	18.	48

'The Telescope [which is an Acromatick of Dollond] answers tollerably well, the Time was taken when I could see the least appearance & I could observe the Satellite decrease & increase for 40s. I suppose there must have been a considerable Error in the Tables as the Time may be depended upon, The Quadrant giving me the Time (as it adjusts well) to the *nearest second* by *equal altitudes.*'

I shall only add that the Quadrant is that of 12 inch Radius by Bird, which the late Captain Cooke had in his last Voyage, lent to Capt Huddart by the Board of Longitude thro' your and my other Friends, good offices,

I remain D Sir very truely Yours
L. Dalrymple

22d. Dec. 1784[1]

Joseph Huddart is thought to have been the first person to have produced a reliable account of persons unable to distinguish colours which he set out in a letter written to the Rev. Joseph Priestley on 15 January 1777. Priestley read this to the Royal Society on the following 13 February and in 1779 Abbe Rozier translated his account into French. Huddart's account was also referred to by John Dalton, the famous chemist, in a paper he read to the Literary & Philosophical Society of Manchester in 1794. Both Dalton and his brother suffered from colour blindness; they were born at Eaglesfield near Cockermouth in Cumberland but J. Dalton went to Manchester to teach mathematics. The letter to Priestley reads as follows:

London, January 15th, 1777.

Sir,

When I had the pleasure of waiting on you last winter, I had hopes before now of giving you a more perfect account of the peculiarity of vision which I then mentioned to you, in a person of my acquaintance in the North: however, if I give you now the best I am able, I persuade myself you will pardon the delay.

I promised to procure you a written account from the person himself, but this I was unfortunately disappointed in, by his dying suddenly of a pleurisy a short time after my return to the country.

You will recollect I told you that this person lived at Maryport in Cumberland, near which place, viz. at Allonby, I myself live, and having known him about ten years, have had frequent opportunities of conversing with him. His name was Harris, by trade a shoemaker. I had often heard from others that he could discern the form and magnitude of all objects very distinctly, but could not distinguish colours. This report having excited my curiosity, I conversed with him frequently on the subject. The account he gave was this: That he had reason to believe other persons saw something in objects which he could not see; that their language seemed to mark qualities with confidence and precision, which he could only guess at with hesitation, and frequently with error. His first suspicion of this arose when he was about four years

---

[1] This is reproduced by courtesy of the Royal Society.

old. Having by accident found in the street a child's stocking, he carried it to a neighbouring house to enquire for the owner; he observed the people called it a *red* stocking, though he did not understand why they gave it that denomination, as he himself thought it completely described by being called *a stocking*. The circumstance, however, remained in his memory, and together with subsequent observations led him to the knowledge of his defect. As the idea of colours is among the first that enters the mind, it may perhaps seem extraordinary that he did not observe his want of it still earlier. This, however, may in some measure be accounted for from the circumstance of his family being Quakers, among whom a general uniformity of colours is known to prevail.

He observed also that, when young, other children could discern cherries on a tree by some pretended difference of colour, though he could only distinguish them from the leaves by their difference of size and shape. He observed also, that by means this difference of colour they could see the cherries at a greater distance than he could, though he could see other objects at as great a distance as they; that is, where the sight was not assisted by the colour. Large objects he could see as well as other persons; and even the smaller ones if they were not enveloped in other things, as in the case of cherries among the leaves.

I believe he could never do more than guess the name of any colour; yet he could distinguish white from black, or black from any light or bright colour. Dove or straw-colour he called white, and different colours he frequently called by the same name: yet he could discern a difference between them when placed together. In general, colours of an equal degree of brightness, however they might otherwise differ, he frequently confounded together. Yet a striped ribbon he could distinguish from a plain one; but he could not tell what the colours were with any tolerable exactness. Dark colours in general he often mistook for black, but never imagined white to be a dark colour, nor a dark to be a white colour.

He was an intelligent man, and very desirous of understanding the nature of light and colours, for which end he had attended a course of lectures in natural philosophy.

He had two brothers in the same circumstances as to sight; and two other brothers and sisters who, as well as their parents, had nothing of this defect.

One of the first mentioned brothers, who is now living, is master of a trading vessel belonging to Maryport. I met with him at Dublin, in December 1776, and took the opportunity of conversing with him. I wished to try his capacity to distinguish the colours in a prism, but not having one by me, I asked him, Whether he had ever seen a rain-bow? He replied, He had often, and could distinguish the different colours; meaning only, that it was composed of different colours, for he could not tell what they were.

I then procured and shewed him a piece of ribbon: he immediately, without any difficulty, pronounced it a striped and not a plain ribbon. He then attempted to name the different stripes: the several stripes of white he uniformly, and without hesitation, called white: the four black stripes he was deceived in, for three of them he thought brown, though they were exactly of the same shade with the other, which he properly called black. He spoke, however, with diffidence as to all those stripes; and it must be owned, the black was not very distinct: the light green he called yellow; but he was not very positive: he said, 'I think this is what you call yellow.' The middle stripe, which had a slight tinge of red, he called a sort of blue. But he was most of all deceived by the orange colour; of this he spoke very confidently, saying, 'This is the colour of grass; this is green.' I also shewed him a great variety of ribbons, the colours of which he sometimes named rightly, and sometimes as differently as possible from the true colours.

I asked him, Whether he imagined it possible for all the various colours he saw, to be mere difference of light and shade; whether he thought there could be various degrees between white and black; and that all colours could be composed of these two mixtures only? With some hesitation he replied, No, he did imagine there was some other difference.

I could not conveniently procure from this person an account in writing; but I have given his own words, having set them down in writing immediately. Besides, as this conversation happened only the 10th of last month, it is still fresh in my memory. I have endeavoured to give a faithful account of this matter, and not to render it more wonderful than it really is.

It is proper to add, that the experiment of the striped ribbon was made in the day-time, and in a good light.
I am, Sir, &c.

On 24 November 1796 Huddart read a paper to the Royal Society on 'Observations on Horizontal Refractions which affect the appearance of terrestrial objects, and Dip, or Depression of the Horizon of the Sea.' The subject must have seemed esoteric even to the members of the Royal Society, and more a subject for discussion in the captain's room at some port hostelry over a noggin of rum. Few people apart from navigators were familiar with the use of a sextant or the tricks that can be played by horizontal refraction.

Huddart made the point that evaporation in the atmosphere can distort the observation of the horizon or of distant objects. In fact, the paper was of more scientific interest than anyone quite realised. The word 'mirage' had not at this date been coined but here the phenomenon was being explained for the first time. By an extraordinary coincidence the most astonishing account of superior mirage in England occurred less than two years later. In July 1798 from Hastings beach on a still hot afternoon the whole French coast from Calais to Dieppe could be seen in the clearest detail for a period of over three hours.

Huddart in his paper described three instances where his vision of distant objects became distorted, and this distortion caused problems in the use of a sextant, the instrument used to measure the altitude of the sun in relation to the horizon. From the reading of a sextant the observer can determine his latitude. The idea of the modern sextant, which brings the observation of the sun into line with the horizon by the use of mirrors, was first conceived by Robert Hawke in 1667. If the horizon, not being a reflected image, is visible along the edge of one mirror and another mirror reflects the image of the sun on to that edge, the altitude of the sun can be arrived at from the angle between the two mirrors. It took an expert in mechanics to put Hawke's theory into practice and that man was John Hadley.

Hadley was born in 1682 and was a mathematician and a mechanist. In 1732 his reflecting quadrant was tested by the Admiralty and became the accepted instrument for determining latitude by observation of the sun.

Hadley's quadrant consisted of a mahogany frame forming an octant, or a sector of forty-five degrees, with a scale engraved upon the circular edge which would have been faced with metal measuring 0° to 90°. An arm called the 'index bar' was fixed on the frame to rotate from the centre of the circle of which the octant formed a sector. This carried a vernier scale which travelled over the scale on the frame. Centred over the pivot of the index bar was a mirror called the 'index mirror' standing perpendicular to the frame so that the face of the mirror was in line with the index bar.

Standing on the frame and perpendicular to it was another mirror with

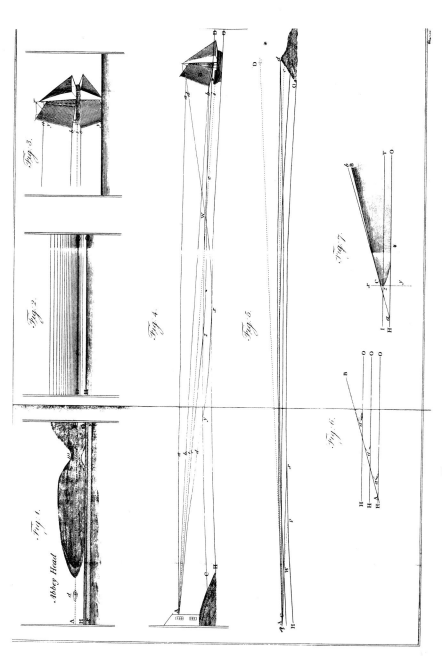

Illustration of Mirage at Abbey Head, Galloway.

the upper half unsilvered and left as clear glass called the 'horizon glass'. The mirrors faced each other and were so arranged that when the horizon glass and the index mirror were parallel, zero on the index bar coincided with 0° graduation on the scale on the frame; the graduations were one sixth part of a degree, making it possible, with the aid of the vernier, to take measurements in minutes. As soon as the observation had been made the vernier was clamped to the frame, so that the angle of the index bar could be read off in degrees and minutes giving the altitude of the sun.

By 1780 quadrants or sextants had a tangent screw on the clamp so that a finer adjustment of the index bar could be made once it was clamped. Other improvements were a telescope through which to view the horizon and a microscope to assist in reading the scale. Quadrants or sextants had shades of coloured glass to reduce the glare of the sun and Hadley's quadrants had a back glass or back horizon mirror to enable measurements to be made of angles greater than ninety degrees, but these were difficult to keep in adjustment and were soon discontinued. Huddart says, 'I could never adjust the back observation of Hadley's quadrant with sufficient accuracy to be depended upon.'

As the angle of incidence is always equal to the angle of reflection a mirror moving through an angle of 45° will measure the altitude of the sun up to 90°, so that what was referred to as a Quadrant was in fact an Octant. By the end of the eighteenth century the sextant replaced the octant.

The text of Joseph Huddart's paper reads as follows:

> The variation and uncertainty of the dip, in different states of the air, taken at the same altitude above the level of the sea, was the occasion of my turning my thoughts to this subject; as it renders the latitude observed incorrect, by giving an erroneous zenith distance of a celestial object.

> I have often observed that low lands and the extremity of head-lands or points, forming an acute angle with the horizon of the sea, and viewed from a distance beyond it, appear elevated above it, with an open space between the land and the sea. The most remarkable instance of this appearance of the land I observed at Macao, for several days previous to a typhoon, in which the Locko lost her topmasts in Macao Roads; the points of the islands and low lands appearing the highest, and the spaces between them and the sea the largest, I ever saw. I believe it arises, and is proportional to the evaporation going on from the sea; and in reflecting upon this phenomenon, I am convinced that those appearances must arise from refraction, and that instead of the density of the atmosphere increasing to the surface of the sea, it must decrease from some space above it; and that evaporation is the principal cause which prevents the uniformity of density and refraction being continued, by the general law, down to the surface of the earth: and I am inclined to believe, though I mention it here as a conjecture, that the difference of specific gravity in the particles of the atmosphere may be a principal agent in evaporation; for the corpuscles of air, from their affinity with water, being combined at the surface of the fluid from expansion, form air specifically lighter than the drier atmosphere; and therefore float, or rise, from that principle, as steam from water; and in their rising (the surrounding corpuscles from the same cause imbibing a part of the moisture), become continually drier as they ascend, yet continue ascending until they become equally dense with the air.* However, these conjectures I shall leave, and proceed to the following observations upon refractions.

> (* Mr Hamilton, in his very curious essay on the ascent of vapours, does not allow of this principle, even as an assistant; though by a remark (page 15) he takes notice of those appearances in the horizon of the sea, and says they

arise from a strong or unusual degree of refraction; the contrary of which I hope to illustrate in the course of this paper.)

In the year 1793, when at Allonby in Cumberland, I made some remarks on the appearance of the Abbey Head in Galloway, which in distance from Allonby is about seven leagues; and from my window, at fifty feet above the level of the sea at that time of tide, I observed the appearance of the land about the Head as represented in Tab. 1 fig. 1. There was a dry sand, *x y*, called Robin Rigg, between me and the Head, at the distance from my house of between three and four miles, over which I saw the horizon of the sea, H O; the sand at this time was about three or four feet above the level of the sea. The hummock *d* is a part of the head-land, but appeared insulated or detached from the rest, and considerably elevated above the sea, with an open space between. I then came down about twenty-five feet, when I had the dry sand of Robin Rigg, *x y*, in the apparent horizon, and lost all that floating appearance seen from above, and the Abbey Head appeared every where distinct to the surface of the sand; this being in the afternoon, the wet or moisture on the said would in a great measure be dried up. I have reason, therefore, to conclude that evaporation is the cause of a less refraction near the surface of the sea; and when so much so as to make an object appear elevated wholly above the horizon, (as at *d* in fig. 1.) there will from every point of this object issue two pencils of rays of light, which enter the eye of the observer; and that below the dotted line A B (parallel to the horizon of the sea H O), the objects on the land will appear inverted.

To explain this phenomenon, I shall propose the following theory, and compare it with the observations which I have made. Suppose H O, fig. 2, to represent the horizontal surface of the sea, and the parallel lines above it, the laminae or strata of corpuscles, which next the fluid are most expanded, or the rarest; and every lamina upwards increasing in density till it arrive at a maximum (and which I shall in future call the maximum of density) at the line D C, above which it again decreases in density, ad infinitum.

Though this in reality may be the case, I do not wish to extend the meaning of the word density further, than to be taken for the refractive power of the atmosphere; that is, a ray of light entering obliquely a denser lamina to be refracted towards a perpendicular to its surface; and in entering a rarer lamina, the contrary; which laminae being taken at infinitely small distances, the ray of light will form a curve, agreeable to the laws of dioptrics.

In order to establish this principle in horizontal refractions, I traced over various parts of this shore at different times, when those appearances seemed favorable, with a good telescope, and found objects sufficient to confirm it; though it be difficult at that distance of the land to get terrestrial objects well defined so near the horizon, as will afterwards appear.

One day observing the land elevated, and seeing a small vessel at about eight miles distance, I from my window directed my telescope to her, and thought her a fitter object than any other I had seen for the purpose of explaining the phoenomena of these refractions. The telescope was forty feet above the level of the sea, the boat's mast about thirty-five feet, she being about twenty to thirty tons burthen. The barometer at 29.7 inches, and Fahrenheit's thermometer at 54°.

The appearance of the vessel, as magnified in the telescope, was as represented in fig. 3, and from the mast head to the boom was well defined. I pretty distinctly saw the head and shoulders of the man at the helm; but the hull of the vessel was contracted, confused, and ill defined: the inverted image began to be well defined at the boom (for I could not clearly perceive the man at the helm inverted,) and from the boom to the horizon of the sea the sails were well defined, and I could see a small opening above the horizon of the sea, in the angle made by the gaff and mast; and had the mast been shorter by ten feet (to the height of *y*), the whole would have been elevated above the horizon of the sea, and from *y* to *d* an open space. This drawing was taken from a sketch I took at the time, and represents the proportion of the inverted to the erect object, as near as I could take it by the eye, the former being about two-thirds of the latter in height, and the same breadth respectively; though at one time during my observation, which I continued for about an hour, I thought the inverted nearly as tall as the erect object. The day was fine and clear, with a very light air of wind, and I found very little tremor or oscillation in viewing her through the telescope.

I have laid down fig. 4 for the explanation of the above phenomenon, in which A represents the window I viewed B the vessel from; H O, the curved surface of the sea; C D, parallel to H O, the height of the maximum of density of the atmosphere; the lines marked with the small letters *a a*, *b b*, *c c*, *d d*, the pencils of rays under their various refractions from the vessel to the eye, or object glass of the telescope.

The pencil of rays *a a*, from a point near the head of the mainsail, is wholly refracted in a curve convex upwards, being every where above the maximum of density; and the pencil of rays *d d*, which issues from the same point in the sail, and passes near the horizon of the sea at *x*, is convex upwards from the sail to W, where it passes the line of maximum of density, which is the point of inflection; there it becomes convex downwards, passing near the horizon at *x* to *y*, where it is again inflected, and becomes convex upwards from thence to the eye. The pencil of rays *b b*, from the end of the boom, passing nearly parallel to the horizon, and near the maximum of density, suffers very little deviation from a right line in the first part; but in ascending (from the curvature of the sea) will be convex upwards to the eye. The pencil of rays *c c*, from the same point in the boom, may have the small part to *c* convex upwards, from *c* to *z* it will be convex downwards, and from *z* to the eye convex upwards.

From this investigation it appears, that two pencils of rays cannot pass from the same point, and enter the eye, from the law of refraction, except one pencil pass through a medium which the other has not entered; and therefore the maximum of density was below the boom, and could not exceed ten feet of height above the surface of the sea at the time these observations were made.

Respecting the hull of the vessel being confused, and ill defined in the telescope, as by fig. 3, it arises from the blending of the rays, from the different parts of the object, refracted through the two mediums; some parts of the hull appearing erect, and some inverted. Suppose the dotted line *i i*, fig. 4, an indefinite pencil of rays, passing from between the inverted and erect parts of the object, or the upper part of the hull of the vessel, to the eye, (for the lower part of the hull could not be observed): the objects cannot appear inverted, except the angles at the eye *a* A *c* and *a* A *d*, exceed the angle *a* A *i*; for the intermediate space could only be contracted by the secondary pencils of rays. The lengths of the inverted, compared with the erect image of the sail, is as the sines of the angles at the eye *a* A *i* to *i* A *d*; and the angle at the eye *a* A *d*, made by the two pencils of rays from the same point near the head of the sail, must be double the angle *a* A *i*, when the inverted image is as tall as the erect. In this case, the sines of the angles *a* A *b*, *a* A *c*, *a* A *d*, fig. 4, are proportional to the altitudes *a b*, *a c*, *a d*, in the magnified view of the vessel, fig. 3.

Under this consideration no inverted image of the sail will be formed, until the angle at the eye, made by the two refracted pencils of rays *a a* and *d d*, exceed the angle made by *a a*, and *b b*, the apparent height of the sail of the vessel; for were those angles equal, the inverted sail would only be contracted into the parallel of altitude of the boom *b*, and render the appearance confused, as in the hull of the vessel.

Respecting the existence of two pencils of rays entering the eye from every point of an object not more elevated than a, or less than i, fig. 3, in this state of the atmosphere, I cannot bring a stronger proof than that of the strength of a light when the rays pass near the horizon of the sea, proved by the following observations.

Going down Channel about five years ago in the Trinity yacht, with several of the elder brethren, to inspect the light-houses, &c. I was told by some of the gentlemen, who had been on a former survey, that the lower light of Portland was not so strong as the upper light, at near distances, but that at greater distances it was much stronger. I suspected that this difference arose from the lower light being at or near the horizon of the sea, and mentioned it at the time; but afterwards had a good opportunity of making the observation. We passed the Bill of Portland in the evening, steering towards the Start, a fresh breeze from the northward and clear night; when we had run about five leagues from the lights, during which time the upper light was universally allowed to be the stronger, several gentlemen keeping watch to make observations thereon, the lower light, drawing near the horizon, suddenly shone with double lustre. Mr. Strachan, whose sight is weak, had for some time before lost sight of both lights, but could then clearly perceive the lower light. I then went aloft, (as well as others,) but before I got half mast up, the lower light was weaker than the upper one; on coming down upon deck, I found it again as strong as before. We proceeded on, and soon lost the lower light from the deck; and drawing the upper light near the horizon, it like the former shone exceeding bright. I again went aloft, when it diminished in brightness; but from the mast-head I could then see the lower light near the horizon as strong as before. This is in consequence of the double quantity of light entering the eye by the two pencils of rays from every point. To illustrate which, we compare the vessel, fig. 4, to a light-house built upon the shore, and A the place of the observer; and having brought down the light so low as to view it in the direction $a\,a$, another light would appear in the horizon at x from the pencil $d\,d$; and had the vessel been still enough to have observed it at this time with a good glass, I doubt not but the two images might have been distinctly seen: as the light dropped, (by increasing the distance) the two images would appear continually to approach each other, till blended with double light in one, and disappear at the altitude i, above the apparent horizon of the sea. But, as explained before, if the strength of evaporation did not separate by refraction the pencils $a\,a$ and $d\,d$ to a greater angle than double the angle that the lamps and reflectors appear under, the two images would be blended, and the strong appearance of light would be of shorter duration. The distance run from the lights, during the time each of the lights shone bright, would have been useful, but this did not occur at the time, nor have I had the like opportunity since. However, I recommend to the mariner to station people at different heights in looking out for a light, in order to get sight of it near the horizon, when it is always the strongest.

Respecting the appearance of the Abbey Head before mentioned, fig. 1, the dotted line A B represents the limit, or the lowest points of the land that can be seen over the sea; for, as above stated, all the objects appearing below this line, are the land above it inverted; and where the land is low, as at d and m, it must appear elevated above the horizon of the sea.

In fig. 5. let H O represent the curve of the ocean, and d the extreme top of the mount visible at A by the help of refraction; the dotted pencil of rays $c\,c$ passing from d to the eye in some part a little below the maximum of density, where inversion begins; therefore no land lower than this can be seen; for any pencil from a point in the land lower than this, must in the refraction have a contrary flexure in the curve, and therefore pass above the observer. Let A D be a tangent to the curve at A, then the object d will appear to be elevated by refraction to D; also let A v be a tangent to the pencil A x at A, then the angle D A x will appear to be an open space, or between D and the horizon of the sea. Suppose a star should appear very near and over the mount d, as at ★, two pencils would issue from every point of it, and form a star below as well as above the hummock *d*. There are always confused or ill defined images of the objects at the height of the dotted line, fig. 1, above the level of the sea, as before mentioned; and instead of the points of *d* ending sharp in that line, they appear blunted, and the Abbey Head is frequently insulated at the neck *m*.

I have viewed, from an elevated situation, a point or head land at a distance beyond the horizon of the sea, forming, as in fig. 6, a straight line A B, making an acute angle B A O with the horizon of the sea. Seeing the extreme point blunted and elevated, I descended; and though in descending the horizon cut the land higher, as at H O, H O, yet the point had always the same appearance as *a, a, a*, fig. 6, though the land is known to continue in the direction of the straight line A B to beneath the horizon, or nearly so, as viewed from the height above.

If then from a low situation we view this head land through a telescope, the inclination of the surface A B to the horizon being known to be a straight line, it will appear as in fig. 7, the dotted line (at the height of the point where a perpendicular *x y* would touch the extreme of the land) being at the limit or lowest point of erect vision. And if a tangent to the curved appearance of the land *a b*, is drawn parallel to the inclined surface of the land A B, fig. 6, touching it at C, the point C will shew the height of the maximum of density, where the pencil of the rays of light, from thence to the eye, approach nearest the sea; for pencils of rays from this land, taken at small distances from C, will form parallel curves, nearly through the refracting mediums, and C will be the point of greatest refraction; for above C, as at B, the refraction somewhat decreasing, will appear below the line *a b*, or the parallel to the surface of the land, and the refractions decrease below the point C; for had they increased uniformly down to the surface of the sea, it would render the apparent angle of the point of land *z* more acute than the angle C *a* O, contrary to all observations.

Thus I have endeavoured to explain the phoenomena of the distorted appearance of the land near the horizon of the sea, when the evaporation is great; and when at the least, I never found the land quite free from it when I used a telescope; and from thence infer, that we cannot have any expectation to find a true correction for the effect of terrestrial refraction, by taking any certain part of the contained arc; for the points *z* C B, fig. 7, will have various refractions, though they are at nearly the same distance from the observer. And if the observations are made wholly over land, if the ground rises to within a small distance of the rays of light in their passage from the object to the eye, as well as at the situation of the object and observer, the refractions will be subject to be influenced by the evaporations of rains, dews, &c., which is sufficiently proved by the observations of Colonel Williams, Captain Mudge, and Mr. Dalby, Phil. Trans. 1795, p. 583.

The appearances mentioned by Colonel Williams, Captain Mudge, and Mr. Dalby, (Phil. Trans. 1795, p. 586, 587,) cannot be demonstrated upon general principles, as they arise from evaporation producing partial refractions. In those general principles, it is supposed that the same lamina of density is every where at an equal distance from the surface of the sea, at least as far as the eye can reach a terrestrial object; but in the partial refractions, the lamina of the expanded or rarefied medium may be of various figures according to circumstances, which will refract according to the incidence of the rays, and affect the appearance of the land accordingly, which I have often seen to a surprising degree. But my principal view is to shew the uncertainty of the dip of the sea, and that the effect of evaporation tends to depress the apparent horizon at *x*, when the eye is not above the maximum of density; and from hence the difficulty of laying down any correct formula for these refractions, whilst the law of evaporation is so little understood, which indeed seems a task not easy to surmount. The effect indicated by the barometer and thermometer is insufficient: and should the hygrometer be improved to fix a standard for moisture in the atmosphere, and shew the variations near the surface of the ocean, which certainly must be taken into the account, (evaporation going on quicker in a dry than a moist atmosphere,) the theory might still be incomplete for correcting the tables of the dip. I shall therefore conclude this paper, by shewing a method I used in practice, in order to obviate this error, in low latitudes.

When I was desirous to attain more accurately the latitude of any head-land, &c. in sight, I frequently observed the angular distances of the Sun's nearest limb from the horizons, upon the meridian both north and south, beginning a few minutes before noon, and taking alternately the observations each way, from the poop, or some convenient part of the ship, where the Sun and the horizon both north and south were not intercepted; and having found the greatest and least distances from the respective horizons, which was at the Sun's passing the meridian, and corrected both for refraction, by subtracting from the least, and adding to the greatest altitude, the quantity given by the table; and also having corrected for the error of the instrument, and the Sun's semi-diameter; the sum of these two angular distances, reduced as above, − 180°, is equal to double the dip, as by the following

EXAMPLE.

The Sun's declination 4° 32' 30" north, and its semi-diameter 15' 58" took the following observation:

		South				North		
The meridian distance of the Sun's nearest limb from the horizon of the sea		78°	36'	30"	=	101°	1'	20"
Refraction per table		−	0	11	=	+	0	11
Distance corr. for refraction	=	78	36	19	=	101	1	31
Error of the Sextant		+	1	32		+	1	32
Sun's semi-diameter		+	15	58		+	15	58
		78	53	49		101	19	1
½ diff. or the dip found			6	25		78	53	49
Altitude reduced	=	78	47	24		180	12	50
Zenith distance	=	11	12	36		180		

					diff	12	50
The Sun's declination N	=	4	32	30	½ = (Dip)	6	25
Latitude of the ship N	=	15	45	06			

I regret that I cannot in this paper insert the dip which I have found in my observations; for I only retained the latitude of the ship determined thereby, as is usual at sea; I generally rejected the error of the instrument, the dip, and semi-diameter, as they affect both observations with the same signs, and reduce the observation by the following method:

	South				North				
Sun's dist. as before	78°	36'	30"		101°	1'	20"			
Refraction	−	0	11		+	0	11			
Dis. cor. for refraction	78	36	19		101	1	31	101°	1'	31"
				+	78	36	19			
Sum of S. diam. dip, & refraction = ½ diff.				Sum	179	37	50			
	+	11	5		180			+	11	5
Carried over	78	47	24	Diff		22	10	101	12	35

Brought over	78 47 24	Diff	22 10	101 12 35
		½	11 5	101 12 36
	90			90
The ½ dist. as before =	11 12 36	½ D. =		11 12 36

It may be observed, that neither the dip, semi-diameter, or index error, can affect the zenith distance of the Sun's centre; and the refraction being small near the zenith, the result must be true if the angles are accurately taken; and it is only necessary to observe, that when the sum of the distances is less than 180°, the half difference must be added to the distances, as by the last reduction. There is a difficulty in making this observation when the Sun passes the meridian very near the zenith, as the change in azimuth from east to west is too quick to allow sufficient time; nor can it be obtained by the sextant when the Sun passes the meridian more than 30 degrees from the zenith; for I never could adjust the back observation of the Hadley's quadrant with sufficient accuracy to be depended upon.

To follow Joseph Huddart's argument requires some practical knowledge of the use of a sextant, as there are certain corrections to be made to obtain an accurate reading. In the first place Dip involves a correction. This results from the observation not being made at sea level, that is to say, the actual level of the water which would provide no field of vision. The higher the point of observation the more extensive the field of vision, because the view is less restricted owing to the curvature of the earth; in fact, the distance of the horizon in nautical miles is equal to 1.06 times the square root of the viewer's height in feet above sea level. If an observation is made at a point one hundred feet above sea level this will widen the angle the sun makes with the horizon and make a difference of about ten miles in calculating the observer's position.

Secondly, a slight correction is needed for refraction, because the light of the sun's rays coming through the atmosphere becomes slightly distorted: refraction is greatest when the sun is low in the sky. Tables are given in nautical almanacs for these corrections. Thirdly, corrections have to be made for any inaccuracies in the instrument as no instrument is perfect and these error sare established when the instrument is tested.

Joseph Huddart points out that with regard to refraction, one cannot be satisfied with a rule of thumb calculation, because there comes a point near the earth's surface where the density of the atmosphere decreases instead of increasing. He attributes this to 'evaporation', which may not be the correct word to use as evaporation means to disperse into vapour whereas what is being referred to is the loss of density in what is already a vapour. Although it was realised at the time that air could be dense and heavier or less dense and lighter this was not attributed to hot air expanding. The cause of air currents was not really understood, although Boyles Law had been established in the previous century and it was known that as pressure eased volume expanded and vice versa.

What is happening in Huddart's observation is that the heat of the ground is expanding the air above it and reducing its density but this increases as it cools and meets the atmosphere above, at the point of maximum density. It is now generally accepted that there are abnormalities in refraction particularly where the temperature of the air and the sea differ, but no satisfactory method has evolved of evaluating them; Huddart, however, shows how the problem can be overcome.

Let us now turn to the actual observations made. In 1793 from his house on the shore of Allonby Bay in Cumberland, Huddart could see across to Abbey Head in Galloway 21 miles away, and from his window 50 feet above the level of the sea at that particular state of the tide there was an area of dry sand called Robin Rigg between him and Abbey Head about three or four miles from his house, over which the horizon of the sea was visible and the sand rose to about three or four feet above sea level. A hummock forming the extremity of the headland appeared to be detached from it and considerably elevated above the sea. However, coming down to 25 feet above sea level the dry sand of Robin Rigg became the horizon and the floating appearance disappeared with Abbey Head everywhere distinct to the surface of the sand. The explanation Huddart offers is that evaporation causes a loss of refraction near the surface of the sea and when this is sufficient it makes an object appear elevated above the horizon.

Two rays of light enter the eye of the observer, a superior one which is direct and an inferior reflected one where the objects on the land appear inverted. The reason for this is that there is a layer of maximum density at some distance above the sea and either side of this the density decreases.

The second observation Huddart made was of a small vessel of about twenty to thirty tons about eight miles from his window. The telescope was about forty feet above the level of the sea, barometer stood at 29.7 inches and the temperature was 54° Fahrenheit: he estimated the height of the mast at thirty-five feet. He observed that the mast down to the level of the boom and the man at the helm were distinct but the hull was contracted and confused and then the image below the boom appeared inverted.

Huddart explains in some detail that the inferior image is reflected from the warm layer of air near the surface, whereas the superior image is seen directly and at the point of maximum density the image will be confused. He puts the point of maximum density in this instance at about ten feet above the level of the sea, that is where the warm air rises from the earth and losing density meets the pressure of the atmosphere from above.

The third observation given in this paper is connected with the inspection of Portland Lighthouse. The lower light was reported to be not so strong as the upper light at near distances, but stronger than the upper light at greater distances. The *Trinity* yacht with several elder brethren on board passed Portland Bill with a fresh breeze from the northward and a clear night. At 15 miles from the lighthouse the upper light, it was agreed, was the stronger, but when they reached the point where the lower light was near the horizon it shone with double lustre. On going aloft at half mast the lower light was weaker than the upper one. They continued sailing until the lower could not be seen from the deck and then, as the upper light was near the horizon, it shone much more brightly, but on going aloft this brightness diminished. However, on reaching the masthead the lower light could be seen as strong as it was before.

Huddart explains this by saying that at a certain point the superior image coming directly to the eye and the inferior image reflected from the surface of the sea become blended into one. Huddart concludes by saying that having established the uncertainty of identifying exactly the dip of the sea's horizon that the effect of evaporation tends to depress the apparent horizon when the eye is not above the point of maximum density. Therefore, it is difficult to lay down an exact principle for establishing dip particularly in low latitudes.

Huddart suggests as an alternative method, taking observations in opposite directions. If the eye is at sea level then the view of the heavens, unless interrupted, forms a complete hemisphere giving a measurement from one point on the horizon to another diametrically opposite 180°, but if the eye is some feet above sea level owing to the curvature of the earth slightly more than an exact hemisphere comes into view and this is the reason for dip.

Declination is a factor that has to be taken into account in determining latitude from observations of the sun; which arises from the apparent movement of the sun during the year from its position over the Tropic of Cancer at the summer solstice, when declination is at its maximum, to its position over the Equator at the autumnal equinox, when declination is minimal and to the Tropic of Capricorn at the winter solstice. If we imagine the celestial equator in the heavens as corresponding with the Equator upon the earth, declination is the number of degrees on any day of the year the sun appears to be North or South of the celestial equator.

In taking readings of the altitude of the sun it is more accurate to observe a limb of the sun that is its edge than to try and fix the centre of the sun and so a correction is required which is taken from tables of the sun's semi-diameter.

The term zenith regards the observer as at the centre of the celestial hemisphere. If we regard this as a vast umbrella over the head of the observer, then the zenith is the point immediately above him. The angular distance of an object in the heavens above the celestial horizon is called its altitude and its angular distance from the zenith is called its zenith distance and added together they must equal 90°.

Having established the altitude of the sun with the aid of a sextant, the latitude of the observer is equal to the Zenith Distance plus or minus the declination of the sun according to the position of the observer. A declination North will be added in the northern hemisphere and a declination South subtracted.

In the example given by Huddart, his nautical almanac gives the sun's declination for the day of the observation as 4° 32' 30" North and the sun's semi-diameter as 15' 58". The meridian distance from the sea's horizon is given as 78° 36' 30" South and 101° 1' 20" North, which after correction is 78° 53' 49" South and 101° 19' 1" North. These readings total 180° 12' 50": therefore the height of the observer above sea level has increased the arc visible by 6' 25" in each direction: to arrive at the sun's altitude this has to be deducted making the altitude 78° 47' 24". The Zenith Distance is the difference between this figure and 90° that is 11° 12' 36" to which must be added the sun's declination to arrive at the observer's latitude, making it 15° 45' 06".

Huddart goes on to point out that when readings are taken in opposite directions certain steps in the calculation can be omitted, but this has not been a practice that navigators have followed. Hadley's quadrant or octant with the use of a back glass made it possible in theory to read angles between 90° and 180°, but the use of a back glass was soon discontinued.

The sextant, which extended the scale of an octant to 120°, superseded Hadley's octant and became generally adopted. This was first introduced by John Campbell, originally pressed into the Navy but later to become a Vice-Admiral, so that the question of reading angles above 120° was precluded.

The interest in Huddart's paper really lies in its being the first attempt to account for the phenomenon of mirage and for the apparent displacement of the horizon, where air and water temperatures differ; it is generally accepted that in certain parts of the world the displacement of the horizon can give an error of ten or even fifteen minutes.

The two contributions to the Royal Society are of a very diverse nature but they do show the ability of Joseph Huddart as a scientist, that is, one whose powers of observation see things that do not follow the ordinary course of nature, which others pass by unnoticed, and having seen them then seek an explanation for the abnormality.

The only common ground between Huddart's two papers is vision: in the one case there is a person with a defect in his sight which had never been remarked on before, and in the other case there is a distortion of the scene observed, which also had never been remarked on before. Huddart does not offer a solution to colour blindness, nor to the effect of mirage, except for possible ways of avoiding it.

The same powers of observation gave rise to his invention explained in Chapter VIII. In this case, he noticed the way a rope broke and most people would have been satisfied that it was in the nature of ropes to break if the strain was too great, but what Huddart noticed was that at first only the outer strands broke and the inner strands then took up the strain until they gave way and eventually only the core was left. From this he satisfied himself that initially it was the outer strands which were taking the strain and the inner strands were just packing on which there was little tension. This led him to find a way of distributing the strain equally throughout the rope.

CHAPTER VII

Navigational Surveys

HUDDART'S RETURN from China in 1786 took him back to Allonby, where, although his wife had died recently, his mother was still living and evidently while there, he was approached by the Senhouses to advise on Maryport harbour, which during the eighteenth century had developed from a haven for fishermen to a busy port. A lifetime at sea and an established reputation as a hydrographer gave him the necessary qualifications for such a task. His report for the harbour improvements is contained in the following letter to Philip Nelson acting on behalf of the Trustees. Of course Maryport was a harbour well known to Huddart: it was here that the *Patience* was built and from here he took her on the first voyage. In fact he must have been in and out of this harbour on many occasions in his early days.

Mr. Philip Nelson.

Sir,

As you have desired my Opinion of Improving the Harbour of Maryport, I therefore Transmit you the following Remarks; And inclose you a sketch to elucidate the same, which at some proper opportunity I request may be laid before the Trustees of the Harbour.

The Present Works which is done in black lines, I have taken from your Plan as the one I had formerly done from my own Survey, I have not by me, & the Parts represented in Red are additional Works.

The greatest error in the former works of this Harbour arises for want of room inside; for as 40 or 50 yards is as narrow as the entrance ought to be for the safety of Shipping entering the Harbour in heavy Gales; The Sea from this entrance will principally diminish in Proportion to the Area within. Jetty's are secondary helps and when Properly constructed will render the Harbour compleat.

It is said the Present Complaint from the Masters is the great Sea thrown into the Harbour in heavy gales of wind from the NWward tho I think it cannot be worse than we have formerly known it; And to remedy this it is proposed to lengthen the Woodwork Jetty from *A* towards *a*. In my opinion this will incommode the entrance of the Harbour & will be a considerable expence for a Temporary relief, & Probably such extream bad Weather as we have had of late may not hapen in the Course of the Winter.

But in case it is absolutely necessary to add something immediately would prefer continuing the Jetty in the same Direction towards *b* when $\frac{2}{3}^{ds}$ the Length will break off as much Sea consequently a saving of $\frac{1}{3}^{d}$ of the

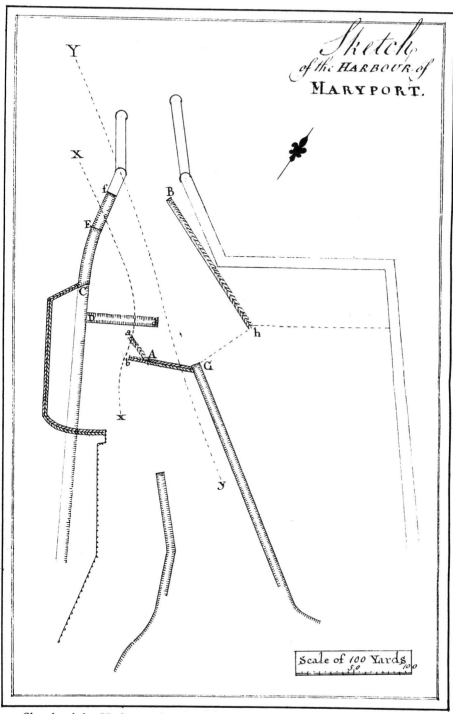

Sketch of the Harbour of Maryport.

Expence; & Ships in my opinion will enter safer as they frequently get to the Nward by scant Winds or bad steerage (as by the Tract *XX*) but by continuing their head way assisted by the Sea Tumbling into the Harbour might weather *b* when they could not be able to get round *a*.

However I think the omission of this work may be dispensed with & the money's better laid out.

The Sand &c wash'd into the Harbour in heavy gales is a perpetual expence & there is no way of Prevention but by running Works out to Seaward both on the South and North Side of the Harbour; which will likewise most effectually smoothen the Harbour & insure more water, Properties most essintialy wanted. For it is in vain to deepen the Harbour without the Works as the first Gale of W.erly Winds will fill it level with the rest of the Coast; If both South & North works are equally extended out to Sea; the Sand &c will be sweept past both Pier heads with strong Winds & Surff, & would not enter the Harbour except in form of Mudd which all docks & Still waters are liable too, nay I think it would be advantageous for this Harbour that the North works extended further to seaward then the South Pier, which would assist the entrance by preventing the River from being forced to the N.ward & the bank from gathering at the South Pier head.

This being premised I would therefore recommend that Next Summer, the addition to the South Pier of 30 or 40 yards of Stone Work be built to extend out to Seaward in the same direction with the Outer Part of that work from *E* to *f* this covers the Present Entrance & will tend to smoothen the Harbour in all winds except to the N.ward of NW b N (which seldom blows hard twelve hours together) and at the same time a Woodwork (which in your opinion will last 20 years Stone being too Expensive in the present Harbour Finances) to begin at *B* & extend in the direction towards *h* so far as prevent the Sand &c entering the Harbour & which two Works will make a safe & Secure harbour in all Winds & Weather.

I have run this North Woodwork to the Northward of the Stone Work that the Sea from the Entrance may expend itself, & I believe when this is done the most Part if not all the Jetty from the N.work may be taken away for the convinience of Ships comming in; But was this new Woodwork to join the Stone Work the Sea would range up the whole length of the Wall. – If in case the Same should wash in between *h* & *G* it may be closed up with a Wood Work; The Sea from the entrance (which will be much expended before it reach that work) striking against it and rebounding will still contribute to smooth the Sea entering the Harbour.

This being done will make a very safe Harbour for the present Ships employed; The South Side above the Stone Work may be next undertaken & a Stone brestwork run up as in the Plan from *C* to widen the Harbour towards the Hurries about 20 yards or as might be found Convenient; & by runing a Jetty head over from *D* to *d* the whole of the Present Harbour will be as secure as a dock. The Ships comming in may conveniently keep the Tract *Y y* & run along side the North Wall, & all the Ships lay to the Southward within the Jetty secure from all winds as well as the Ships entering the Harbour.

I am not an advocate for increasing the debt, but supposing a Thousand Pounds or two was borrowed to compleat the Stone work *E f* & the Woodwork *B h* next Summer I believe the Interest of this Sum would be saved by keeping out the Sand &c, the removal of which is attended with great expence; And that more Ships would be induced to use the Harbour & inable you to sett apart £200 per Annum to discharge the aforesaid Sum, & the South side & Jetty might be carried on with the Remainder of the income.

– Query; whether might not this be a saving in the long run.

However, supposing some inconvenience may attend the speedy execution of these Works; The Owners of Shiping who have ventured considerable Sums on the good faith of the Trade being continued & Harbour improved; deserve their Property kept as secure as circumstances will Permit, & to neglect which would be highly criminal; for the time may be at no great Distance when Shipping may be more valuable.

Having no Interest in either the Harbour or Shiping of Maryport, I may therefore be supposed to be unbiased; it is only the regard I have for the Place I formerly sailed from on my first launching out that makes me anxious for its Prosperity; & if I have contributed any thing towards it, I shall think myself amply rewarded for the employment of a Liesure Hour.

I am

Sir

Your Most Obedient
Humble Servant

Allonby 25.th September

1786   J. Huddart

The report was completed in September 1786 and in November of that year Huddart had to rejoin his ship on her voyage to China, which proved to be his last voyage. But it was nearly two years before he was back in England again so that further steps in the matter were the responsibility of the Trustees.

On his retirement Captain Huddart found himself filling the rôle of a consulting engineer. The knowledge he had gained in his thirty-odd years at sea and in carrying out surveys for his charts was much in demand by those undertaking improvement works to harbours and inland navigational waterways. A seaman's knowledge was more important in the days of sail than it would be today, as sailing ships had to have room to manoeuvre in all conditions of weather, whereas a powered craft can go wherever there is sufficient depth of water regardless of wind or tide.

Having no professional standing as a civil engineer, Huddart made no charge for his advice, though the preparation of his reports was detailed and exacting work and not without a heavy responsibility. Of course he expected his expenses to be paid to which was usually added an honorarium.

In 1789 his reputation for giving advice on harbour improvements had reached Whitehaven as in December of that year he received the thanks of the Trustees for his improvement plan to the harbour which was considered the best submitted; but during 1790 there was evidently a feeling that it was too far reaching and opinions over the plan were divided.[1] However, the improvements were proceeded with which consisted of adding two return piers at the port, the eastern one being built first, which had the effect of deflecting the westerly seas into the western part of the harbour and so the western return pier was built which closed up and deepened the harbour mouth and caused heavy seas, with the result that further work had to be done as set out in the following report and this appears to have provided a satisfactory solution.

---

[1] Huddart's plan is unfortunately no longer in existence.

To Robert Blackeney, Esquire.

Dear Sir, – I have received your favour of the 28th ult., inclosing a plan and suggested improvement for the northern part of the harbour of Whitehaven, requesting my further consideration of this subject at the request of the Trustees. I was desirous to view the harbour in its present state (in order to ascertain whether the effects of the late works were what I had reason to expect,) before I gave an opinion upon the tongue or breakwater for stilling the north harbour, which I have done; and taking the whole into consideration, I give it as my opinion that the North Tongue should begin at the right line joining the extremities of the New Quay, and the North Pier or quay continued, leaving 38 yeards clear, &c., between the North Quay and the Tongue, at its south-west angle. From which point the Tongue to be extended in a right line to join the old Bulwark at 50 yards distance from the north-west angle of the sugar house yard, as by the inclosed plan, in which the North Tongue (with an additional breadth to the Bulwark), is coloured red, and which additional breadth may be further extended down the Tongue as occasion may require for business. I have mentioned 38 yards of clear opening for better accommodation, presuming that the north harbour will then be so still as not to occasion any damage to the shipping therein; but if a further reduction of waves is thought necessary, it may be obtained by adding to the length of the Tongue, as represented by dotted lines, at any further period. It is also my opinion that this Tongue will not sensibly affect the old harbour, and will render the whole area of the North Harbour perfectly secure for shipping.
– I am, sir, your most obedient,

Allonby, 27th October, 1804.   J. Huddart.

In March 1791 the Directors of the British Society of Fisheries passed a vote of thanks for Huddart's survey of the islands and the coast of Scotland.

In the latter part of the eighteenth century great strides were being made in British agriculture with the enclosure of commons, the rotation of crops and drainage of swamps. Under an Act of Parliament of 1781 a big drainage scheme of the Fens was initiated, probably through the influence of Sir Joseph Banks who was an active Lincolnshire landowner. In July 1793 Huddart was engaged by the Boston Corporation to survey the harbour and adjacent rivers. This was necessary to improve the outfall of the surface water from the surrounding land.

The general state of the Fen country can be gathered from Daniel Defoe, who, writing early in the eighteenth century, tells us:

The Fen Country begins about Wainfleet which is twenty miles south of Grimsby and extends itself to the Isle of Ely south and to the grounds opposite Lynn Regis in Norfolk East. This part is properly call'd Holland for 'tis a flat, level, and often drowned country like Holland itself; here the very ditches are navigable, and the people pass from town to town in boats as in Holland: Here we have the uncouth musick of the bittern, a bird formerly counted ominous and presaging and who as fame tells us (but I believe no body knows) thrusts its bill into the reed and then gives a dull heavy groan or sound like a sigh, which it does so loud, with a deep base, like sound of a gun at a distance, 'tis heard two or three miles (say the people) but perhaps not quite so far. Here we first saw Boston, a handsome well-built seaport, at the mouth of the river Witham. The tower of this church is without question, the largest and highest in England; and it stands in a country, which (they say) has no bottom, nothing is more strange, than that they should find a foundation for so noble and lofty a structure; it has no ornament, spire, or pinnacle on the top, but is so very high, that few spires in England can match it, and it is not only beautiful by land, but is very useful at sea to guide pilots to that port and even into the mouth of the river Ouse: for in clear weather 'tis seen quite out at sea to the entrance of those channels, which they call Lynn Deeps and Boston Deeps, which are as difficult places as most upon the whole eastern shore of Britain.

. . . The town of Boston is a large, populous and well-built town full of good merchants and has a good share of foreign trade, as well as Lynn. . . The country round this place is all fenn and marsh grounds, the land very rich, and which feeds prodigious numbers of large sheep, and also oxen of the largest size, the overplus and best of which goes all to London market: and from this part as also from the downs or heath above mentioned comes the greatest part of the wool, known as a distinction for its credit, because of its fineness, by the name of Lincolnshire Wool: which is sent in great quantities into Norfolk and Suffolk, for manufacturers of those counties and indeed to several other of the most trading counties in England. These fens are very considerable for their extent; for they reach in length in some places fifty miles, and in breadth above thirty: and as they are so level that there is no interruption to the sight, any building of extraordinary height is seen a long way for example Boston Steeple is seen upon Lincoln Heath near thirty miles Peterborough and Ely Minsters are seen almost throughout the whole level so are the spires of Lynn, Whittlesea and Crowland seen at a very great distance, which adds a beauty to the country.

The system for draining the fens was to bank up the rivers, so that they would not overflow on to the land at high tide, and the surrounding land could then be drained into channels. To drain the water from these channels, it had to be lifted into the rivers where the level of the river was above that of the drainage channels.

The drainage of these channels was carried out with wind pumps which operated as conventional windmills: that is to say, they each consisted of a brick tower spreading at its base to add to its stability with a wooden capping that could revolve on the top of the tower. The wooden capping carried sails which reached nearly to the ground with a rotating weather vane to keep the sails facing the wind. If the wind changed it would catch the weather vane and start it rotating and the vane was so geared that by rotating it revolved the wooden capping until the vane was out of the wind and the sails were facing the wind. The sails had louvres on them which could close or open according to the strength of the wind. The motion of the sails was transmitted by a crown wheel to a vertical shaft running to ground level where another shaft carried the motion of the sails horizontally outside the building. Here the operation was the reverse of a water wheel, and instead of water from a higher level turning the wheel, water from a lower level was scooped up from the channels and lifted to a higher level by the motion of the wheel, so that it could be discharged into the river. This was a system developed in Holland in the previous century and effectively drained a large part of that country. Defoe, writing of the fens, says:

. . . here are some wonderful engines for throwing up water, and such as are not seen to be anywhere else, whereof one in particular threw up (as they assur'd us) twelve hundred tons of water in half an hour and goes by wind sails. 12 wings or sails to a mill:

All this was of no purpose unless the water from the rivers could be made to flow into the sea which, in this case, meant the Wash. Where Huddart was asked to make a survey we often find John Rennie working on the same project with a detailed engineering plan. Rennie was Huddart's

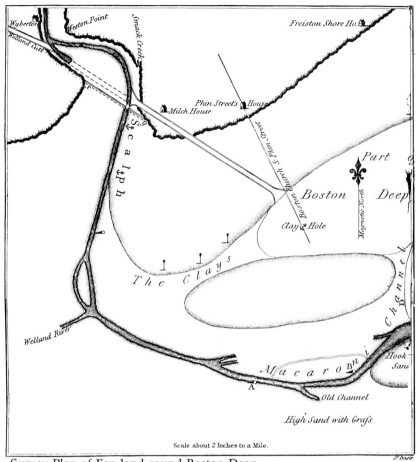

Survey Plan of Fen land round Boston Deep.

junior by twenty years and like Huddart he was the son of a farmer, who owned the farmsteading of Phantassie in East Lothian.

Rennie had established himself as a mechanical engineer through his association with Boulton and Watt by his work on the Albion Mills. On the retirement of John Smeaton, the architect of the Eddystone Lighthouse, Rennie stepped into his shoes as the civil engineer planning and supervising the canals which were then being built. Rennie's early association with James Watt convinced him of the value of steam power and he was anxious to use steam power to pump the water out of Bottleshaw and Soham Fens. Steam power had already been accepted in the Cornish mines, where conditions were so intolerable that anything which alleviated them was welcome but it was different elsewhere.

The Luddites saw their jobs being replaced by steam power and the use of steam met with the same resistance that automation and the microchip does today. Wind pumps required incessant attention and each pump provided a home and a job for the man who maintained it. However, Rennie's views prevailed in the end. In December 1821 his Son writes:

I also examined the new steam pumping apparatus, which had lately been erected for draining Soham and other fens. This, although proposed by my father in 1786, was the first of the kind that had been erected. It consisted of a scoop wheel, with a perpendicular lift, worked by a condensing engine. It answered its object completely, and has been imitated by numerous others with equal success in different parts of the fen and lowland districts. Yet in many places it has been found very difficult to induce the fen proprietors to combine together in order to effect a natural drainage, which would be better and less expensive; they prefer to act independently of each other, and adopt the steam wheel. Still, even with this, the main outfalls must be improved to their fullest extent, otherwise the water cannot run off; and when the floods in the adjacent rivers rise so high that the banks are endangered, the pumping must be discontinued, otherwise the banks will break, and then a greater injury will ensue. Nevertheless, the steam pumping apparatus is an immense improvement on the old windmill, which could only work when there was a wind.

There were some seventy-five thousand acres of land which lay under water for the greater part of the year: and it seems to have been a double problem of draining the land and improving the navigation of the River Witham which runs through Boston and of the Welland, where there was insufficient fall to maintain the flow of the river. Huddart's problem and the one on which he drew up his report was to increase the flow of the rivers and at the same time to improve their navigability.

The report, a copy of which follows, was in favour of a cut which took the Witham from near Wyberton straight into Clay Hole through its former channel of the Clays.

CAPTAIN HUDDART'S REPORT
TO
SIR JOSEPH BANKS, BART

SIR,

AGREEABLE to your request, that I would take an opportunity to visit the entrance of *Boston Harbour*, and the *Deeps*, and give my opinion, whether an intended Cut to bring the River *Welland* from its ancient course down to *Spalding Set Way*, to join the *Witham* near *Wyberton*, would injure the navigation to *Boston*: I have therefore, in compliance with your request, been at Boston, and taking the opportunity of strong spring tides, to go down the River, and by a few sets to determine the situation of the Buoys, Becons, &c.

I herewith inclose you a Sketch thereof, and beg leave to report my opinion thereon. From the enquiry I made respecting the ancient navigation to Boston, I have reason to believe that the River once ran round by the Clays; and I was informed that a report prevails that it ran by the Point within the Scalp, and which might be the case, but being a long time back, cannot be depended upon. In proceeding down the River, I took a set upon each point at the entrance of Boston River, or the Witham, and then down by the only channel, the lower part of which is called the *Macaroni*, or New Channel, I suppose to distinguish it from the Clays; and on our arrival at the Buoy marked C in the Sketch, we found the sand extended across at D, and the River directed its course on the south side of the Long Roger into Lynn Deeps; from which we may conclude, that the Long Roger joins the Scalp, and that there is no channel over into Boston Deeps at low water. The pilots we had with us did not expect to find the sand dry at D; therefore I conclude this sand is increasing, and probably the channel may never more attain that course, if left to chance. We observed, upon coming up of the flood tide, when covering the sand or bar at D, that the tide rose nearly of the same height on both sides, viz. from Lynn and Boston Deeps covered D at an hour and an half flood.

I have not a doubt but from the great length of the Long Roger, that there will be always a channel or swatchway further to the eastward through this sand, from Lynn into Boston Deeps (or probably more than one, but if so they will not be so good) but I suspect these swatchways will be liable to have a north-west and south-easterly direction, on account of the tide of flood setting up stronger on the Norfolk coast, than up Boston Deeps; therefore, when the bar at D grows up so high as not to admit ships, it will be very inconvenient to navigate from Boston Deeps through this channel into Lynn Deeps, for vessels bound to the Harbour of Boston, provided there is water over the Flats by the track of the River. The Scalp is a bank more difficult to be moved by the tide, than any of the other sands; which I apprehend principally arises from vessels throwing out ballast upon it; for on the part where they lie, it is mixed with gravel &c but to the eastward it appeared to be sand.

From the Scalp to the Buoy A is a considerable breadth of flat sand, and here the Rivers may be very subject to change their course, or divide into branches, which lessen their effect to scour a channel; and what even large rivers are subject to, in various parts of the world, which fall into the sea upon a flat shore.

The rest of the sands are much higher, and I suppose the Clays to have about five feet less water over than the bar at D, or entrance into the Macaroni Channel.

As these flat sands accumulate and grow higher, they will be subject to raise the bed of the River, which will have a bad effect upon the navigation to Boston; for, by decreasing the fall, the River will be too languid to clear away the silt; and in course of time, by imperceptible degrees, the navigation will be lost to the Scalp, the channel will be subject to vary, sometimes better, and at other times worse; but, upon the whole, it is my opinion, that the sands will continue to increase, for the mud which is brought in by the flood and deposited at high water slack, will in part remain; for the ebbs are not so strong, and therefore not equal to take away as much as is brought by the flood; for the freshes, during a great part of the year, are inconsiderable, and at all times, compared with the quantity of salt water, whilst the banks are covered, and after they are dry, not sufficient to scour out a deep channel, in so great a length and little fall. The Witham proceeds from a little below Wyberton House, to the opposite shore, and keeps the eastern or same shore in a curved direction round that bay which I shall distinguish by Smack Creek Bay, not knowing its name; and afterwards, in nearly a direct course, towards the Scalp Buoy, a little below which it divides into two branches, but joins again before the junction of the Welland. The western branch of this division seemed the larger, and inclined in a curve to the eastward, and continues past the junction of the Witham, without sensibly altering its course.

If the Welland does not alter the direction of the Witham on its first meeting it cannot afterwards; for what direction soever the combination takes, it will continue that course till affected by some other. The quantity of water from the Welland seemed very trifling, I do not think more than one foot deep, and narrow; that of the Witham had water for the boat. I think the quantity, more than ten to one, therefore, had this small effect upon it. But this difference cannot arise from the country drains, but from the salt water; for I was told that the drainage by the Welland is more than the Witham, but there were no freshes coming down by either of them after this dry season of any signification, and the smallness of the drainage of Spalding Set Way proves to me that the sands are high, and a pretty regular descent. Therefore the floods and ebbs will rise and fall with an easy current, and as soon as the tide is retired from the sands, very little remain to come down. I only saw another small run of water above the Scalp Buoy, which I believe would not have wet a person over the shoes. Therefore it appears to me that the principal, and almost the whole of the back water, is from Boston Harbour, and which is the principal source in keeping the navigation to the Scalp.

Was the tide prevented from flowing up the Harbour to Boston, the nagivation of the Scalp would soon be lost, and probably not a great many years after that might endanger the drainage of the country. But though the Harbour of Boston receives from the sea a considerable quantity of back water, being pretty wide in several parts of it, yet time and experience proves, that, assisted by the drainage, it is not sufficient to keep down the bed of the River, as said before, over such an extent or Sands, and, as the River silts up, most prove effectual. Between the junction of the Welland and Witham, and the Buoy A, they divide at one place into three parts; but I believe very little water goes over the Flats to the northward of B, the principal channel running between A and B, which are pretty high banks. I think it doubtful whether or no the channel, if left to its own course, will ever run northward of B, wherever the Rivers may join; nor is this part of the channel between A and B likely to shift much to the southward; for at a small distance are the highest sands extending from the Holland shore, which I observed to have grass upon it (as marked in the Plan.) This shews that these sands are so high, that the tides have not influence to move its surface so as to prevent its growth, and by which means the grass will assist in retaining the silt, and these sands rise quicker, whilst the tides in general cover them, until they are covered with spring tides only, and so become Marsh land.

Therefore, as said before, this part of the channel will probably never incline much farther to the southward, the high sands acting as an embankment, and therefore the alteration proposed will have little or no effect upon this part of the channel, either one way or other.

From Wyberton to the Scalp the channel takes a different course in winter, to that which I have before described, being as I found it in summer. It keeps the western or Wyberton shore in the winter, when the drainage is strong, till near the Point, and then continues that direction across to the eastern shore; and afterwards, being turned to the southward by meeting the opposite shore, proceeds, as at present, past the Scalp.

A part of this winter channel may be seen in the Sketch, which remained not silted up to E. Such alterations in channels are always the consequence, wherever they are crooked, unconfined, and the tides from any cause subject to vary in their force, not only in rivers, but banks of sand at sea. For, from a long course of winds from one quarter tending to increase the floods and retard the ebbs, or vice versa, the channel, or rather the banks that environ the channel, are altered; which often continue going on till a new channel is formed, probably, at a considerable distance from where the old one ran. In the case before us, the tide of flood, in the summer months, being stronger than the tide of ebb, keeps the northerly direction till it is forced round by the shore of Smack Creek Bay, and then gives a direction, which it continues towards Wyberton; but in winter the land floods, which not only join the ebbs, but have their principal effect at low water, directing its force towards, and keeping a southerly direction past Wyberton, is forced to the eastward by that shore, and continues that direction till it falls into the same channel as in summer, near the opposite shore, above Milch House Point, and continues the same to the Scalp.

This will be clear by observing its form in the Plan; and supposing a continual influx, there will not be a dissenting opinion, but it would form the summer channel; and if a constant ebb or outfall, would form the winter channel, where the ground is of a shifting quality. The prevailing tides therefore, in course of time, produce the same effect.

Having treated of the present state, and given my opinion respecting the consequences which may happen in time to the navigation, I shall now consider, whether the case may be worse, provided the Welland is brought into the Witham, near Wyberton.

The junction of the Welland may make an alteration in the situation of the winter channel above described, according to the angle it makes with the Witham and quantity of back water, till they enter the old channel near the opposite shore; but as the joint effect to scour a channel must be greater than the Witham alone, I conceive it cannot be worse, but tend to improve the navigation from this junction to the place where they join at present, as their junction will not tend to alter the situation, except as above described, or within the points of land. From the place where they join at present to the entrance into Lynn Deeps, I have already given my opinion, that the direction will not be liable to be changed for the worse, and the quantity of back water being equally the same, the force to scour a channel will be also the same; therefore I give it as my opinion in toto, that the navigation of Boston will not be rendered worse by this intended Cut. I am also of opinion, that whatever method be used for the improvement of this navigation, by keeping up a channel into Boston Deeps, that this Cut will materially assist by adopting any plan which has presented itself to me under this consideration; for the Welland joins the Witham too far to the southward, at present, to give any assistance. And having given my opinion respecting the Cut, I beg leave to add my opinion respecting the improvement of this navigation. The general obstruction to rivers and harbours upon sandy shores arises from the extent of the sands from where the river is confined to the low water and the shallowness of the sea. For some distance beyond the low water to seaward this lessens the velocity of the river or back water, suffering it to spread or divide into different branches, by running so much upon a level, and form bars and obstructions about the entrance; when, if the fall was greater, it would scour the deeper and more certain channel.

It therefore occurs to me, that the most advisable methods would be either to divert the channel into its ancient course by the Clays (for I give up the idea of removing the Scalp) for two reasons; it being of a substance not easy to be removed, and the best laying for ships in the present situation; or otherwise to make a Cut through the point by the Milch House in a right line, extending from the intended junction into the Deeps, as represented in the Sketch, and coloured yellow; and this being, in my opinion, the most effectual method, shall confine my observations to that only. It must be understood that Clay Road, or Clay Hole, and the upper part of Boston Deeps, represented in the Plan, cannot be depended upon as correct; for I never saw the line of low water, or took any soundings to determine the same; but being told that Boston Church and Phineas Street's House, in one, was the anchoring in Clay Hole, in about 8 or 10 feet low water, spring tides, I ventured to sketch the upper part of Boston Deeps and Clay Road from this information and my own idea; for I was also deprived of a cross set for the white Buoy, which would have determined in some measure the south side of the Deeps at that place.

The scale I reduced by the mean distance from Boston to Wyberton, taken from the only two plans I had, which differed widely between themselves, and therefore cannot be depended upon; but from which I made the sketch two inches to a mile, thinking it not necessary, on my present business, to measure a base; therefore, before any Cut can be determined upon, an exact survey should be made of the upper part of the Deeps. This sketch is therefore no farther useful, than to convey my general ideas; and which are, that from the junction, the Rivers ought to proceed near the track of the winter channel, and in a direct line, through the Point into Boston Deeps. The tides, flowing in a direct course, are not subject to alter the channels, having the same effect upon the sides both upwards and downwards, and therefore will keep the same channel both winter and summer, and not liable to the obstructions thrown up frequently in curved channels. The advantage to be gained by this Cut, will arise from the short distance giving it a greater descent for the low water spring tides in Boston Deeps. It must be many feet below the bed of the River within the Point, and the upper part of both the Deeps of Lynn and Boston are upon the same level at low water; therefore the descent will be in the reciprocal ratio of the length of the two channels, and in which the unconfirmed part need only be considered in both the intended and present channels. The back water arising from the tides in Boston Harbour, assisted by the drainage of the country from the Welland and Witham, appear to me abundantly sufficient, with this descent to scour a channel, in a short time to receive ships of two to three hundred tons, and would certainly improve the navigation to the quays at Boston; but could speak with greater certainty if I had taken a more accurate survey. I suppose that eight or ten feet deep below the surface of the marsh or high water spring tides will be very sufficient for this Cut; and after the embankment is made from X to Y, if the earth prove the same as it appears to be, I doubt not but the channel to Boston, in one year, will be better than it has been for a century past; but, depending upon the tenacity of the soil, may take more or less time to scour it. The breadth of the Cut requires a farther consideration: for if the Cut be made too broad for the back water, it will not scour it so soon nor so deep; and if too narrow, the tides may be too rapid, and not so convenient for the navigation: and this will partly depend upon whether the Welland navigation is to be supplied by the tides, or kept at a certain height by locks; nor have I the least apprehension of any obstruction to the navigation from a bar at the entrance into the Deeps. This being only a Sketch for your consideration of the improvement, shall only remark, that if this plan should be adopted for the improvement of trade, and the drainage of the country secured, that gates being put in the embankment from X to Y, for ships to pass at high water, the old channel may be used till there should be sufficient water in the new one, and afterwards an excellent birth for ships to discharge at to the southward of the embankment; for ships might then lie in the best of the water, and not be effected by the tide, which could be no stronger than at the quays at Boston. At present they are obliged to haul upon the Scalp to prevent their washing by the tide; for if they lie in the bed of the River, the strength of the tide will undermine them; or, as the seamen term it, wash them hollow at one end or both, as they may lie end on or broadside to the tide, and subject them to receive damage; but after the tide is prevented by the embankment, the ships will lie much safer at the Scalp till time may silt it up, or a convenient dock might be made either below the embankment or in Smack Creek Bay, and the excavation made, in a great measure.

Humbly Submitted,

September 2d, 1793. J. HUDDART

REPORT

The thanks of the Boston Corporation were conveyed to Joseph Huddart in a letter from Sir Joseph Banks who had called for the report and the Corporation presented Huddart with a cup bearing the following testimonial of their appreciation:

> This cup was presented to Capt. Joseph Huddart by the Mayor and Corporation of the borough of Boston as a Testimony of their gratitude for his useful service in exploring at their request the state of the Channels leading from the Westward into the deeps near the junction of the currents of the Rivers Witham and Welland.

July 1795

The reverse side of the cup bore the coat of arms of the town of Boston.

The River Witham which flows through Lincoln and reaches the Wash at Boston had become silted up and its bed above the level of the surrounding countryside with the consequent flooding. Arthur Young, the Secretary of the Board of Agriculture, visited the District in 1793 and found the freeholders of the high lands adjoining Wildmore and West Fens pasturing their sheep on the drier parts during the summer months; but large numbers of them were dying of foot rot:

Nor is this the only evil; for the number stolen is incredible. They are taken off by whole flocks, as so wild a country (whole acres being covered with thistles and nettles four feet high and more) nurses up a race of people as wild as the fen.

The people in the neighbourhood lived in rush huts or boats: in the East Fen 2,000 acres were constantly under water. Sir Joseph Banks owned a good estate at Revesby near Tatters Hall (Tattershall) with a mansion known as Abbot's Lodge standing on elevated land above the fens. He had other houses but he visited Revesby regularly, keeping open house and entertaining lavishly. He was popular and good humoured, taking an active part in local affairs.

Banks was sufficiently public spirited to wish to pursue a scheme for drainage of the extensive fen under the view of his windows and make it more profitable for its owners.

Arthur Young visited Sir Joseph in 1799 at Revesby and says in his report on Lincolnshire: 'He had the goodness to order a boat and accompanied me into the heart of the East Fen, which had the appearance of a chain of lakes bordered by great crops of reed.' Sir Joseph called meetings of the local landowners: those of Wildmore Fen met at Horncastle on 27 August 1799 and a resolution was adopted to employ John Rennie to investigate and report at a subsequent meeting.

In Napoleonic times the difficulty of obtaining supplies of food from abroad was a significant factor and it was important to extend England's growing capacity. When the drainage of Wildmore East and West Fens was completed the total cost was £580,765: 60,481 acres were reclaimed having an annual value of £110,541. But the Boston Corporation who controlled the Witham were staggered at the estimate of £50,000 for the works Rennie proposed and decided to proceed no further but by 1826 the harbour was practically silted up and the Boston Corporation now had to do something about it, and they called in John Rennie's son, later Sir John Rennie, to remedy the situation.

John Rennie the younger referred to his father's report of 6 October 1800, which in turn was based on Huddart's report of 2 September 1793, and indicated the lines of direction in which the Welland and Witham entered the Wash tended to silt up both channels and he suggested that the two river outlets should be united into one and diverted into the centre of the Wash at Clayhole which, at the same time, would greatly increase the depth and enable a large area of land to be reclaimed for agriculture.

One of the problems with land reclamation is that any harbour at the mouth of a river where the waters are discharged tends to silt up, because it has relied on the scour of the tide ebbing and flowing over the land that is flooded at each tide. This was the case with Boston and the drainage works which were carried out higher up the Witham were at the expense of its lower reaches. The Boston Corporation could not afford a scheme on their own and found the River Commissioners unwilling to support them, so that a modified scheme had to be carried out.

Huddart was also involved with the Eau Brink Cut on the River Ouse. The River Ouse made a long circuitous bend above Lynn for about five miles to St Germans Bridge and between these points the channel followed an irregular course, interrupted by sand banks which were constantly changing. In some places the river was a mile in width divided into small

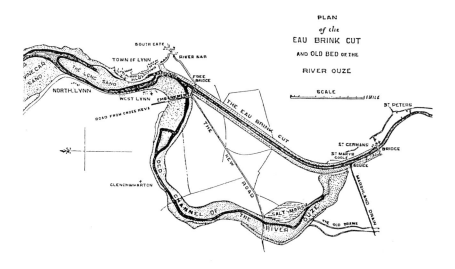

Plan of the Eau Brink Cut.

streams; the course of the river was so obstructed that during floods the surface water could not escape with the ebb tide and as soon as the tide started to flow again the surface water was forced back inundating the surrounding countryside. The result was that valuable agricultural land was lost to reeds and sedge.

In the neighbourhood of Downham Eau the corn had at times to be reaped from platforms moved by boats, and boats also had to be used to gather fruit from orchards. In Marshland Fen the ground was so soft the horses had to be fitted with wooden boards over their shoes to prevent them from sinking into the soil.

Until the Ouse could provide a proper outfall no interior drainage scheme was worth pursuing. A scheme had been advanced to make a cut from St Germans Bridge to Kings Lynn and thereby straighten the channel of the Ouse, saving two miles of navigation and gaining a fall of five feet. This scheme had been planned nearly a century earlier but had met with opposition from the inhabitants.

In spite of the objections from the Kings Lynn inhabitants an Act of Parliament was passed in 1781 to carry out the improvements and lay a tax of four pence per acre on the lands which were expected to benefit. Certain guarantees were built in for Lynn harbour and the riparian owners. The Act decreed that there should be two engineers, one for the drainage interest, who was Robert Mylne, the architect of Blackfriars Bridge, and one for navigational interests, who was Sir Thomas Hyde Page, RE. These engineers were to decide the direction and dimensions of the proposed Eau Brink Cut which was to commence below St Germans Bridge and terminate a short distance above the boat wharf at Kings Lynn.

However, they differed so materially that Huddart had to be called in as arbitrator, and when he had made his award it was found that the whole of the appropriated funds, amounting to £80,000, had been spent on litigation and getting the Act of Parliament passed, so the matter fell through. However, the state of the fens could not remain as they were and everyone was convinced that the scheme awarded by Huddart was the only answer.

A new Act was therefore obtained, increasing the tax on the lands sufficiently to cover the estimate originally made by John Rennie, who was appointed engineer-in-chief and an executive committee was appointed consisting of Lord W. Bentinck, Sir A. Hammond, Charles Browne and Thomas Hoseason. Jolliffe and Banks were awarded the contract.

As soon as it was completed the low water mark at the upper end fell five feet. The winter of 1821–2 was exceptionally wet and but for the opening of the Eau Brink Cut a large area of the fens would have been under water. The work was carried out in exact conformity with Huddart's design. Sir John Rennie who succeeded his father as chief engineer in 1820 writes in 1821:

> I went to Lynn to examine the works and was astonished to find great the effects which had been produced by the Eau Brink Cut. Instead of the circuituous old shallow course full of shoals and obstructions of every kind, there was a fine straight deep channel, two miles shorter than the old one of the proper width bordered by strong banks of the full height; the floods passed without difficulty and the navigation was so much improved that lighters and barges going up the river from Lynn saved several tides.

In November 1794 Huddart received the thanks of the Commissioners for Customs for his survey of the port of Hull with a view to the construction of a new dock. The report reads as follows:

COPY OF THE REPORT OF

J. HUDDART, ESQUIRE

RELATIVE TO THE MAKING OF A NEW DOCK

AT KINGSTON UPON HULL

To the Hon. the Commissioners of His Majesty's Customs,

MAY IT PLEASE YOUR HONORS,

In compliance with the request of the Honourable Board, communicated to me by Letter from the Secretary, dated the 25th May, requesting my Opinion on the most fit situation, under all circumstances, for constructing a new Dock at Hull: I proceeded thither, and having collected all the information in my Power, in which I have been attentively supplied by the Collector of the Port of Hull, with Papers and Plans of what has been proposed, as also by Meetings of the Dock Company, by the Committee of the Corporation and Merchants of the Town, and by the Corporation of the Trinity-House of Kingston-upon-Hull; and having read those Papers, and considered of the propriety of the Propositions of those Gentlemen, and made my own observations, I beg leave to report my opinion to the Honorable Board.

The situation of the Town of Kingston-upon-Hull, being upon a Plane extending for some Miles to the East, North, and West of the Town, nearly upon a level with the Humber at High Water Spring Tides, (excepting the excavations made by Hull River, and other small Drainages and eminences thrown up by Art) therefore as the soil is nearly the same, the expence in making the excavation for a Dock cannot be widely different in any situation near the Town of Hull.

The situation of the Humber and Hull Rivers, are what I shall next consider: The Humber continues its depth along the Shores, both to the East and West of the Town of Hull, at a very convenient distance to form an entrance into a Dock: I am therefore of opinion, that the principal entrance into a New Dock, ought to be from the Humber, for the following reasons;

The River Hull, from which the present Dock has its entrance, is narrow and generally crowded with Ships, Craft, Raft, &c. that often impede the passage of Ships for several days, especially in Neap Tides, when large Ships have not water into the Dock: and as more than half the disbursements of the Ships in general is accumulated in Port, (exclusive of what is termed Port-charges) every convenience to promote despatch, will have its due weight in reducing the Freight, and thereby promoting the increase of Trade and Revenue.

In entering the Dock from the Humber, scarce a Tide would be lost, even in the Neaps, in Docking the largest Ships in the Trade, for without making the excavation deeper than the present Dock, if the Lock at the Gates into the Humber, is deep enough to receive the Ships in Neap Tides, (and which I find from the rise of Tide in the Humber is practicable) and water is reserved in the Dock in Spring Tides, assisted by a back water from the Country, if thought necessary to supply the waste, would lift the Ship to enter the Dock at the lowest Tides.

The reserving the water in the Dock at Spring Tides, to enable them to Dock in the Neaps, would have the advantage of lessening the quantity of silt deposited in the Docks; for though the quantity of Mud in the Humber appears to me less than in Hull River, yet by the present practice, large quantities must always be brought in; for it is common to empty the Dock every Tide, of a considerable quantity of Water which has deposited the principal part of its silt in the Dock, and is again filled with muddy water the next Tide; and so every Tide deposits silt in proportion to the quantity of Water received, and the mud in it; but by keeping the Water in the Docks up to the full height, (except what the Lock requires to bring Ships, &c. in and out of Dock) the Docks would not receive more than a tenth part of the silt they do at present; for when the Tides have been at their height, at the Spring, and every succeeding Tide falling off, they would not receive any Water by the Tide in the Dock for several days, and when they do, it will be near High-water slack and not so muddy. I mentioned this at the Dock gates; they returned no other reason, but that the Lock was sooner filled to the level of the Dock, and Vessels sooner brought in; however this difference would be but a few minutes, for the water runs strongest when the difference of its height in the Dock and Lock is greatest, and the tedious part in filling the Lock is, when the Water becomes nearer upon a level and runs slower.

It is said the Proprietors of the sufferance Quays on Hull River, will object to a Gate or entrance from the Humber; but any disadvantage to them must be principally ideal, and should have no weight; for they must bring, as at present, any Ships or Craft to their Quays, and with less incumbrance, as the River will be clearer of Shipping, Craft, &c. in their way in and out of Dock; and which cannot add to the interest of those Proprietors, having no legal Business to transact at their Quays. Therefore my opinion is, that they cannot be materially injured, and should not therefore interfere with the general good, which would be produced by an entrance from the Humber.

Some objections to it are given on account of the strength of the Tide in the Humber: I apprehend those who advance this as a reason forget that the Tide slacks at High Water, and at any time of the Tide, when the Gates ought to be opened, there will be no more inconvenience in passing into, and out of the Dock, into the Humber, on account of Tide, than out of Hull River into the present Dock.

In general, Ships may sail directly into Dock from the Humber at High Water, when the Gates are all open, and no Bridge to interrupt. Yet heavy gales of wind may sometimes render it difficult; but it ought to be considered, that in such particular cases, the Navigation of Hull River will be more commodious by clearing the mouth of it, of many Ships, Craft, Raft, &c. which used to lay there, waiting to go into the Humber, they now preferring the more convenient passage out of the Dock; and I doubt not but Ships entering by Hull River, will not be liable to damage themselves and others, as they are at present, and will certainly have the advantage in choosing the passage that is most convenient and safe at all times.

In taking into consideration which is the most fit situation for a New Dock, the two principal objects that occur to me are, conveniences for the benefit of Trade, and security of Revenue, (for the difference in the expence between one place and another near Hull, of a Dock of certain dimensions, to contain about 100 sail of Ships, I think cannot amount to more than £500; and if near the Humber, the earth would be dispensed with to make the Fore shore, in doing which, I apprehend, the Corporation would be glad to lend their assistance, if on the S.W. side of the Town; and whether the Dock is on the East, of West-side of the Town, the entrance above-mentioned may be made from the Humber.)

Convenience for the benefit of Trade, depending much upon the nearness of the seat of business to the Counting-House, Warehouses, &c. of the Merchant, by reducing the Land Carriage, and being more immediately under his inspection, to see that his work is not neglected and prevent fraud; I am of opinion, that the West-side of the Town is the next fit situation to answer this desired purpose universally. The length from that end of the Dock near White Friar, or Beverley-Gates to the Humber, is about equal to the length of the present Dock: and the Dock Company having a lot of Ground granted them by his Majesty, (formerly the Walls and Ditches of the Town) by purchasing some addition to which, a continuation may be made of the present Dock to the Humber, to contain what number of Ships may be thought necessary. Or rather, the whole ought to be divided into three Docks, to communicate with each other by Gates, and by way of distinguishing them, shall call them, the Old Dock, the Middle Dock, and the Humber Dock: The best division will be by the two direct Roads, leading into the Country from White Friar and Myton-Gates, over Draw Bridges, where the Gates may be fixed for communication between the Docks. The Town of Kingston-upon-Hull, would then be surrounded by Docks and Navigable Rivers, consequently the Merchants and Inhabitants would enjoy the most fair and equitable disposition for individuals at large; for though the Merchants in High-Street, may be the most considerable at present, occasioned by the former situation of the Town and Harbour, yet it is but fair, that others, (who in a growing Town which bids fair for great increase of Trade) should have equal advantage, by an opportunity to fix upon a commodious situation to conduct their business. The transporting of Ships, Craft, Raft, &c. from one extreme of the Docks to the other, would be practicable at all times, and might pass into the Humber, or Hull Rivers at High-water, to general advantage.

I have before mentioned, that keeping up the water in the Docks to its height at High-water, as much as circumstances will allow, would greatly lessen the quantity of silt deposited in the Docks; which silt is an universal impediment and heavy expence in clearing it out of all Docks and still Harbours supplied by Tides, but much more so in muddy Rivers, and whether this recommendation is complied with or not, the above-mentioned disposition of the Docks may be applied to clearing away the silt; the Middle Dock will be found to collect very little, in comparison with the others, for the Tide in passing the Dock Gates from the Humber, and Hull Rivers, on entering the Dock where the width is extended, looses its velocity as it proceeds upwards, and begins to deposit the silt in greatest quantity near the Gates, and proportionably less towards the head of the Dock, where very little is carried and the water clear. The middle Dock being supplied from the heads of the Old Dock, and the Humber Dock, by Water, which has deposited the greatest part of its mud, brings in very little, therefore the expence of clearing the Middle Dock will be trifling, if done by the Machine; but the whole of the Docks, if properly constructed for the purpose, will assist in clearing each other. The Middle Dock being considered as a reservoir, or back water, may be applied alternately, or as occasion may require, to clear both the Old and Humber Docks, by making a proper disposition for that purpose, when it is intended to run the sluice,

It might be some saving in the purchase of Ground, if the Middle Dock is confined to the property already in the possession of the Dock Company, between White Friar-Gate and Myton-Gate; by allowing ten yards for Quay on the Town-side, and five or six yards on the West-side; it would then contain room for from thirty to forty sail of Ships; and the Corporation having some Ground adjoining that belonging to the Dock Company, between Myton-Gate and the Humber, which probably might be had on reasonable terms, by the addition of which the Humber Dock would contain about double that number, and this additional Dock room may be thought sufficient at present. But I could wish it to be understood by the Honorable Board, that I do not mention this contraction of the Quays and Middle Dock, but on the principal of saving, for it is very probable that, in the course of a few years, more Dock room may be wanted, and narrow Quays are inconvenient, and not favorable to the security of the Revenue.

In respect to making a Dock in the Garrison Ground, it is allowed, that Gates may be made into both the Rivers Humber and Hull, but there would be an inconvenience in transporting Ships, &c. from one Dock to another, which would often take two Tides to perform it, especially from the Old Dock to that in the Garrison Ground. It is also much further from the seat of Business, though (as some propose) a Bridge may be thrown over Hull River near the Dock; but a Bridge would much incommode that River.

There are many advantages and objections thrown out for and against those two situations by the Parties, most of which, in my opinion, have little weight; that of Fire is the most alarming, in the situation the Dock was in last Winter, when they scarcely had room to move a Ship; for spare room in Dock is the best preservation against a general Conflagration. If there is sufficient space left to transport Ships from one end to the other of the Dock (which should always be the case) and a Ship should take Fire; this room may be occupied by Ships removed from the Fire; and if the Dock Company have in readiness several Creepers with each a small Chain, of about ten fathoms long (which I think they ought) to throw on board and hook the burning Vessel, and haul her by Ropes made fast to the small Chain, into a clear birth; for it is probable, that after her moorings are burnt, the Wind might force her among other Ships and prove fatal, which the small Grapnails and Chains would prevent; and which might always be replaced, should the hold the Creeper had, be loosened by the Fire, so long as there was a timber head above Water. They would also be useful in placing the Vessel in the most advantageous situation for the Engines to play upon her and reduce the Fire. This is the best resource I have thought of, and adds one more reason for keeping the Water up in the Dock to float the Ships, and in which situation, are much safer than in Tide Harbours; though it is of little moment respecting the two different situations for a Dock.

Respecting the security of the Revenue in the two different situations of a Dock, I am of opinion, that the West-side, has the preference, and that the Duty on the East-side, would require a greater number of Officers to execute the same Business, by reason of its distance, and being separated by Hull River from the lawful Quays. But as each individual of the Honorable Board, and the Officers of the Customs at Hull, are much more competent to judge of this matter than I am, shall say no more on this subject.

If the Town is surrounded, the Water to supply it will require to be conducted under the Dock; but in this there is very little difficulty or danger.

Humbly submitted,

J. HUDDART

HIGHBURY TERRACE,
August 6th, 1793.

Huddart's advice of making the dock entrance from the Humber was followed and a powerful steam engine had to be employed to pump the water from the coffer-dam in front of the Humber entrance, which had been constructed to enable the cill to be made and the lock gates to be fixed.

The work was begun in 1803 and finished in 1809, providing a dock 900 feet long by 370 feet wide covering 7½ acres, and was capable of holding about seventy square-rigged vessels. The entrance lock communicating with the tidal harbour opening into the Humber was 42 feet wide and 158 feet long with a cill 6 feet below low water springs.

The engineering work was again carried out by John Rennie and in the course of this project he invented a dredging machine consisting of a series of rollers armed with spikes that raked the bottom, followed by buckets and spoons to lift the deposit operated by means of a walking wheel between two barges: but the idea proved tedious and inefficient and a fresh idea was taken up of an endless chain with buckets operated by steam power. This was able to raise 300 tons of mud and gravel in a day from a depth of 22 feet.

In June 1795 Huddart received the thanks of the Trustees of the Harbour of Swansea for his advice on the improvement of the Harbour. His services were first advocated at a meeting of the Trustees on 2 September 1793. John Smith, one of the Trustees, proposed:

> From enquiries he had made he thinks Captain Huddart the most competent and proper person for the business; Mr. Smith conversed with him and also with Mr. Wyatt, surveyor to the Trustees at Ramsgate Harbour. If Captain Huddart comes down he will expect his expenses to be paid, and leave it to the trustees to make him what present they think fit for his trouble, for that, as he intends to things of this sort principally for his amusement, he never makes a charge. Mr. Wyatt said that his charge for such surveys is five guineas per day during his absence from London, besides his expenses.

The Trustees accepted Mr Smith's proposal and requested him 'to have a further conversation with Captain Huddart and if he continue to think Captain Huddart a proper person for making the survey of this Harbour' engage him, proposing to make him a present of fifty guineas beyond his expenses.

On 4 August 1794 the line of the embankment on the town side of the river had not been fully determined and a sub-committee was formed to meet Captain Huddart with the proprietors of the Swansea Canal and other proprietors of the Port to mark out the line in the most advantageous manner.

At the September meeting Captain Huddart was requested to report:

> To what extent he would recommend the improvement of the River and Harbour of Swansea with the best method of conveying the same into execution, including those works which the Trustees are directed to do by present Act of Parliament, viz, to deepen widen and make straight by a cut or channel the Western Bar; to make stop Gates at, or near as reasonably may be to a place where there is now a ferry: to erect Walls or Piers, Bays and Slips at the entrance at the Harbour and River for the safe laying for ships: to clear the bed or Channel of the River by having it deepened, widened, scoured and cleansed of all annoyances.

Huddart made his report from London on 27 September 1794, which was received by the Trustees at their meeting of 6 October. This is summarised as follows:

> He says that having gained a general idea of the harbour, especially the outer one, known then as Fabian's Bay, he had formed the opinion that 'upon lowering the bar and increasing the water into the harbour, depends the principal object of improvement, for in its present state great detention must accrue to ships of burthen.' Singularly enough he had an example of this danger upon his visiting Swansea on the 5th August, 1794, when, he says, 'I found only 8 feet of water in the harbour; and on the evening of the 31st July, a vessel of about 13 feet draft of water, in sailing out of the harbour grounded upon the bar, where she remained until the 10th August, when the tides rose to take her off, and every ship in the harbour loaded to that draft of water, and ready to sail at that time, must suffer the same detention.' And he immediately expressed the opinion that 'the water cannot be materially deepened in the western channel without a continual expence attending it, from its being liable to be filled up from the effect of the sea; until the works or piers are extended further out to seaward on both sides of the channel,' the westward one from Black Point, and the eastward from Salt-House Point. In urging the necessity of these piers he avowed four principal objects, viz:- (1) 'The depth of the water to be acquired, (2) the stilling of the outer harbour in gales of wind, (3) the convenience for ships in sailing into and out of the harbour in various winds and weather, and (4) the expense attending the erection of the same.'

> Respecting the water to be acquired, he wrote: 'I give it as my opinion that when once the channel or bed of the river is deepened to the depths mentioned, it will continue, so long as the tide is suffered to flow up the river as at present, it being sufficient to clear away the silt from the bed of the channel, and the stilling of the harbour will prevent the sea from bringing in any heavier materials within the ends of the piers.' Having laid down this dictum, he states that the contraction of the entrance by the east and west piers would increase the current between them, and would secure about 20 or 30 inches more of water, or 14½ feet at the lowest tides, for ships to sail or arrive in safety, and so would admit a collier of 300 tons, if properly constructed for the trade, and he would also obtain a fall of about 2 feet from the ferry pool to the pier heads, which would be sufficient to keep the channel clear.

> The breadth of the channel to be deepened might in the first instance be 50 or 60 yards which could be increased when revenue permitted. Captain Huddart was meditating the continued use of the river for layerage without the introduction of docks, although the Trustees were empowered to introduce them in their Act, nevertheless it is evident that such a project was even then suggested, for Captain Huddart observed that 'should the river be embanked for a floating dock, sluices will be necessary to clear away the silt out of the channel, which will deposit in the outer harbour.'

> Recognising that there was then in progress a receding of the water in the Mumbles Road, which was obliging ships of burthen to lay further out and

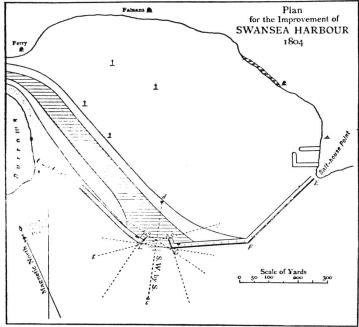

Captain Huddart's Plan of Fabian's Bay.

more exposed, he pointed out that this would not materially affect the Port of Swansea, as the loaded ships might be hauled down into the outer harbour and berthed under either of the piers in good water, for there was a sufficient bank of the river within and at the foot of the pier side for this purpose, and thence they would be ready to push out and save the wear of cables, which would be necessary in lying in the Mumbles Road. 'The ground near the extremity of the eastern pier will afford at present 13 feet on the lowest tides, and when larger ships frequent the Port, this ground may be taken away or deepened to the depth of the channel if required about 2 feet more, and extended from time to time as the number of large ships may require berthing,' and there was a further advantage that the inner harbour would be cleared of the loaded ships bound to sea.

Captain Huddart recommended the immediate construction of the two piers simultaneously, which being done, the principal inconvenience of the harbour would be removed, the ballast would no longer remain a burthen, and the detention of vessels from 200 to 300 tons for water would be at an end.

The prevailing state of the harbour finances was, he admitted, a bar to progress, and he suggested that material should be prepared, and the work begun upon the western pier. The out-goings of the harbour he estimated at £900, which was 'about equal to the revenue of the harbour collected by a rate of 2d. per ton upon the shipping as appears by the books.' He, therefore, recommended application to Parliament for an increase of duty upon registered tonnage to 6d., the yield of which would probably encompass the necessary improvement, and popularize the Port by making it free of access, and not liable to detention for want of water; for as he says, 'Dispatch is the life of trade, and is the general principle, next to safety, that gives one port the advantage over another, provided the internal situations are much the same, and in the end will find its account.'

Captain Huddart concluded his report by an observation upon the great resources at Swansea, enjoyed from the 'Internal produce of iron, coal, etc., in the neighbourhood, which appear almost inexhaustible, and he urged that 'if the harbour is rendered commodious, the trade will increase in those staple articles, and the merchant is not in the worst situation for the export trade and many articles of inland consumption.

This report was printed in pamphlet form and circulated by the Trustees, who added the following observations:

It is very evident that by obtaining an increase of about 5 feet of water in the Harbour of Swansea as proposed to be done by Capt. Huddart's plan, vessels of 300 tons burthen will be enabled to proceed on their voyages on the lowest neap tides, whereas in the present state of the harbour, small vessels even of 60 tons burthen are frequently beneap'd, therefore, by completing the improvements according to Capt. Huddart's recommendations, most essential advantages will be rendered to the Port of Swansea as well as to every consumer of coal in Cornwall, and likewise vessels of every other port with which any commerce may be carried on, and when it is considered that a small impost of 1s. per ton on shipping by register measure, together with a trifling payment on coal and copper ore will produce the above effect, it is confidently expected that the measure will be unanimously supported by every person connected with the Port of Swansea.

The Trustees recorded a vote of thanks to Captain Huddart and resolved to ask his acceptance of a hundred guineas for his expenses and by way of gratuity for his time and trouble. A special Committee was appointed to carry out an examination of the site of the proposed western pier and whether or not it should incorporate an embankment made by Mr Morris of slag from his copper works. The Committee found the site was gravel and that a wall should be built with a wing and should be a single wall backed with gravel and slag, 28 feet at the lower end and 20 feet at the upper end.

Captain Huddart visited Swansea again in February 1804 at the request of the Trustees and found the results that he forecast of his suggested improvements had proved correct and he made a second report, which was appended to a pamphlet dated 1804 entitled 'Swansea Harbour: Extracts from the Report of Joseph Huddart Esquire, Addressed to the Trustees, Showing his plan for the Improvement thereof, dated 1794.'

Huddart made the following observations in his second report:

I find that the river Tawe, and the shore by the side of the river, from the head of the western pier to the sea at low water, has not undergone any sensible alterations; that the sand, to the extent of about 90 yards west of the river, and to 270 yards southward of the pier head, is worn down (in some parts) nearly one foot since that period. The sand to the eastward of the river has accumulated, I think, one foot or more, occasioned by the erection of fishing weirs (one of which is only about 70 yards from the river side, bearing south 40° west 750 yards from Salt-house Point); and although at present they have not affected the channel or bed of the river, yet they are injurious to the free navigation of the port; but it is my opinion, that if those obstructions are removed, the sands will be reduced by the effect of the sea to their former level, and that no erections or obstructions from high-water to low-water be allowed nearer the river Tawe than one mile.

I have also examined the river from the pierhead to the Ferry-pool; the bar is somewhat increased, and the ground at the pier-head lower than in 1794; the difference being 4 feet 10 inches; at present the fall from the bar to the pier-head is 5 feet 6 inches eighth, which tends to confirm my former report, that a permanent depth of water into the river cannot be secured but by the completion of the outer harbour by the eastern pier, and which is of the first consequence to the port of Swansea.

Huddart accompanied his 1804 report with a plan in which a short jetty was added to each pier-head. These jetties were to prevent waves running up the inside of the pier and thus helped to make a calmer water within the harbour. The piers were 30 feet in width at the top and the length facing the entrance of the harbour was 75 feet and rounded off at the ends marked '*ba*' and '*ab*' on the plan. To enable ships to moor against the pier he suggested snatch blocks, that is to say, blocks of a single sheave in which the largest cables could be hooked in rather than run through: these were to be at the points '*a, a* & *b, b*'.

Huddart was in favour of the channel between the piers being dredged to a width of 60 yards as far up the river as Ferry-pool, and the excavated earth being used for the work on the eastern pier. Huddart advised the Swansea Corporation not to let the riverside buildings:

> In the present situation of the harbour before the eastern pier is erected I cannot recommend it, as the waves in southerly winds would range higher against the wall than at present, when they are more retarded and expended upon the beach (or river bank); I also think that the Corporation had much better retain this property in their own possession, for should foreign trade be introduced, and ships employed that would not take the ground well, the most eligible situation for a wet dock is from the upper end of the western pier towards the Ferrypool, and if taken from the harbour, executed at the least expense.

Huddart's foresight eventually became reality with the building of the South Dock on this site.

In May 1805 the work commenced and the Trustees submitted to Captain Huddart the suggestion of terminating the pier-heads with right-angled corners to strengthen the wall, on the grounds that 'if projections or sets-off were made in the outsides of the walls terminating in points at right angles, they would tend to strengthen the pier and throw the force of the sea from the pier wall into the bay.' However, this suggestion did not find favour with Huddart, who replied 'although the proposed projections may strengthen the wall, yet under the consideration of the effect of Waves in Gales of Wind and the Tides, they would be detrimental.'

A further question on which Captain Huddart was consulted was the replacement of the existing Mumbles lighthouse, which was coal-burning, with an up-to-date lighthouse. Presumably the existing light was, in fact, a coal-burning cresset on a tower, which was not only expensive to maintain, but inefficient for navigation.

A decision was taken by the Trustees in December 1794 to give notice of their intention to apply at the following session of Parliament for leave to bring in ' a bill for erecting a lighthouse on the Mumble Head to be furnished with Reflectors on the best principle, and Argand Lamps, and it is intended that all vessels passing the proposed Light House and using the advantage of the Lights shall pay per Ton by measurement.'

Before making their application they communicated with Huddart who, as one of the Elder Brethren of Trinity House, was the best person to advise whether the proposal 'would not still be of further advantage to the Trade of that Port' to which Huddart replied:

> A Light on the Mumbles must be very interesting [sic] to the safety of the Trade in general which frequent the Navigation of the Bristol Channel; To

have a known light in sight is of much comfort to the Mariner, affording a greater certainty of attaining a Port of Safety in bad weather, and at all times a Check upon the distance run; but this Light on the Mumbles will be more particularly useful in avoiding the Sker Weathers and Helwick Sands by a Compas bearing and to the Safe Anchorage in the Mumbles Road.

I am, therefore, of opinion that not only Bristol, but all vessels bound, or forced by stress of Weather, into or out of Barnstaple and Caldy and to all Ports and places to the eastward of them on either shore up the Bristol Channel, should contribute to the support of a light on the Mumbles; except such coasting vessels as navigate the Severn, and do not proceed to the westward of Bridgwater or Cardiff. Ships being frequently drove from their intended Port, or out of the Tract of their Voyage by Gales of Wind, it, therefore, seems reasonable to me that vessels from or to Milford Haven which round the Land's End as well as those from the St. George's Channel bound round the Land that may put into Milford Haven by contrary winds, should contribute; as it may frequently happen that those Vessels being forced up Bristol Channel may receive great benefit from this light especially if improved to an Oil Light. It was upon this consideration that the Trade of Liverpool was ready to contribute to the support of a Light on the Long Ships.

Huddart was an advocate and even a crusader in the use of revolving lights which, with the aid of the newly introduced Argand lamps, enabled a beam to be shone at distinct intervals, thereby making it possible for mariners to identify the lighthouse by the beam it cast. The system had been initiated in the Scillies lighthouse. The use of Argand Lamps with reflectors also made it possible to cast a beam a far greater distance than any normal light would carry.

On 5 April 1796 it was resolved to proceed with the lighthouse bill, but the question of approaching Trinity House was not pursued. It was not until 1 November 1975 that Trinity House took the lighthouse over from the harbour authority. The 55-foot brick tower designed by William Jennegan and first used in 1794 continued as the lighthouse, being administered by the harbour trustees.

In March 1796 Huddart, after surveying the harbour of St Agnes in Cornwall, furnished the proprietors with a plan for a new jetty; but no details of this survey appear to have survived.

In 1800, at the request of the Magistrates and Council of Edinburgh, Joseph Huddart undertook a survey of the harbour of Leith. This matter appears to have been initiated by John Rennie, to whom Huddart wrote on 21 July 1800 as follows:

Highbury Terrace. 21st July 1800

Dear Sir,

Having perused the Letter from Mr. Sibbald, and also the observations of Captain Liddell with the Plan for the improvement of Leith Harbour, and giving it every attention as far as my abilities could suggest from this and other information, you have sent me, having never been at Leith, I offer the following remarks upon the aforesaid observations.

That Captain Liddell's observations upon the danger and difficulties in entering the Harbour are very just respecting the tide setting to the eastward at the East Pier Head etc. and to remedy which proposes a Pier to be built in an East or N.N.E. direction, which gives a great latitude in the direction, but taking it as represented in the Plan, viz. about N.N.E. and the head of this new Pier S.S.W. from the head of the Eastern Pier, and the present Western Pier taken down would not alter the force or direction of the Tide or be of any advantage until the ship had entered the Piers, when in some cases it might be useful. A good Capstan upon the head of this Pier, would also be very useful, in case of ships grounding upon the eastern side of the channel, without the Pier head. However a Deadman sunk in a proper situation, with a buoy, would be a good substitute in the cases he mentions. But I am of opinion that the Harbour would be more agitated in strong northerly winds by this alteration in the Western Pier, at least as far up the harbour as the Ballast key, and would not afford any safe security for berthing of ships. Respecting the last observation of Captain Liddell, it is certainly very convenient, and safe, to have shoal water for a ship to bring up upon the ground in strong N. and N.Werly winds. I should suppose that the present harbour may afford such situation near the intended entrance of the proposed Docks, without the Ballast Key in smoother water, then if the alteration was made.

Hence my opinion which you desire upon the observations of Captain Liddell is that the alteration by building the proposed Pier will not afford any advantage adequate to the heavy expense, for it would not tend to acquire a better channel or more water to the Harbour, the want of which is the foundation of those risks in sailing into, and out of, the Harbour of Leith.

The great extension of Flat Shore without the Pier Head, will render it an expensive operation, to gain sufficient water for large ships, at the present entrance; nothing less than extending double piers can render it sufficient for large ships, and permanent, for probably not more than one foot increase of water could be gained by sluices, and that kept up at a very considerable expense. It therefore appears to me that the most effectual plan for the improvement of the Harbour and accommodation of the Trade of Leith is to have the principal entrance to the proposed docks for large ships near Ankerfield where the shore having a good descent to seaward affords the means of mentaining a good and safe entrance.

I am, Sir,
Your most obedient,

(Sgd.) J. Huddart.

Mr. John Rennie.

On 3 November Huddart made a survey and report. Unfortunately no details of this survive, but his suggestions were approved and carried into effect, for which he received the thanks of the City conveyed by the Lord Provost. In 1804 Rennie furnished plans for new quays and new docks, which were not fully carried out: but two large docks 1,500 feet long, and two small ones 750 feet long were constructed along the shore between the old tidal Harbour and the village of Newhaven.

In January 1803 Captain Huddart received the thanks of the Directors General of the Inland Navigation for the 'Consideration and Application' he gave to the improvement of the harbour of Dublin.

On 4 March 1804 Joseph Huddart laid the foundation stone to the East India Docks and this event affords an opportunity to look back at the growing problems of operating the Port of London, particularly as far as the East India Company was concerned. In the seventeenth century the East India Company had its dockyard with a comprehensive organisation to monitor the unloading of vessels which had been to foreign parts; however this had, by now, been abandoned.

During the eighteenth century an enormous increase in trade had taken place. Taking the Port of London as a whole the foreign-going British tonnage increased five times and the foreign tonnage increased three times not counting the vast coastal trade. In 1798 the total number of ships entering the Port of London was 13,553 with a total tonnage of 1,877,536, which caused considerable congestion in the river. On arrival ships had to moor a long way down river, East Indiamen usually unloaded at Blackwall whereas the Company's warehouse was at Leadenhall Street.

The lengthy process of discharging into lighters meant that it took a month to discharge an East Indiaman of 800 tons of cargo. This situation can be seen from the following details of the harbour journal of the *Royal Admiral*, which anchored in the Thames on 6 July 1788:

Sunday July 6th 1788
At 3 P.M. Came too with the best Bower about ¼ of a mile above Gravesend – got the Guns out.

Monday July 7th
At 10 A.M. weighed and dropt up into Longreach – At 2 P.M. Came too with the best Bower in ¼ 5 Fathoms at low-water veer'd away and moored Ship, half Cable on the best Bower and a whole cable on the small Bower – Got the Powder out and sent down Top Gall't yards.

Tuesday July 8th
Employ'd delivering Tea on Acct. of the Honble Company – Received on board 18 Fellowship Porters to work the Ship out.

Wednesday July 9th
Loaded two Hoys with Tea on Account of the Honble Company and some private trade – Loos'd the sails to dry and black'd the Bends.

Thursday July 10th
Employ'd as before – Got the Longboat out Booms & Sails.

Friday July 11th
Employ'd as before.

Monday July 14th
Employ'd delivering Tea on Acct. of the Honble Company.

Tuesday July 15th
At 3 P.M. Unmoor'd Ship and hove short – At 6 A.M. weighed – At 1 P.M. Came too with small Bower at Blackwall lash'd along side the Worcester and took up the small Bower Anchor at 10 P.M. Cast off and dropt up to Deptford.

Wednesday July 16th
At one A.M. lash'd along side the Monsieur Frigate below the low watergate – At daylight Moored Ship with small Bower to the Hood – Unbent the Sails and loaded a Lighter with Tea on Acct. of the Honble Company and Private Trade.

Thursday July 17th
Sent the best Bower and Sheet Cables to the Warehouse.

Friday July 18th
Got the Top Gallant masts down and unreev'd the running rigging.

Saturday July 19th
Got the lower and Topsail yards down – Employ'd unrigging and sending the stores to the Warehouse – A.M. wash'd the Gundeck.

Monday July 21st
Employ'd unrigging and loading Lighter with Tea on Account of the Honble Company.

Tuesday July 22nd
Sent the Main & Mizen Topmasts ashore – Stript the lower masts – At 6 P.M. Came along side the St Helena Hoy.

Wednesday July 23rd
A.M. Loaded a Hoy with Tea on Acct. of the Honble Company and some Private Trade.

Thursday July 24th
Employ'd as necessary.

Friday July 25th
Employ'd as necessary – P.M. Came along side the Robert Lighter.

Saturday July 26th
Employ'd loading a Lighter with Tea on Account of the Honble Company and some Private Trade – P.M. wash'd the Gun deck.

Monday July 28th
Loaded a Lighter with Tea on Account of the Honble Company and some Private Trade.

Tuesday July 29th
Employ'd delivering Cargo on Acct. of the Honble Company.

Wednesday July 30th
Loaded a Lighter with Tea on Acct. of the Honble Company.

Thursday July 31st
Employ'd delivering Cargo on Acct. of the Honble Company.

Friday August 1st.
Employ'd as yesterday.

Saturday August 2nd
Wash'd the Gun deck otherwise employ'd as necessary.

Monday August 4th
Employ'd delivering Tea on Acct. of the Honble Company.

Tuesday August 5th
Employ'd as yesterday.

Wednesday August 6th
Employ'd as before.

Thursday August 7th
Employ'd as before.

Friday August 8th
At noon came on board the Inspectors and cleared the Ship.

If ships could be docked the time taken in going to and fro with lighters would be saved and the inevitable loss of stores, gear and cargo to the hordes of thieves who swarmed the crowded reaches of the Thames between London Bridge and Blackwall would be avoided. These consisted of an odd assortment of plunderers, many of whom must have been put out of business when the docks were surrounded with walls 25 foot high.

In the first place there were the River Pirates, who might weigh the ship's anchor, set it adrift and make off with it, or they might steal the rigging while the crew were asleep. Then there were Night Plunderers, who were usually watermen working in gangs of four or five; they specialised in plundering lighters or craft in which goods were stored prior to going ashore. They were usually in league with the watchmen and shared

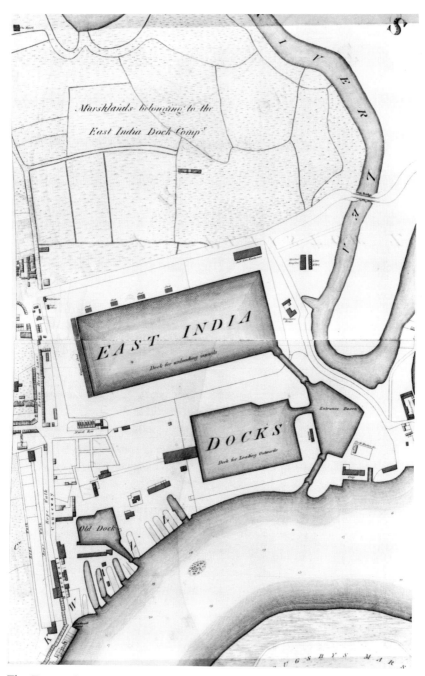

The East India Docks.

the plunder with them, though the watchmen would also ensure that it was not their lighters which were plundered. Another variety were Light Horsemen, who made night raids on West India ships, acting in concert with the ship's crew. They got on board by making a payment of thirty to fifty guineas for the sweepings, that is, the sugar that remained in the hold after the ship had been discharged, but, once on board, they opened as many hogshead of sugar and coffee as possible: the ships suffering a loss were known as game ships.

Another form of theft was carried out by the Heavy Horsemen, who offered to work on West India ships without payment and once on board they filled their pockets with sugar, spices, rum and anything else worth stealing. They wore under-waistcoats with pockets all round, as well as pouches tied to their legs.

To complete the picture of river theft, there were the Game Watermen and Game Lightermen, who helped themselves to the cargo they were shifting; Mudlarks who prowled the mud with the pretence of beach combing, but actually received goods from thieves on board the ships; Scuffle hunters who stole from the crowded quays; and Copemen who were the receivers.

In 1794, the merchants of London, realising the problem and the over-crowding of the Thames, sought the asistance of Trinity House to survey the river from the Tower to Blackwall; Huddart, then one of the Elder Brethren, was given the task, which resulted in a proposal to build the London docks. In 1796, there was a parliamentary enquiry into the condition of the Port of London, at which Huddart gave evidence, as did William Vaughan, a merchant and director of the Royal Exchange Corporation.

In 1798 the Thames Police was established to check the wholesale depredation which was going on; but so long as ships discharged into open lighters and the goods were then landed on open quays, piled up in no sort of order, the surveillance of the police was bound to be limited. The only satisfactory method was to build proper docks which were walled in and as yet docks hardly existed in the Thames.

There was a small dock known as Greenland Dock, which had been constructed by the South Sea Company. Daniel Defoe, writing early in the eighteenth century, says:

> The South Sea Company have engaged in Greenland Fishery, and fitted out a fleet of twelve great ships, which they have built new from the stocks, and have made that great wet dock between Deptford and Redriff the center of all that commerce and buildings, the works and the management, of that they call cookery; that is boyling their blubber into oyl. Tis well if they do not make stink enough, and gain too little, especially to the neighbouring places of Deptford and Redriff.

The other existing dock was Perry's Dock. Perry was a ship builder who built his private dock to get his shipping out of the river and placing them and their cargo under lock and key.

John Rennie, being the most experienced civil engineer of the time, was consulted in 1798 to devise a plan for the docks. The West India Dock which occupied the isthmus connecting the Isle of Dogs with Poplar was designed and built by William Jessop, ward and pupil of the famous Smeaton; while John Rennie was responsible for St Katharine's Dock, which bordered on the Tower of London and the London Docks.

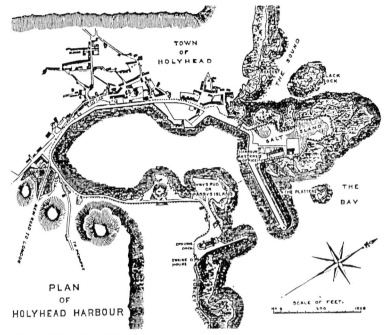

Plan of Holyhead Harbour.

Shortly after this, in 1803, a company was formed by Act of Parliament with a capital of £660,000 called the East India Dock Company and Huddart was appointed a Director, while Ralph Walker, who started life as a sailor and became an eminent civil engineer associated with John Rennie, undertook the work.

The site chosen was immediately west of the River Lea near the point at which it enters the Thames. At that time there were two small docks with wooden walls, Brunswick and Perry's Dock, and these had to be purchased and included in the scheme.

The honour of laying the foundation stone was intended for William Pitt, the Prime Minister, but, in his absence, the duty was delegated to Joseph Huddart. The foundation stone bore an inscription stating that it had been laid by Joseph Huddart FRS and the names of the engineers John Rennie and Ralph Walker also appeared in the inscription. The docks were completed and open for business on 4 August 1806. Huddart supported Walker in the erection of a perimeter wall 25 feet high, although he thought that unnecessary expense had been incurred in the amount of masonry used. The docks consisted of one entrance lock into the Thames 210 feet long and 47 feet wide with a cill laid 7 feet below the level of low water spring tides.

This lock was connected with a triangular entrance basin covering 4½ acres on the west side of which it communicated, by another lock, with a dock expressly provided for the outward bound vessels called the 'Export Dock'. This dock measuring 760 feet in length and 463 feet in width was situated along the north bank of the Thames and covered 8½ acres. At the north end of the entrance basin was the 'Import Dock', measuring

1,410 feet in length and 460 feet in width covering 18½ acres and having a depth of 22 feet below mean high water at spring tides. The Import Dock extended along the south side of East India Dock Road and the total dock area was 50 acres.

The Company was governed by twelve directors with William Cotton as the chairman and there were three dockmasters who lived at the docks. Before vessels were allowed to enter the docks, they had to dismantle their lower masts, and they had to take off guns, ammunition and stores while they lay at their moorings. It had always been the practice for powder and guns to be taken ashore before unloading commenced.

Before being permitted to enter, a report had to be made by the Captain to the Dockmaster of the amount of water the ship had been leaking every twelve hours for the previous three days. All ships from the East Indies and China unloaded their cargoes within the docks unless their draught was such that some cargo had to be discharged to reduce their draught.

On the outward-bound journey the East Indiamen loaded in the Export Dock or in the River below Limehouse Creek. Imported goods were taken away by the Company's caravans to their various warehouses in Fenchurch Street, Haydon Square, Coopers Row, Jewry Street, Crutched Friars, New Street, Leadenhall Street and elsewhere.

Not only did Rennie's plans give security to the cargoes, but he worked out details for the introduction of labour-saving devices. In 1808 he recommended that all lifting cranes should be worked by steam; however, labour-saving innovations met with the same unwelcome response as they do nowadays, and it took a long time for his ideas to be implemented – one suggestion that went unheeded was the introduction of railways round the quays.

Walled-in docks protected the cargo of ships discharged at the quay side, but there were still chances of a ship being plundered as she made her way up river. However, now the task of the River Police was much easier and the chances of plundering a ship's cargo were limited. There was an instance in 1812 where a cargo of valencia silk and ostrich feathers was trans-shipped to a hoy under the supervision of the London Customs. When the master was absent a gang boarded the hoy and plundered the cargo.

Valencia silk was unique in England and such silk was found to be worked in a mill in Somerset; its origin was then traced to the White Swan in Ratcliffe Highway, otherwise known as Paddy's Goose. The publican was persuaded to turn King's Evidence and the gang were arrested; three were hanged and another was transported for life.

John Rennie's Docks opened a new era on the Thames and in London's dockland, which continued throughout the nineteenth century until the middle of the twentieth century, when docks built for sailing ships from 1,000 tons to 1,800 tons no longer served a useful purpose and eventually had to be abandoned and redeveloped. These were not the only monuments to Rennie's engineering to suffer, Rennie's London bridges had to submit to the same fate: the elegant nine-arch Waterloo Bridge with its Doric pilasters built to set off the magnificent waterside facade of Somerset House not only suffered structurally in the nineteen-twenties, but became hopelessly inadequate with the emergence of motor traffic, having only a three-lane carriageway for vehicles and pavements 7 feet in width to carry the hordes of commuters which swarmed daily over the bridge.

The Union with Ireland in 1800 brought a demand for a closer communication between Ireland and Great Britain. The nearest point from Dublin across the sea was the Isle of Anglesey; but Holyhead was the only possible place for a harbour on the island. It had deep water, but no pier or jetty or anything to adapt it for a harbour. Added to this it was not only inaccessible by road but also involved crossing the Menai Straits.

As far back as 1802 Rennie had been requested to report on the possibilities of Holyhead. In May 1808 Joseph Huddart had the task of surveying Holyhead as a possible harbour with the alternative of Pwllheli which was more accessible by land, but not so well placed for a crossing. He also had to report on the positioning of a lighthouse, for which he recommended South Stack, a rock off the extreme western point of Anglesey. There had been proposals as far back as 1665 for a light at this point, but Charles II had refused to grant a patent.

On the strength of Huddart's report, a lighthouse was erected at a cost of £12,000 and designed by Daniel Alexander. The tower was 90 feet in height and the light was 200 feet above mean high water. The lantern which was fitted with twenty-one Argand lamps and reflectors revolving on a central pillar, first showed a light on 9 February, 1809. The chasm between the rock and the mainland was spanned by a cable 70 feet above sea level, which carried a moving basket for transporting goods or passengers to the lighthouse.

Captain Cotton, the Deputy Master of Trinity House, makes the following report:

> It is one of the best constructions, in point of effect and utility, constituting the safety of intercourse between the capital of Ireland and England; it is discovered half-seas over[1] by the splendour of its appearance, being a revolving light, situated on the South Stack, an island near the Head of considerable height, and with which communication is kept up by a rope bridge: but at some future day an iron one may be substituted, a model of which is at Trinity House.
>
> This light from its moderate height and insular situation, is never obscured by clouds (while that on the opposite side of the Channel on the Hill of Howth was so frequently, as to cause its removal) and it is admitted to be a model for future structures in similar situations.

In the same year, Rennie was requested to make plans for the harbour and these were approved by the Government, the work being started in 1810 and completed in 1824. Rennie's plan was to use a natural inlet where the cliffs came down to the sea with the town on the west side. The entrance to the inlet was sheltered with rocks and by Salt Island.

Rennie's work consisted of connecting Salt Island on its western side with the mainland and extending a pier 1,150 feet eastwards from the landward side of Salt Island parallel with the coast of the mainland running due east. The depth of the water at the end of the pier at low water spring tides was 14 feet. To construct the entrance of the harbour a 60-foot jetty was built from the main pier running due north. The pier and the jetty were protected by a flat stone paved slope of rough stone laid at an inclination of 5 to 1. The quay was curved on the face at one-fifth of the height. The thickness of the masonry was about 10 feet strengthened at the back by

---

[1] I.e., midway on the sea crossing.

strong counterforts 15 feet apart. The foundation of the wall was laid below the water by means of long stones inclined to each other.

After his survey of Holyhead Huddart was requested by the Government to survey, in conjunction with Rennie, the Harbour of Howth on the Irish side of the crossing for packets: the Harbour was opened for packet traffic in 1819.

The work of providing a road to Holyhead was given to Thomas Telford and also that of connecting Anglesey with the mainland, which he did with his famous suspension bridge, was completed about the same time as the Harbour.

The construction of the Martello Towers from Folkestone to Seaford was an outward and visible sign of a much deeper and inward concern over British defences, at a time when Napoleon was overrunning every country in Europe and the British fleet was stretched to its limits.

A Commission of Civil Officers of the Navy was appointed to consider means of improving the output of work in the Naval Dockyards, which lagged behind similar establishments run by private enterprise and other Governments have subsequently been faced with the same problem.

On 14 May 1807, John Rennie, who also had been engaged on the problem, delivered his report. He found the Royal Dockyards, that is to say, Chatham, Woolwich, Deptford and Sheerness on the Thames, and Portsmouth, Pembroke and Plymouth, in a state of decay and silted up, with the exception of Plymouth where deep water and a rocky terrain had not given rise to silt: but here the objection was the exposure of Plymouth Sound to the south-west gales. Portsmouth was in a deplorable state; the depth of water over the bar during the period of a century had been reduced from 18 feet to 14 feet and the harbour works were in a state of decay. He considered the docks inadequate and badly laid out, having been run up in haste with no overall plan.

Rennie offered the following comment on Portsmouth:

> Let any stranger visit Portsmouth Dockyard the head establishment of the British Navy he will be astonished at the vastness and number of buildings and perhaps say 'What a wonderful place it is' knowing nothing of the subject. But I compare the place to nothing else than a pack of cards with the names of different buildings docks etc. marked upon them, and then tossed into the air, so that each in falling might find a place by chance – so completely are they devoid of all arrangement and order.

It was a damning report at a time when Napoleon was saying 'let us carry our victorious eagles to the Pillars of Hercules.'

In September 1808 Huddart visited Portsmouth with Mr Mylne – presumably Robert Mylne, the architect of Blackfriars Bridge on the Thames. This was not his first visit; as far back as 1796 he had been to Portsmouth and in December 1798 he had been written to by James Watt of Boulton & Watt requesting details of the largest dock at Portsmouth; no doubt this information was required to enable a steam engine to be constructed for emptying the dock by steam power instead of horses.

On this occasion, Huddart reported on the proposal to make an entrance to the harbour by a canal from Stokes Bay. If it is right to assume that the bars which built up across the entrances to Portsmouth Harbour, Langstone Harbour and Chichester Harbour were caused by a backwash as the tidal water from Spithead passed Gilkicker Point south of Gosport, then an entrance from Stokes Bay using Stokes Lake (or Haslar Lake) as part of a canal would provide a solution, but evidently the idea was never pursued.

Dear Sir,

I observe in your letter to Lord Melville, that you mention the diminution of water on the Bar of Portsmouth Harbour and as I was examining this Bar (with the Master Attendant and others) in the year 1796 when viewing the Encroachments at *Gosport* I thought it would not be unacceptable to *you* to express my Ideas on this subject the Entrance being naturally in a slow but progressive state of Decay.

The Master Attendant, Pilots and others may inform you that the first Quarter Ebb coming down Channel fills Portsmouth Harbour, which arises from the observing the great increase of Velocity of the Tide of Flood in the last Quarter: but this is occasioned by the small extent of the Area of the surface water in the Creeks at Low-Water compared with the Area as it covers the Mud Lands which are very extensive in Portsmouth Harbour, and which continually rise by the deposition of Mud and lessens the Velocity on the Bar, and Entrance &c., and which is the cause of this diminution.

In the Year 1796 Mr. Mylne and Mr. Jessop were with me, and an Idea of a Back Water from Langstone Harbour was suggested, and at Dinner with Sir Charles Saxton Commissioner, Mr. Jessop mentioned this Idea with Sluices to admit Water from Langstone Harbour, General Bentham replied that the same thought had struck him in coming from London the day before.

As I always considered Portsmouth as the Key to this Island the extent from Spithead to Yarmouth rendering it a continual Harbour for the safety of any number of Ships, and the Harbour so contiguous, I have turned the Improvement in my mind, & the taking of water from Sluices while Langstone Harbour remained open to the Sea would be of little avail, not worth consideration. If embanked from the Sea and a Large and Open Channel opened between the two Harbours, the Depth on the Bar would be encreased, by the encreased velocity of Tide; but the velocity of the latter part of the Flood would add to the present difficulty of getting out except with a leading Wind, and the deposition of mud on the covering Lands would again lessen the depth as before. The Continuance of a wall on the S.W. side of the Channel from the Point, would give deep water over the Bar, but the encreasing velocity would remove the bed & a part of which would be brought into or towards the Harbour by the Floods, & the rest taken without the wall & form a second Bar, except extended into deep water, at a heavy expense, & it occurred to me the best mode for securing the benefit to the Public from Portsmouth Yard to extend a Canal from Stoke Lake into Stoke Bay, a steep shore & a short distance between Low Ground, & at a less expence than either of the Modes before mentioned & which would permanently secure the easy passage of Ships with their Stores so long as there is sufficient water to transport them across the Harbour to the Yard.

When at Portsmouth on the Gosport business in Sept. 1808 I mentioned this to Mr. Rennie & went with him over the Ground from the Lake to Stoke Bay, & found no difficulty. Some Conversation at the Trinity House took place last Thursday & I mentioned this cut to Sir Andrew Hammond, who said he had not heard of this before.

I do not think it adviseable to encrease the number of Naval Arsenals except in the instance of Northfleet, on account of the difficulty in the River above Long Reach, I see no advantage in the Harbour of Falmouth, above what it is at present, I have been informed that some Ships of the Line have taken the Ground in that Harbour, there is scarcely width in the Channel to bring up Large Ships in a Gale of Wind or to birth a great number but if a Breakwater is properly constructed in Plymouth Sound it would render great Benefit & Security to our Navy.

Copy of a Letter to Mr. Rose April 9th 1810.

Signed J. Huddart

Above £1,200,000.

Stamford Street Jany 3. *1814*

My Lord

In consequence of the Conversation with which your Lordship honoured me on the 23rd. ult., I have looked out the papers and Observations relating to *Mr. Huddart*'s Plan for a New Entrance to Portsmouth Harbour from Stoke Bay, & which Plan I cannot discribe better than is done by himself in a Letter which he wrote to Mr. Rose dated the 9th of April 1810, a copy of which he sent to me on the 2nd of August of the Same year, with liberty to use it as I might Judge adviseable, I have therefore with this transmitted a copy of the said letter for your Lordship's use.

It appears from Mr. Huddarts letter, that his only object was a New entrance to Portsmouth Harbour, conceiving as any skilfull person does who has examined the Harbour attentively, that it is in a gradual State of decay, & that at no very distant period, unless encroachments on the shores of the Lake are prevented, & proper attention in other respects is paid to the preservation of the Harbour, there will not be a Sufficient depth of water on the Bar for a Ship of the Line to go into or come out of it – It was however no part of Mr. Hudarts plan to have a Wet Dock in Stoke Lake for laying up Ships in Ordinary, & indeed it is my opinion, that the damming up of that Lake would be extremely prejudicial to the Harbour.

The Shore covered with Water in Stoke Lake west of Gosport Point is – (every tide) about 150 acres, thus if the whole Space in Portsmouth Lake is nearly five thousand acres as it is said to be, this would be a diminution of 1/32 part, a diminution which in a very few years would render the Harbour unfit for the reception of Ships of the Line. I cannot therefore suppose a plan of this sort would be sanctioned by your Lordship, unless an adequate space for the Tide to Cover, was to be provided somewhere else equally advantageous, & this would occasion a very Serious expense & indeed if Such an Idea was to be entertained a better Situation might be found for a Wet Dock than Stoke Lake – If Stoke Lake is not to be taken for a Wet Dock but to be made the Medium of communication between the Harbour & a Wet Dock, this might be done without injury to the Harbour, but from the rough Estimates I have made, a Wet Dock any where between Stoke Lake & Stoke Bay, would cost at least one third more in preportion to its Capacity than a Dock at Northfleet, & when Done, would be so remote from the Dockyard as very much to abridge its advantages, a Wet Dock should if possible have a direct communication with the Graving Docks, Masts & Storehouses &c, so that the Superintendance of the Ships should be within reach of the Officers of the Dockyard, which cannot be the case if a Dock is made on the Gosport side of the Harbour & Ships laid up there.

I have the Honor to be

My Lord

About £2,000,000   Your Lordships Most Hble Serv.

John Rennie

The Right Honble
Lord Viscount Melville.

In August 1808 Joseph Huddart, accompanied by John Rennie and Mylne, was requested by the Admiralty to report on Woolwich Dockyard.

Rennie and Mylne had already paid a visit there on 27 July, choosing the time when spring tides were at their highest, but Huddart was unable to accompany them. He had been paying a visit to Gilsland in Cumberland to take the waters and improve his health and probably had not returned by the end of July. Rennie, as the engineer who had to work out the particular details in these Government contracts, played the dominant role in preparing the reports while Huddart and Mylne were there in an advisory capacity. Huddart's nautical knowledge was always valuable on these occasions.

Woolwich was condemned by Rennie in his report of 1807. He considered it to be too high up the river and incapable of enlargement. There was a considerable accumulation of mud there owing to obstructions in the river, and, no doubt, this was the reason for Huddart being called in to give a second opinion. Rennie's son, later Sir John Rennie, says:

> In the spring of 1814 my father, being desirous that I should be initiated into the practice of marine and trigonometrical surveying upon a large scale, sent me, under the direction of the late Mr. Francis Giles, who had then been appointed by Mr. Rennie to make an extensive survey of the different places where it was practicable to construct proper artificial harbours on the south-west coast of Scotland. . . . (1815) I also about the same time assisted Mr. Giles in the survey of the Thames in the vicinity of Woolwich Dockyard, the accumulation of mud in front of which was so great at that time that it threatened to render that dockyard useless. The evil to a certain extent has since been remedied by removing a number of the projections which interfered with the currents of the ebb and flood tide, according to the plan laid down by the late Mr. Rennie, although as he clearly pointed out, it would be impossible to improve the river to such an extent in front of Woolwich and Deptford dockyards as to render them fit for the construction and accommodation of large vessels of war; and therefore he recommended that they should be abandoned and sold, and that a proper establishment should be made at Northfleet capable of accommodating at all times of tide any number of the largest vessels of war at that time in the navy, or that might be built hereafter . . .

Later Sir John Rennie says that among the works he had executed was the great basin, two building slips for first rates, mast slip, and the river wall in front at the Royal Dockyard Woolwich, costing £340,000.

John Rennie the elder had condemned all the Royal Dockyards in the Thames and advocated that they should be abandoned and replaced with a single dockyard at Northfleet capable of handling all naval vessels and fully equipped to do so. This scheme had the support of Pitt but by the Autumn of 1815 Napoleon had been defeated and Pitt had died. The incentive to launch out on a grandiose scheme faded away into patching up and making do with the existing establishments.

In August 1815 Joseph Huddart received the thanks of the Lords Commissioners of the Admiralty for the assistance he gave in the survey of the Royal Dockyard at Sheerness.

Sheerness is situated on the north-eastern corner of the Isle of Sheppey at the mouth of the Medway commanding the entrance to that river and the Thames. No doubt it was of strategic importance in Elizabethan times, but the range of guns had reached a distance to make its position vulnerable from an invading fleet. Sir John Rennie writes:

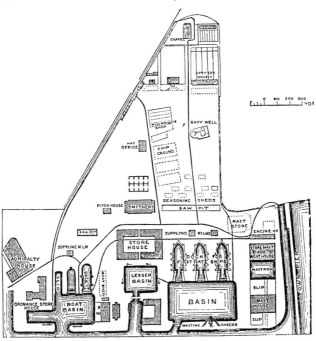

Plan of Sheerness Docks.

The most difficult and anxious work, however, at that time (1813) was the new dockyard at Sheerness, designed and partly carried into effect by my father. He originally, in the year 1807 recommended that the old dockyard, which was composed only of some old wooden slips imbedded in the mud, a few storehouses, a wretched basin, and some timber jetties, should be abolished. He said that it was on the lee or wrong side of the harbour, that the foundation for the new works was of mud and quicksand, that the space, on account of the buildings in the old town was very confined, and, therefore, that to make a good dockyard there would be very expensive, and he thought it would be far better to make a new complete establishment at Northfleet, just above Gravesend, and to get rid of Woolwich, Deptford, and Steerness altogether.

But with Pitt's death this suggestion fell to the ground.

As before, Huddart having made a report, the practical details became the province of Rennie. The plan decided upon was to use the river frontage of the Medway extending from Garrison Point to near the old Town Pier of Sheerness of a length of 3150 feet including the entrances and enclosing within it three basins.

One basin to the North 480 feet long and from 90 to 200 feet wide containing a surface of about two acres, 4 feet below low water spring tides with two frigate docks, a building slip and boat slips. A central tidal basin of 220 feet square of the depth of 2 feet below low water with storehouses around it for the reception and delivery of victualling and other stores. On the South-western end of the dockyard a basin 520 feet long and 300 feet wide covering an area of 4 acres provided on the East side with dry docks for ships of the line, having cills, the bottom of the basin being laid 9 feet below low water spring tides. On the West of this basin were mast ponds, mast locks and workshops, while to the East of this basin were saw pits, timber berths and officers houses covering in total 64¾ acres.

After the defeat of Napoleon in 1815 the House of Commons was reluctant to spend large sums of money on naval and military works. However, it was essential to have a repair yard at the mouth of the Thames. The total number of pennants flying at the end of the war was 1,000 with 127,000 sailors and marines. There was also a greater depth of water at Sheerness than at any of the other dockyards. It was therefore decided to repair Sheerness, which, in fact, resulted in rebuilding it.

The work was commenced in 1815 and Lord Melville laid the first stone at the north end. The total cost was £3m, of which £1,700,000 went in engineering works and the rest in the purchase of land and the erection of buildings.

With regard to the completion of the works at Sheerness Dockyard, Sir John Rennie writes as follows:

> These, as I have said, has been wholly designed by my father upon an entirely original and novel plan of hollow walls, which he first carried into effect at Great Grimsby Docks, in the year 1786. These walls though composed of a mass of materials of the same weight as ordinary dock walls, were distributed over a wider area, and pressed less heavily upon the surface in proportion to their extent, and therefore the soft, sandy foundation upon which they were built was able to bear them without yielding; the increased friction also produced by the increased surface of their base enabled them to withstand with greater effect the lateral pressure of the earth behind them; thus a double object was gained, namely, security against both vertical and lateral pressure.

> When my father died on the 4th of October, 1821, the northern half of the new dockyard, including the sea wall, the great basin, the three large dry docks at the west end, and the mast ponds and locks had been nearly completed; so that it only remained to fix iron gates for the dry docks and those of the mast and boat ponds, which had already been designed and ordered, and were put into their places under my direction. This portion of the dockyard, although comprising the most extensive and costly part, was not the most difficult. The most arduous task still remained, namely, the construction of the northern portion. Here was the greatest depth of water, varying from 25 to 30 feet at low water of spring tides, the worst foundation, and the situation was most exposed to northerly and easterly winds. These obstacles were felt so strongly by my father, that he originally contemplated carrying out the works by means of the diving bell; but as so much experience had already been obtained by the employment of cofferdams in similar constructions, where they had been very successful, it became a question for my serious consideration whether it would not be better to use cofferdams for the northern portion of the dockyard, instead of employing the diving bell, which would necessarily require much more time. After consulting with the enterprising contractors, Messrs. Jolliffe, Banks, and Nicholson, who had completed the works already made, and Mr. John Thomas, the experienced resident engineer, we came to the unanimous conclusion that it was perfectly practicable to construct the remainder of the works by means of cofferdams; and although it would be rather more expensive, nevertheless they could be done much better and far more speedily than by the diving bell; and, indeed, they told me that my father had expressed the same opinion before he died; and that there was little doubt but that if he lived he would have recommended cofferdams instead of the diving bell. I consulted my brother George upon the subject, and he was of the same opinion. We resolved to recommend that the remainder of the works should be completed by cofferdams, and the Admiralty approved of our recommendation. Messrs. Jolliffe, Banks,

and Nicholson therefore undertook the contract for these works at the sum of £845,000 and gave ample security; and they were most successfully finished for the sum of £845,000 in round numbers, or at about £9,000 beyond the contract price, our estimate being nearly £900,000; so that they were actually for about £45,000 below our estimate, and fully three years sooner than they would have been if the diving bell had been used.

CHAPTER VIII

The Rope Manufactory

THE CROWNING achievement of Joseph Huddart's life was his invention of rope-making machinery. Huddart's achievements in the rope-making industry were equal to the achievements of Hargreaves, Arkwright and Compton in the spinning industry. Rope making was an important industry owing to the enormous amount of sailing vessels afloat.

Rope at this time was made out of hemp and occasionally horsehair was used in certain sorts of cordage. Cannabis, to give it its botanical name, required the sort of rich silty soil that can be found in Lincolnshire and parts of Somerset. Defoe tells us: 'Here are the greatest improvements by planting of hemp, that I think is to be seen in England, particularly on the Norfolk and Cambridge side of the Fens, as about Wisbech, Wells and several other places, where we saw many hundred acres of ground bearing great crops of hemp.' It was usually sown in May at the rate of one bushel to an acre, a bushel being the equivalent of one and a third cubic feet. It was gathered when mature and dried in stooks like other crops.

When dry, the hemp had to be dressed by skutching and heckling. A shutcher was a sort of mallet shaped like a rolling pin which was used to thresh the hemp and a hackle or heckle was a hedgehog-like comb fixed to a bench through which the hemp was drawn to separate the lines or long pieces from the tow. By the end of the eighteenth century these processes would have been carried out mechanically with the aid of water power. The lines were drawn into a continuous sliver and spun into yarn right-handed producing a sort of coarse string, while the yarn was twisted left-handed into strands. A hawser-laid rope consisted of three strands laid up right-handed and a cable-laid rope was three-hawser laid ropes laid up left-handed.

The traditional rope walk comprised a long low building with a hook at one end which could be rotated by a wheel. The workmen had the strands or spun yarn wound round their waists with one end attached to the hook. As they walked backwards from the hook they twisted the strands in one direction while the hook rotated in the opposite direction. This resulted in the rope being laid up with the yarn at the core of each strand remaining slack, as only the yarn on the outside of each strand was pulled tight.

Joseph Huddart, on his voyage from India to China through the Sunda Straits, found that he had to anchor frequently and on weighing anchor, he realised that the outer strands of the anchor cable were the ones that parted. He decided to investigate this and on cutting open a piece of rope he noticed that the whole strain was thrown on the exterior yarns of the strands. The yarns being originally the same length, the outer yarns became shortened by twisting and, therefore, carried the strain whereas the inner yarns were loose and kinked and bore little strain. As the angle at which the strands were laid up increased, so the strain on the outer strands increased and the strength of the rope lessened.

It had long been accepted that a selvagee, where strands lie parallel to each other without being twisted, was stronger than rope with an equal amount of material, and selvagees were used to bind shrouds to chain plates, but they absorbed water. Huddart addressed his mind to constructing a rope that was impervious to water but, at the same time, gave each yarn the same proportion of strain, so that all the material in the rope bore an equal strain. In order to do this each yarn had to be given a length proportionate to the angle it described and to its distance from the centre of the strand.

After his return to England, Huddart constructed a machine in his garden to put his principle into practice. He explained his plan and described the principle of his improvement to a Mr Barnes, a ropemaker in Maryport, Cumberland, not many miles from his native village of Allonby, who assisted in the first experiments. Barnes did not have the capital nor Maryport the trade to make the idea a business proposition; but the use of some of the ropes which were made, in neighbouring colleries under Huddart's supervision, satisfied him that his principle was a real improvement.

He then offered his invention to the East India Company for use by their ropemakers, but as so often is the case there was a reluctance to change from the established practices, especially by the workmen.

The invention was then offered to the Admiralty, who referred it to their practical officers; but they were prejudiced against any innovation coming from the merchant service and particularly against machine-made ropes. How often must this story have been repeated through the years! There is a bright idea – yes, but no-one wants to burn their fingers putting it into practice, or there are those who crab it because they have not thought of it themselves. Joseph Huddart tended to sheer away from taking financial gambles and yet what bigger gamble could he have made than building the brig *Patience* on borrowed money, which at the age of twenty-eight he had to man with a crew, navigate himself and carry on a profitable trade.

However, this Admiralty contact did bring about an unexpected result. One of the Lords of the Admiralty, Admiral Gambier, was impressed by Huddart's invention and suggested to him that, rather than forsake the idea, it might succeed as a private venture, if he could get a few men with capital who would enter into partnership to form a rope manufactory.

Huddart accordingly found three partners, Sir Robert Wigram, Charles Hampden Turner and another called Woolmore who was supported by a syndicate, and although Huddart was reluctant to go into business he could not see his friends risk their fortunes without doing like-wise. Thus, on 16 February 1800 the partnership of Huddart & Co. was formed.

Huddart, who was still living at No. 12 Highbury Terrace, Islington, took a cottage near a farm at Limehouse where the rope-making works were established. East Enders will identify its position from Joseph Street, Huddart Street and Turner Road. Limehouse got its name from the Lime kiln and associated buildings on the South side of Limehouse Dock; in the eighteenth century this was as far as London reached, with only a scattering of buildings along the River and a ropewalk. North of Limehouse

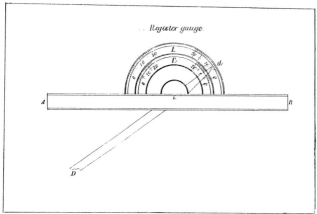

Register gauge for Huddart's Rope-making Machine.

Dock was Saint Ann's Church looking out on fields, where Huddart listened with delight to a lady performing on the organ; about two hundred yards to the North of the church was the rope factory, extending for about a quarter of a mile approximately along the line of Burdett Road. The plan shows the contemporary layout.

The yarn was spun by a yarn-spinning machine probably supplied by Messrs Blyth and as it was spun it was wound onto a winch. The invention used a series of bobbins set up on racks onto which each yarn was wound by use of a winding machine. The patent specification indicated seven racks of bobbins with twenty bobbins on each rack, but this number was varied according to the thickness of the rope which would be laid up from the strands passing through the machine. The word 'bobbin' has so many connotations that it probably conjures up different images in different minds and today the word 'reel' would be used, as everyone is familiar with a cotton reel; the bobbins were the same thing on a larger scale. There were two types of bobbins, one onto which the yarn was first wound. This was tapered slightly and supported on a spindle at its wider end, which was keyed into a pulley wheel to supply the power to rotate it. At the narrower end, if we regard the bobbin as a truncated cone, a wooden arm was fixed which rotated with it and led the yarn off it and carried it through the hollow of the spindle of the bobbin.

Each bobbin was spring loaded to preserve the tension of the yarn as it wound off in the same way as the tension is preserved in a modern sewing machine. There would be racks of possibly a hundred bobbins with the yarn being drawn away through the centre of each spindle and through a tarring machine. After this, it was wound onto a second type of bobbin, cylindrical in shape instead of being a truncated cone.

The yarn having been tarred by the first process, it then had to be twisted by the next process and led into what was called the register. Therefore, when sufficient yarn had been wound onto the second type of bobbin, each was housed in a metal casing or canister supported on spindles enabling it to revolve, which were then set up in racks. The bobbin inside the canister was free to rotate on an axis at right angles to the spindle of the canister so the yarn could unwind and be drawn off through the hollow of the spindle of the canister. The bobbin was again spring loaded to maintain the tension

A.D. 1799. Aug 20. N° 2339
HUDDART'S Specification   *I. SHEET.*

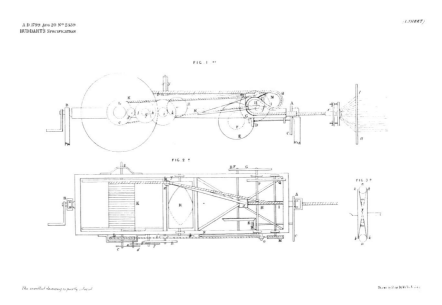

The enrolled drawing is partly coloured   *Drawn & Printed by H. Ma Nichi &c.*

Drawing attached to Huddart's second Patent for Cordage Machinery.

of the yarn as it was drawn off and as the canister revolved, it twisted up the yarn, and squeezed out surplus tar.

The yarn from all the bobbins gathered at a central point at what was called the 'register' and this takes us to the third process of the invention. The register was a sheet of metal perforated with holes about two inches apart like a colander, with one central hole and the others ranged in concentric circles around it. There was also a small replica of this with the holes pierced as nearly as possible to each other, but apart from the central hole at a slight angle from the circumference. The two plates were set up so that the central holes were in line with each other and each yarn was drawn through first the hole in the larger plate and then the corresponding hole in the smaller plate. The distance between the plates determined the angle at which each yarn met, they being brought together in the form of a cone, so that when the strands were laid up the outer yarns lay on the outside of the strand and the central yarn formed its core. From the register plates the yarn was drawn through and compressed in a cylindrical tube made in two half sections longitudinally and funnel shaped at the end the yarn entered, with mechanism to compress the two half sections together.

For the purpose of the first patent it was assumed that the strands would be laid up by hand. This patent was granted on 24 May 1793 for 'A New Mode or Art of Making Great Cables and other Cordage so as to Attain a greater Degree of Strength therein, by a more Equal Distribution of the Strain upon the Yarns.'

To determine the angle of the outer yarns a register gauge was devised, not as part of the working machinery but as an accessory. This was similar in appearance to a school protractor fixed to a stock AB with a straight edge and with a rotating arm Dd, pivoted at i. The part forming a protractor was engraved with two semicircular arcs divided into two concentric graduated scales and the arm rotated round these scales. The outer scale was marked 'L' for laying and the inner scale 'R' for registering and the scales were based on the mean stretching of yarn founded upon experiments.

To use the register gauge the stock was laid parallel to the centre strand and the revolving arm determined the angle of the outer strand: the foreman having decided the laying angle he set the arm to correspond with the registering angle shown on the scale marked 'R' and the distance between the registering plates had to be adjusted in order to give the outer yarn this angle.

The sharper or more acute angle at which the strands were laid up the more impervious they were to water, but at the same time, the sharper the angle the less was the strength of the rope. It was also found the more regularly the rope was laid up the better it coiled.

To complete the process of drawing the yarn through the register it was first intended that this should be done by hand in the traditional manner of a ropewalk, but the register had to remain fixed. A way had to be devised therefore of laying the rope up with a stationary machine and this was covered by a second patent. Instead of there being a rotating hook from which the men laying up the rope walked backwards, the machine which drew the yarn through the register itself revolved, being supported at both ends by gudgeons or pivots. The strand from the register passed through one of the pivots, which was hollow, being drawn and twisted at the same time, and this twist was transmitted back to the register tube. The machine also wound the strand as it came through onto a drum.

At this period, which was the dawn of mechanical engineering, it was no small achievement to construct a machine, such as the laying machine, which, although it weighed nearly twenty tons, had to revolve on its bed supported by only two bearings. The exact details of this mechanical process can be seen from the following extract from the Patent specification and its accompanying drawing. The second patent was granted on 19 September 1799 and described as 'An Improved Method of Registering or Forming the Strands in the Machinery for Manufacturing Cordage'. The letters of reference used in the specification correspond with those in the drawing.

> The register and tube, Fig. 1st, must, instead of being drawn along the yarns, be fixed at any convenient distance from the bobbins; the machine, the frame of which may be of wood or iron, revolves round its axis upon the gudgeons at A and B, that gudgeon next the register at A (being perforated to receive the strand from the register tube x, described in my former Patent), and works in the centre of a fixed or sun wheel A, which, by the machine revolving, gives motion to the planet wheel C, Fig. 1st and 2d, in the machine, and the machine and the bevel pinion upon its axis D, which carries the bevel wheel E, and upon its axis the spur wheel F; this wheel F carries the wheel G, and upon its axis the wheel P, and the whirl H, which has a groove to receive the strand from the perforated gudgeon, and after passing about two-thirds round this whirl to wind in like manner upon the whirl I of the same diameter, connected by equal wheels P and Q, upon their axes, to give equal motion to

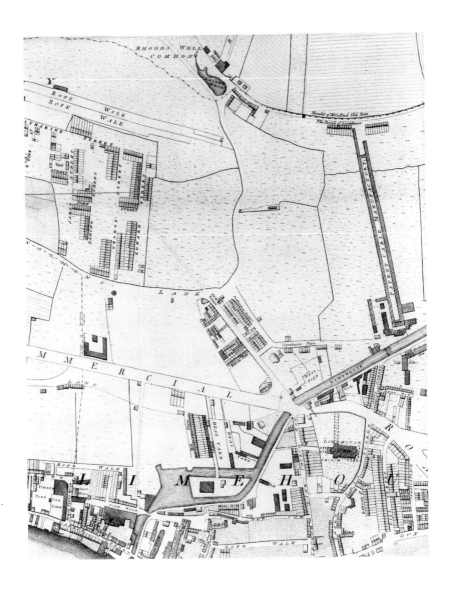

Plan of Limehouse showing Huddart & Co.'s Patent Cordage Manufactory.

the whirls, so that the friction of the strand in the grooves of the whirls may not suffer it to slide over them (or the strand may wind over more whirls to increase the friction if necessary) in its passing to the reel K, which has a motion communicated to it by a band passing round L, a whirl, upon the axis of a crank applied to one end of the reel, and M, a whirl upon the axis of one of the former whirls I; this band must be sufficiently tight to give the reel a power to prevent the strand from sliding round the whirls H and I, which it passes over, and yet so easy as to allow itself to slide round the whirls L or M, when the reel, by the increase of its diameter from the strand being wound upon it, would draw more than the whirls H and I give, which are to regulate the quantity or length of strand, and for the adjustment of which a clip that moves upon the centre N, with friction wheels o, o, is provided to be tightened by a screw pins or otherwise (which to prevent confusion is not represented in the Drawing) to draw the legs N, O, N, O, nearer together. In order to vary the angle or degree of twist, and form strands of different sizes by the same machine, the wheels F and G, which works in each other, are provided in pairs (the sum of the two radii of each pair being equal), which vary in numbers one or more teeth in each wheel, and may be extended to as great a variety as necessary by shifting those pairs and applying them to either axis. This difference in number will increase or diminish the ratio between the revolutions of the machine and that of the whirls, which determines the length of strand to be drawn each revolution. Now, the length of one turn and the circumference of the strand being given, which forms a right-angled triangle, the triangle is given, and therefore the angle of registering found which may be compared with the register gauge; or the ratio may be varied by different sets of the whirls – and I applied to their axis, each set of different diameters from another set. Or if the groove in the whirls is so formed that the width of the outer part k, k, Fig. 3rd, is equal to the diameter of the largest strand intended to be registered on the machine, and the sides of the groove by right lines meeting at the axis or centre of the whirl at l, the machine will register all strands at the same angle when the same shifting wheels are applied. The smaller strand m, passing round that part of the whirl at the distance l, m, from the centre, will draw a less length of strand in the same ratio to the circumference as the larger strand n to its distance from the centre n, l, and circumference, therefore the angles of registering will be equal in various sized strands registered by the machine. It is necessary to have a traverse to pass the strand more regularly round the reel, and particularly to ascertain the turns and fraction of a turn, if any, that the strand makes in winding from one end of the reel to the other, in order to acquire the length of strand registered. This may be performed various ways now in practice, by communicating the motion from the axis of the crank which carries the reel, by worms or tooth and pinion to a heart and lever, or otherwise to guide the strand over; but my Invention is by the application of a cylinder R, which makes half a revolution, while the strand is winding from one end to the other of the reel, and by its spiral ridge or groove upon its surface, which moves the lever a, b, upon the cylinder, by friction wheels or pin at the under side of the lever or otherwise, the strand passing between the rollers x and y at the end of the lever, and returns the strand again to the end of the reel where it begun, while the cylinder moves through the other half of its revolution, which is communicated by wheels and pinions from the axis of the crank or reel to the cylinder. In this Drawing, Fig. 1st and 2d, where c represents the wheel upon the axis of the lever, and carries d with the pinion e, and the pinion e carries the wheel f and pinion g, which carries the wheel h and pinion i; this pinion i carries the wheel k, fixed upon the axis of the cylinder R, which by two pinions in it may give motion to an index to shew the number of shells of strand wound upon the wheel and ascertain the length of the strand. The wheel C and D, or any other pair, may be made to shift and vary the revolution of the cylinder, according to the size of the strand, as before described, and having registered the required length upon this reel, it may be shifted by drawing the pin S (which is secured by a forelock or otherwise); the strands are then to be run upon the laying ground and hardened up by the hooks to the required angle, as described in my former Patent, and then topped or laid into a rope in the common way. I must remark, that the tube A of the register, instead of being in two parts to compress the strand, may be of solid metal, without much injury to the performance, as from the compressibility of the strand and the evenness of size, when composed of many yarns, it will pass the tube very uniformly; and also, if the strands are smaller than the hole in the perforated gudgeon at A, which will generally be the case, it will be necessary to have friction wheels between the machine and the tube x, to confine the strand in the axis of the tube, continued to prevent any vibratory motion in the strand, which will render a long tube necessary, as the ratio of the yarns is given at the mouth on first entering the tube, and its length is only to preserve the direction of the strand. The fore board of the register in Fig. 1st may be dispensed with if the yarns from the bobbings come to the register at a sufficient distance to keep them from being entangled by the fibres, which it was intended to prevent, and if a sufficient number of turns is put in the yarns before winding, there will not be any necessity for keeping up the twist in registering, if performed by this machine, when the distance is short between the bobbins and register. The bobbins may be run either perpendicularly or horizontally, and the machine may also revolve with its axis parallel or perpendicular to the horizon, as the situation may require.

The patented machinery produced only strands which still had to be laid up to make a rope and the fourth process in the manufacturing was to lay three strands up into a rope and for this purpose a Laying Machine was devised. This followed the same principle of giving the same twist to the same length of rope as it passed through the machine and a uniform angle at which the rope was laid up and the same compression as it went through the laying machine. This could never have been achieved with gangs of labour.

Three machines, on each of which the strand was wound, revolved round a central pillar on which a sun wheel was fixed and a planet wheel transmitted to each machine a counter turn to each strand. By revolving round a common centre the strands were twisted into rope as a regulated length was drawn off with each revolution, thus preserving uniformity throughout the rope. The sun and planet wheel was a means of transmitting a circular rotating motion into an oscillating motion or vice versa. In most cases the same result could be achieved with a crank, but probably the sun and planet wheel set up less vibration at a time when engineering skill was in its infancy. In this case, it enabled the rotation of a single pillar to be transmitted to three machines.

Each strand from the reel or cylinder on which it was wound passed over two riggers united by equal wheels, and so formed as to prevent any slipping of the strand; and the riggers on each machine were united by a combination of wheels to one wheel on the centre pillar, so as effectually to prevent any one strand being longer than another in the rope; a resistance to movement of this centre wheel was given by a friction block attached to it, the pressure being regulated by a spring giving a uniform tension and compression to the strands as they were formed into rope.

In a rope laid up by hand the twist would be passed up a hundred and thirty fathoms of rope by use of a sledge, but with the machine the same length of rope was subjected to the same tension as it passed through the machine. A rope consisted of three strands laid up together: a cable consisted of three ropes laid up together and the same process was followed for laying ropes up into cables.

Previous to the formation of Huddart's Ropery at Limehouse, no means had been adopted for determining with accuracy the heat of tar. Those who were in the habit of superintending the process of tarring the yarn formed their opinion of the heat of the tar by its appearance or by spitting on it. This did not satisfy Huddart: and having by various experiments, ascertained what heat was requisite in order to tar every fibre of the hemp, he gradually raised the heat of the tar to 400 degrees Fahrenheit, when it entirely destroyed the strength of the hemp. He then had a copper tube, closed at the bottom, fixed in the heated tar and reaching down to the bottom of the tar kettle, and in this tube was suspended a thermometer to give the temperature of the tar. Workmen were directed to keep the temperature of the tar between 212 and 200° Fahrenheit.

The size of cordage is measured by its circumference and the word 'rope' is usually applied to cordage above one inch in diameter or three inches in circumference. Yarns are twisted together to form a strand and three strands laid up to make a rope: this is described as hawser-laid and if four strands are used it is described as shroud-laid. If three ropes are laid up this is described as cable-laid. Manilla, Coir and Sisal, which came from tropical countries, were not available in the eighteenth century and until the introduction of nylon, hemp was still regarded as the best material for use at sea.

The principle of distributing the strain equally to every yarn now having been achieved, Huddart sought a further improvement by making the strands more compact and less compressible to avoid the strain put on the exterior yarns in the process of twisting. He considered the advantage of warm registering, that is, forming yarns into strands as they came out of the tar kettle. Forming strands at a low temperature after they had been tarred affected their compactness on account of the rigidity which resulted from tarring. It was consequently necessary to register them at a higher angle and thereby reduce their strength.

Warm registering was the subject of correspondence with the Navy Board, the firm's best customer. In the first place the Board was approached for some of the hemp recently arrived from India on which to experiment.

Honble Gentlemen,

Upon application at the India House For some of the Pakt (Packet), lately arrived from India, we find your Hon. Board, has taken the only parcel, as yet offered for Sale – We are anxious to make some Experiments upon this article, particularly on our *warm registering* machines – We should feel obliged if you would permit us to have a few Tons from His Majesty's Stores upon which we should make certain Experiments to ascertain its Quality and properties.

We are Hon. Gentlemen,
Your Ob. Servants

Huddart & Co.

Limehouse
17 April 1802

To the Hon. the Comms.
of H.M. Navy.

The Board's decision was unhelpful.

20 April 1802 Acquaint them that from the small quantity of this Hemp which We have procured it is not in our power to spare them any part of it.
Board.

Then in October 1803, the firm wrote offering to supply cordage made of the warm registering process. The letter reads as follows:

Honourable Gentlemen,

In answer to yours we beg to acquaint you, we are ready to manufacture cordage after our improved plan of *warm registering* on the following Terms.

To return Cordage for Hemp . . . . . . @ £16 per Ton.
To return 24 Tons Cordage for £21 Tons Hemp £22 per Ton.
We think it necessary to acquaint you that as we do not put so much Tar into our cordage as is in common Cordage, so we cannot undertake to deliver more than 24 Tons for 21.

The Extreme Strength obtained by our process, safely enables a reduction in size, far exceeding the extra price paid for manufacturing.

Our orders at present being considerable, we cannot undertake to supply your Hon. Board, with more than 25 Tons per Week and this we should recommend to be of large stock, say Cables, Shroud Hawsers and large Ropes.

The Shroud Hawsers, we certainly recommend to be 4 Strand Shroud laid, – which makes them most considerably stronger, and less *capable* of stretching.

We have further to observe that as our Cordage *increases* in Strength, in proportion with its size whilst common Cordage *decreases* in proportion of Strength with its Size so is the benefit resulting from our mode greater in large than small cordage.

We are Honourable Gentlemen
Your most Obedient Servants

Huddart & Co.

Limehouse

The Hon the Comm[s.]   4th Oct 1803.
H.M. Navy.

The Board made the following internal memo:

Mr. Derrick to state what the terms are with other ropemakers who manufacture cordage on Belfour's principle.

The memo in reply states:

No ropemakers have made cables or cordage in the present War on Belfour's principle. In the late War Messrs. Wells Perry were the only persons who made Cables on Belfour's principle, and they were allowed £17-10- per Ton, which was £3-10-0 per Ton more than was allowed for common mode of working. Nothing but Cables have been made by contractors on Belfour's principle: and 24 Tons were delivered for 20 Tons of Hemp.

Belfour's principle involved registering the yarn, but without the perfection or the success of Huddart's invention in positioning each yarn. The Board's decision was minuted as follows:

4 Oct 1803.

The Board agrees to employ Messrs. Huddart and Company to work up 21 Tons of the King's Hemp into Large Cables of 22 and 23 inches and Shroud Hawsers of 4 strands for service of Battleship Rigs of which they are to deliver 24 Tons and be paid The Hon. Commrs. H.M. Navy 22 per Ton.

Acquaint Messrs. Huddart & Co. We have given the Orders to issue the

Hemp but as We observe they return 24 Tons only of the Cables for 21 Tons Hemp desire they will let us know whether the said 24 Tons cordage is nett and free from Bands Spun Yarn &c.

Board.

Acqt them as above.

Then to Mr. Foster – who will observe that the Hemp has been ord-d to be issued.

Huddart & Co.'s reply follows on the 10th October:

Honourable Gentlemen

At the End of your Letter of the 6th present Month, ordering some Warm Registered Cordage, to be manufactured by us, we observe your desire to know whether the Quantity to be delivered is free from Bands, Spun yarn &c, – In answer we have to acquaint you, that we are not in the Habit of spinning our Yarn, after the manner prescribed by your Contracts, so are we unable precisely to give you an acc[t] – our Mode is not to top our Hemp so fine as to spin yarn of the size of 21 – but we make our Yarn to the Size of 18, whereby we are satisfied we procure Yarn of equal if not superior Strength, and at much less Loss of Hemp.

We should therefore be glad if your Hon. Board would allow us to manufacturer the Cordage now ordered in our *own way* – without Reference to Bands, Spun yarn &c – We shall readily give you a precise acc[t] of the produce of the Hemp, by the mode now requested we are certain you will find a considerable abatement in the Loss on the Manufacture.

We are Hon. Gent[n]
Yr most Obed Servants

Huddart & Co.

Limehouse
10 Oct 1803.

The Hon. the Com H.M. Navy.

In response the Board makes the following decision on the 11 October.

The Board agree to this proposal – Acquaint the Officers at Deptford.

Board.

On 26 November 1803 follows a letter in Huddart's handwriting defending the process of warm registering, which the unidentified Mr Chapman seems to have misunderstood.

Honble Gentlemen

In reply to you favor of the 23[d] Ins[t] requesting an explanation of an extract from Mr. Chapmans Letter, we have to remark; that the information he has given you is unfounded, for we dont depend upon what we call the scraper for cleaning the central part of the Strand of the superfluous Tar, this is regulated at the Head of the Kettle, in place of the nipper in the common Mode. But the strand being still hot and the Tar very Fluid, continues afterwards to ooze out by the Twist in the Strand, it was therefore necessary to use a scraper to clear the outside of the Strand.

In Tarring by the Haul, as soon as it has passed the Nipper the yarns become loose & swell having very little twist, & retain the whole of the tar they pass the nipper with, & if the Tar is seen to spring in a Rope when made with cold yarns, it will have a greater proportion of Tar than we can retain in our warm Registering on account of Less vacancy amongst the yarns.

Before delivering you our Tender we examined our Accounts of Hemp Received & Cordage Made & we found we had not used so large a proportion of Tar in the Warm as we had done in the Cold way, & by which it appeared we could not deliver you 24 Tons of Cordage from 20 Tons of Hemp.

However from the Last delivery it appears to have held out to that quantity. The Hemp was of a finer Fibre, than the Greatest part of ours which will always retain more Tar with the same Press.

I am Honble Gentlemen
For Huddart & Co.

Your Most Obedient
Humble Servt

26th Nov 1803

J. Huddart.
The Honble the Commissioners
of His Majesty's Navy.

The Board's Memorandum is as follows:

See Mr. Chapman's letter It is just sent in

2 Dec 1803.

Send to Mr. Chapman a copy of this letter and acquaint him We have given directions for a Contract to be drawn out for him to manufacture His Majis-s Hemp into Cordage at the rate of 22 per Ton, and to deliver the same proportion of Cordage as Messrs Huddart Viz: 24 Tons 5cwt. 1qr. 6lb for 20 Tons Hemp; that the quantity of Hemp to be first issued to him may be 40 or 50 Tons as may be most convenient to him, and that We shall require Security for the value of the Hemp – but if the cordage when delivered is too full of tar it will be objected to.

Let a Contract be drawn out accordingly

Board.

By this time it had evidently occurred to the Board that instead of paying for the warm registering to be let out to contract this could be done in their own yards: this appears from the following letter written by Huddart's partner Charles H. Turner.

26 March

Honourable Gentlemen

In answer to yours of the 10th Capt Huddart would certainly have sent you a working model of his Registering machine had he had one – but that not being the case, he was unable to comply with your request.

It has always been Capt Huddarts wish, and equally that of his Partners, that H:M: Navy should have the full Benefit of his Improvements in Rope-making, and as the *warm registering* embraces the object in its fullest Extent, he has no objection to the application of it in H:M: Rope Grounds.

Experience warrants us, in saying, the *warm registering* mode, is by far the *most compleat*, the *most expeditious* of any in use – it requires no alteration to any of the present Establishments, but can readily be adapted to use of H:M: Rope Yards.

If after this your Hon: Board, require it, we can have no hesitation in getting Estimates prepared by Mr Rennie (Engineer) of the expense of the necessary Building & machinery; which we take leave to say, must be *very trifling*, compared with the Extent of the object, and can be compleated in a few months. If this Estimate is wished for, we must thank you to acquaint us, the probable Quantity of Cordage required at each Yard.

We have to repeat our willingness to give any further Information; and shall readily assist any Enquiries either to your Hon: Board; or at our own Manufactory, by such ocular demonstration as the subject requires, which we think far preferable to any Model we can get made for you.

Should your Hon: Board with to adopt the Improvement now offered, Capt Huddart will certainly give such assistance as may be necessary to carry it into Effect – and we have only further to state, that two considerable Rope makers have already added the necessary machinery to the end of their Rope Grounds which has been in constant use, without any stoppage whatever, and much to their satisfaction.

Hon: Gent^m I am for
Capt Huddart, Partners
Yr most Humble Sert
C:H. Turner

Limehouse
26 March 1804

The Hon: the
Comm^s: H:M: Navy

The operation of the laying machine has already been discussed, and this laid strands into rope and ropes into cables: to do the same job by hand, it took a team of seventy or eighty men to lay up a cable. Three gangs twisted the strands into ropes and a further gang twisted the three ropes into a cable giving the ropes a counter turn as they were laid up into a cable. The force used to compress the ropes together was a sledge weighted according to the size of the rope.

Any short coming in the handling of the rope by the gangs or any irregular movement of the sledge resulted in an imperfect rope. There was a tendency to err on the side of twisting the ropes too much which made them rigid and difficult to coil and could reduce their strength. William Cotton, one of the partners who joined the firm, writes as follows:

Huddart's views were carried out with the full concurrence and assistance of his partners; no expense being grudged which he deemed necessary. But it should be observed, that Huddart was always scrupulous of increasing expense when it was to fall on others; and few manufactures on a large scale, were ever formed in which so little unsatisfactory expense was incurred by the work being done twice over; and for this advantage the partners were much indebted to Huddart's indefatigable industry, and scientific knowledge.

Every machine, before its construction was commenced, was accurately laid down on paper. The size of the reels and the other parts for holding the rope was fully ascertained, in order that there might be no unnecessary space in the machine, and unnecessary power required to drive it, and the strength of every part was determined by accurate calculations.

Huddart not only determined the principles on which his machinery was to be constructed, but he performed the duty of a skilful and ingenious mechanic. He was his own draftsman, and the superintendent of the work under execution. When a registering machine was to be made by one of the most skilful engineers and mechanics of his day, various schemes were considered for improving the construction; but they ended in the conviction, that it was best to adhere to that which had been laid down by Huddart.

The laying machine, weighing nearly twenty tons and resting entirely on one bearing, has long been considered one of the most beautiful pieces of machinery in the world for perfect proportion of its parts, and the gracefulness of its motion. This first laying machine was constructed from Captain Huddart's drawings, and principally during his absence from London; and when set to work, no alteration was found necessary, except the substitution of rollers on the quadrant on the top of each machine, instead of horizontal rollers, over which the strand had to pass, in order that the surface of the rollers might move in the same direction as the surface of the strand, and prevent that friction from the adhesive nature of the tar which had a tendency to throw the strand off the roller. And when a second laying machine was made by Huddart, and a third after his death, experience and consideration did not suggest any deviation from his plans, or any material alteration in their execution.

When Huddart was upwards of seventy years of age, and was greatly interested in the construction of the laying machines, he was anxious to determine what effect was produced on the angle of the strand as laid in the rope, by the elasticity of the strand, about three feet long between the machines and the point where the strands were united together; and he was sitting on the top of the machine, which was moving round at a considerable velocity, with a piece of chalk in his hand, and holding it against one of the strands in order to mark the spiral, formed by the revolution of the strand and its motion up to the spot where it was to be united to the other strands. His mind was so absorbed by the object he had in view, that he was quite unconscious of any danger.

All this machinery needed motive power to drive it, and until the latter part of the eighteenth century the only power available was either wind or water power. For work that could be done intermittently, wind power could be made use of, but for a continuous operation water power was the only solution. However, it was now possible to operate machinery by steam, which may have brought with it William Blake's dark satanic mills, but it opened up possibilities that never existed before.

John Rennie who designed the machinery for the invention had been associated with Boulton and Watt and realised the value of steam power. He was born in 1761 and at the age of twenty-one he toured the manufacturing districts to improve his knowledge of engineering practice; his friend Doctor Robinson gave him a letter of introduction to James Watt, who took a great interest in him and, in fact, a lifelong friendship sprang up.

The name of James Watt as the inventor of the steam engine needs no introduction, but, in fact, the use of steam power was already not unknown and it was from carrying out repairs to Newcomen's steam engine in 1764 that he started to experiment on his own. James Watt had some doubt as to the advantage of driving corn mills by steam, but in March 1783 a company was formed in London for erecting a large corn mill known as the Albion Mill to be driven by steam with one of Boulton and Watt's engines. Progress with the work was slow. Watt wrote to Boulton:

> Our millwrights have kept working at the corn mill ever since you went away and it is not yet finished; but my patience is exhausted. I have told them that it must at an end tomorrow done or undone. There is no end of millwrights once you give them leave to set about what they call machinery: here they have multiplied wheels upon wheels until it has now almost as many as an orrery.

It was in this situation that young Rennie came to the rescue: he knew something about mills: he had spent his college vacation repairing mills. This supported by a favourable recommendation from Dr Robinson got him the job of planning and supervising the erection of the machinery at the Albion Mill. Rennie has gone down in history as a civil engineer and the works for which he is remembered are Plymouth Breakwater and the

London Bridges, but his first employment was in mechanical engineering. He was certainly the best man to design Huddart's machinery and introduce a Boulton-Watt engine to drive it.

The standard type of engine made by James Watt at the period consisted of an overhead beam made of iron plates bolted together or of wood which was pivoted in the middle operating like the arm of a pair of scales. One end of the arm was connected to the piston rod and the other end to a rod transmitting the motive power. The piston and piston rod operated up and down in a vertical cylinder and this provided the motive power.

High-pressure steam could not be used because a boiler could not be constructed strong enough to withstand a high pressure, technology had not advanced that far. Instead, when the cylinder had filled with steam a jet of cold water condensed it, thereby causing a vacuum which sucked the piston downwards. The pressure of steam from the boiler on the upper side of the cylinder gave additional force to the stroke.

Thus the sequence of events was as follows: at the beginning of the power stroke the inlet valve above the piston was open, allowing the cylinder to fill with steam above the piston and the exhaust valve was open allowing the steam below the piston to reach the condenser and be reduced to water, thus causing a vacuum below the piston. The force of the steam above the piston and the vacuum below provided the motive power. As the stroke of the piston was completed, the inlet valve having already closed, the exhaust valve closed and the equilibrium valve opened. This valve allowed the steam above the piston to pass below the piston on the upward stroke. The valves were operated by linkage to the beam by a somewhat complicated arrangement of levers and weights.

The boiler was not under high pressure but was more of an oversized kettle producing steam. The movement of the engine was fairly leisurely with little vibration. To produce a rotary movement from an oscillating or up-and-down movement, Watt favoured his sun and planet wheel, which consisted of a cog on the free end of the rod transmitting the power. This was the planet wheel and this travelled round a large cog – sun wheel – connected to the driving belt and in so doing rotated it. A crank would have served the same purpose.

In order to put heavy machinery in motion without retarding the steam engine, or give a sudden velocity to the machinery, a friction block was introduced, the power of which was regulated by a spring adjusted by screws, by which it was possible to give a gradual movement to the machine without any risk to the shafts and wheels or strain to the engine. The engine required five or six horse power to keep it in motion.

The same boyhood fascination with which the young Joseph had constructed a model mill now masterminded a unique piece of machinery which was to set the pattern of rope manufacture for the years to come; but before heralding Joseph Huddart as the father of rope manufacturing the claims of one Belfour have to be dismissed.

It is unlikely that Huddart at the time was aware of it, but on 27 March 1793, just two months before he registered his first patent, John Daniel Belfour of Elsinore in Denmark had already patented a method of making cordage which attempted to distribute the strain equally throughout the yarn in a rope, and this he followed up with further patents on 1 June 1798 and 17 May 1799.

This method bore a close similarity to the principles that have already been described but, as will be seen in the succeeding chapter, fell far short of them in operation and seems to have achieved little success in Britain commercially. Huddart and his partners, on the other hand, could count on the Navy as their principle customer and as soon as the patent rights ran out his method was universally adopted for making rope.

CHAPTER IX

The Patent Contested

WHEN JOSEPH Huddart first worked out his invention and before he marketed it, he applied for a patent, which was granted on 24 May 1793. One is apt to associate Letters Patent with modern times, but their origin goes back through the centuries. The right became really established by the Statute of Monopolies in 1624 which swept away the abuses of Queen Elizabeth I and gave:

> grants of privilege for a term of fourteen years or under thereafter to be of the sole working or making of any manner of manufacture within the realm to the true and first inventor or inventors which others at the time of making such letters patent and grants shall not use so as also they be not contrary to the law nor mischievous to the state, by raising prices of commodities at home or to the hurt of trade or generally inconvenient.

According to Blackstone, the eighteenth-century jurist, Letters Patent are 'so called because they are not sealed up but exposed to open view with the great seal pendant at the bottom'. So far as inventions were concerned the matter came under the jurisdiction of the Court of Chancery as one of its miscellany of functions.

Originally it had been on the Lord Chancellor's advice that patents were granted by the Sovereign, and in Huddart's time the procedure which had to be followed dated back to the reign of Henry VIII.

Apart from having to attend before the Master in the Chancellor's Office, three attendances had to be made at the Home Office, and there were also attendances to be made at the Law Officers' Chambers, the Patent Bill Office, the Signet Office, the Lord Privy Seal's Office and the Great Seal Patent Office. In fact, there were ten stages which had to be gone through including twice having to have the personal signature of the Sovereign. Needless to say, fees had to be paid at various stages, which amounted to over £300, and where favours were sought it was an accepted part of eighteenth-century life that bribes in some form or other had to be paid to those whose compliance was solicited or to those who waited upon them. The Letters Patent were then enrolled in the Court of Chancery, that is to say, a copy was made on the Court's parchment scrolls, which can still be seen today.

As ill luck would have it, in this case J. D. Belfour, as mentioned previously, had already obtained his first patent for a similar invention only weeks before. This position gave a certain Grimshaw with a ropery works in Sunderland a pretext to evade Huddart's patent rights on the grounds that he was not the first and original inventor of this type of cordage. It followed, of course, that if Huddart were not the first inventor Belfour was: but that did not deter Grimshaw. Belfour was a merchant living in Denmark and unlikely to intervene even if he became aware of the infringement.

Belfour's invention sought to distribute the stress equally between the yarns in each strand and thereby achieve greater strength in a rope or cable: but his method of doing so was far from perfect and was cumbersome compared with Huddart's power-driven machinery.

Belfour required the yarn to be wound onto reels which were set up in a rack, with iron bars fixed across the rack acting as spindles for the reels. The specification, of course, gave more exact details on the methods of construction. About thirty fathoms of yarn was wound onto each reel (a sixth part of a cable's length) to provide the first strand. Each reel was spring-loaded to control the tension of the yarn as it was drawn off and there were a sufficient number of reels in the rack to provide the amount of yarn to make up the first strand.

In ropewalks a travelling, heavy, wooden structure, known as a sledge, was mounted with a hook, which was rotated with the aid of a crank or by using weights, for twisting the yarn. The sledge moved down the strand as it was laid up, but with this invention the sledge had to be stationary in order to twist the yarns as they were drawn off the reels, and so preserving equal tension.

Before being laid up the yarns passed through a separating machine – a sort of grating – and in place of Huddart's register Belfour introduced what he called a 'top minor' which he described as resembling a sugar loaf – a rare commodity in the modern kitchen – but nevertheless a wooden cone rounded off at the top. The thicker end, that is to say, the base of the cone, had a series of teeth housed in a surrounding iron band each about two inches long, and in thickness an eighth part of an inch; these were fixed a quarter of an inch apart so as to form a circular comb. The top minor was supported by two handles and held in position by workmen so as to guide the yarns as they were drawn off and twisted into strands.

Belfour's patent was a rough and ready way of attaining the same object as Huddart's patent achieved, but it was only with heavy cables that this method made a significant difference in the breaking strain.

When Huddart brought out his first patent we do not know how he intended to twist the strands, as the register had to remain stationary, but it must be presumed that the strands would have been pulled through the stationary sledge with a moving contrivance to carry the strands down the ropewalk as they were laid up. However, he must have realised the difficulty of this process and the necessity to carry it out mechanically, so the first patent remained experimental until the second patent introduced the laying machine, which was ready at the commencement of the partnership business.

The second patent not only made the whole idea practical, but enabled the complete manufacture of rope to be carried out mechanically without any handling by labour gangs. Belfour did introduce improvements in June 1798 and May 1799, among other things using a plate similar to Huddart's register plate as his top minor, but he made no attempt at mechanisation. In fact, the whole operation was labour intensive and the quality of the cordage produced fell a long way short of that laid up by Huddart's manufactory. It is clear from the Navy memoranda already referred to that

Belfour's principle was used only for heavy cables and then solely by one firm and that by the year 1801 it had ceased to be used at all.

Grimshaw's attempt to take advantage of Huddart's invention resulted in litigation. The case that ensued made legal history, and established the principle that attaining a particular purpose by the application of known things is that which constitutes an invention and if the end, effect or result attained thereby be new or useful the invention is such as will entitle the inventor to the sole right of vending it for a limited time. Huddart won his case with the nominal damages of one shilling, but his sole right to the benefit of his ideas was established. The well-known lawyer, Erskine, appeared for him and Gibbs appeared for the defendant.

The case was heard by Lord Ellenborough, who had been raised to the position of Lord Chief Justice the year before. He had previously held various legal offices and had been the leading counsel for Warren Hastings in 1788. He was the fourth son of Edmund Law, the Bishop of Carlisle.

In the judgement that follows verbatim Lord Ellenborough points out the importance of protecting inventions and that they consist in the adoption or combination of common elementary materials for the execution of a particular purpose beneficial to the public. The Lord Chief Justice goes on to make the point that no patent can be claimed for something already in another patent: and that a specification has to be enrolled as a public record giving sufficient information to enable a person skilled in the subject to accomplish the object of the patent, but the insertion of unnecessary material will vitiate the specification.

The Lord Chief Justice then considered Huddart's evidence of infringement of his patent and John Rennie's evidence. We then turn to the defendant's case that Huddart's invention was merely a repetition of Belfour's invention. However, Belfour did not use a tube to compact the yarns, with the result that they were not held in the same position throughout the strand, which was essential to the principle that every yarn bears an equal strain. It was on this basis that Huddart's claim succeeded. Lord Ellenborough's judgement reads as follows:

> This is an action to recover damages for the violation of a patent entitling the plaintiff, for a limited period of time, to the monopoly of an invention, which he states to be new, and beneficial to the public. This is a species of property highly important, as it respects the interests of the individual, and with him also the interests of the public; on the one hand, persons who are really the means of promoting any beneficial object should be protected for the period the law allows, and they should have the benefit of the article so invented; and, on the other hand, in case they are not the inventors, that they should not lock up from the public, for that limited period of time, that invention, which, if they are not the inventors, they have no priority to, and which ought to be open to the public. In inventions of this sort, and every other through the medium of mechanism, there are some materials which are common, and cannot be supposed to be appropriated in the terms of any patent. There are common elementary materials to work with in machinery, but it is the adoption of those materials to the execution of any particular purpose that constitutes the invention; and if the application of them be new, if the combination in its nature be essentially new, if it be productive of a new end, and beneficial to the public, it is that species of invention which, protected by the King's patent, ought to continue to the person the sole right of vending; but if, prior to the time of his obtaining a patent, any part of that which is of the substance of the invention has been communicated to the public in the shape of a specification of any other patent, or is a part of the service of the country so as to be a known thing, in that case he cannot

claim the benefit of his patent; and in claiming the benefit of a patent, it is required that there shall be enrolled a specification, which shall convey to the public a corresponding advantage with that of the individual whose sole right is protected for that time, so that any person looking at a specification, who is skilled in the subject, may be able to accomplish the end; and if in stating the means necessary to the production of that end, he oversteps the right, and appropriates more than is his own, he cannot avail himself of the benefit of it. I don't mean if he states a bobbin which was in common use before, but if he states any particular thing before in common use, applied in a new manner to the production, and effecting a new end, that is part of the substance of the invention. And if he states that which of itself is not new, but old and known to the world, though it was unnecessary for him to do so, having done so, he has overstepped his right, and has included in his invention that which is not his invention; in that respect his patent would be void. It is for you, applying these observations to the present patent, of Mr. Belfour and of Mr. Huddart, to say whether this is a new invention, whether the springs are substantially a part of the invention, and if they be, whether they are new. It is likewise to be considered whether the tube is a new invention: and the next consideration, supposing you should be of opinion that it is a new invention, and old means adapted to the production of a new effect, whether the defendant has been guilty of an infraction of the patent; and I premise these observations for your better understanding the evidence.

The first piece of evidence is a letter, dated 'Patent Ropery, near Sunderland, 21st August, 1779. Our Mr. Grimshaw has just got home, and has informed us of your friendship to him, for which please to accept our thanks. He also informed us, that you have a patent for improvements in rope-making, and that you were so obliging as to say, that we might use your methods (at our ropery only) without premium, provided that the gentlemen concerned with you had no objections. As we are anxious to forward any improvements in the manufacturing of an article of so much importance to this maritime country, we take the liberty of requesting you will please to inform us, whether we may consider ourselves at liberty to proceed in the adoption of your inventions.' Now, to be sure, no argument arises upon the face of this letter, that they knew and admitted that the invention of Mr. Huddart was a new invention, unless they were perfectly cognizant of all its parts at that time. But that does not appear from this letter; it does appear, that this man had visited their manufactory, and after he had got home, he wished to have the liberty of using their invention; that liberty is refused by a letter of the 29th: 'Gentlemen, your letter of the 21st has been communicated by Captain Huddart (who is now on a survey) to the other gentlemen in the concern. Apprehensive a grant to you might lead to an invasion of our patent from other quarters, in justice to ourselves, after the considerable expense that has been incurred, we feel ourselves under the necessity of refusing your request.' These letters are in 1799. Now, there is a letter since, so late as 15th July, 1800: 'Gentlemen, after your application to Captain Huddart, for liberty to use his patent methods of making ropes, and our refusal to permit the same, it has greatly surprised us to receive information (as we have lately done), that you have introduced those methods of making ropes into your manufactory without our license, and even against our consent; and that you use and vend ropes so manufactured in considerable quantities, in violation of the exclusive privileges granted by the said patent, and consequently to our great loss and injury. We should be sorry to be engaged in a litigation on this subject, especially with your house. It would give us great pleasure, if you could satisfy us that we were misinformed: but fearing that is not the case, and being resolved to protect our property in the most effectual and decisive manner, and to suffer no encroachment on, or violation of, those rights which we constantly respect in others, we think it proper to give you notice, that unless you henceforth desist from the use of Captain Huddart's patent above mentioned, and make us proper acknowledgments for what is past, we shall immediately cause the necessary proceedings to be instituted against you for our protection in future; and to obtain a compensation in damages for the injuries we have already sustained.' This is a letter giving them notice, that necessary measures would be taken against them, to obtain a compensation in damages. In answer to this, there is a letter of the 23d July, in the same year: 'Sir, we have received your letter of the 15th instant, and as we believe that we have not introduced into our manufactory any methods for making ropes, in which you are entitled to an exclusive privilege, we conclude you are misinformed on that point; but, being equally with yourselves desirous of avoiding litigation, if you will inform us the instances, or in what parts you suppose us to have infringed on your patent rights, we may, perhaps, be able to convince you, that there is no foundation for the charge. At the same time, to show you how little we are disposed to be litigious, we have for some time past remarked, that there are parts of Captain Huddart's specification strictly within our prior patents, which we have refrained from noticing, because we would avoid contention as much as possible.' Then there is another letter of the 14th July, 1801: 'Gentlemen, being informed that you carry on your manufactory of ropes in a secret manner, and as you refuse me admission when I called upon you at the ropery, and having seen some ropes that were made by you, I am convinced by the inspection of these ropes as well as by your secret manner of conducting your business, that you are making use of my patent method of registering the strands of cordage, as described in the specification of my patent of the year 1793, and am therefore desirous that your manufactory should be inspected on my behalf by my friend Mr. John Rennie, engineer, whom I introduce for that purpose. Your answer and conduct on this occasion will enable me to determine in what light to consider you and your proceedings in this matter, and unless I shall hereafter be better satisfied with the fairness and rectitude of your transactions than I am at this time, I shall commence and carry on against you such proceedings in law or equity, or both, as counsel shall advise.' That letter is no further material, than as it contains this complaint against them, and desiring to see their manufactory, which was refused.

The first witness called on the part of the plaintiff is Mr. Stodday, book-keeper to the defendants, who has been in that situation better than six years. He says, 'From 1797 to 1800, he was acquainted with their manner of making ropes; they then made ropes in the common way, in an open rope-walk; he is not acquainted with the manner in which they now make their first strand; a rope is composed of three strands; I was advised with before in the common way; although I live with them as before, I do not know in what mode their ropes are now made; I am not acquainted with the manner of making Mr. Huddart's ropes.' Upon cross-examination he says, up to 1800, the defendants made their strands in the common way, in a rope-walk. To be sure, no imputation lies upon them for not communicating to their own workmen so important a discovery, as that the business of a rope-walk should be carried on in so small a space as is represented. 'A common rope-walk,' he says, 'must be the full length of the yarn; they make it now in an enclosed place not the twentieth part of a rope-walk.' Upon being re-examined, he says, he saw the strands after they were made, and in opening out the strands, he observed a difference between the ropes made by them and the common ropes. In those, he says, made by his masters, the yarns all bear an equal proportion of strain, which is not the case with common ropes.

Mr. John Rennie is then called: he says, he is an engineer by profession; that he is acquainted with the subject of rope-making; that, by the old mode, the yarns for the strands are cut of the same length; they are stretched on the ground, previous to being twisted. When the twisting took place, some of the yarns took one station in the strand, and some another; those nearest the outside, passing over a large space in the operation of twisting, were necessarily brought to a considerable degree of tension, while the yarns towards the centre of the strand become puckered up. The effect was, that when a strain was put upon the rope, the external yarns sustained the weight, and those towards the centre sustained no part of the weight; when the strain, therefore, was put upon the rope, the outside yarns having been brought to a great degree of tension, naturally gave way first; those in the next degree of tension gave way next, and so on, till the centre yarns, which were originally puckered, came to bear the weight. The number of yarns being diminished, of course those in the centre were unable to sustain the weight. He says, the common rope gave way in the manner I have stated; in the wearing of a rope the outside yarns wear first, then the second set of yarns, and so on; a much less weight would break them in this state than would otherwise break them; and this continued, that is the unequal strain continued, down to Mr. Huddart's patent. He says, 'I have examined the patent and specification with attention; it appears to me to have provided a perfect remedy for this defect by a new method. The specification and drawing annexed to it will enable a man of science to understand the method, and how it should be carried into effect.' He says, 'I have attended to the manner of constructing strands upon Mr. Huddart's plan.' He assumes that the yarns to be manufactured have been usually put on bobbins; they are then passed singly through a plate, which is called a register plate, composed of holes formed in concentric circles; they are then passed through a cylindrical tube, which may be either solid or composed of two semicircular pieces; the tube is the most essential part of the invention; the yarns passing through the register plate are formed into one strand by this tube; being disposed in concentric circles, they take the same relative position in the tube which they had before in passing through the holes, and in that state of relative position the strand is composed of concentric circles or shells of yarns, the outside shell being of a larger diameter; the second shell or layer being of less diameter than the outside layer, the yarns are so much shorter; each layer diminishes gradually till they come to the centre, which consists of a single yarn the length of the strand. I have examined some that have been so manufactured, and the strand being composed of compressible materials, if it were broke in the state in which it came from the registering machine, the centre yarn would break first, that next to the centre would break second, and the outside yarn would break last; the outside shell of yarns surrounding a considerable body of hemp when it is brought to a degree of tension, the outside yarns compress the body of them within, and by this compression the angle is diminished, and they become longer; the centre yarn being at its full length snaps first, then the next, and so on. In order to prevent this difficulty, Mr. Huddart has contrived a mode of what he calls setting up or hardening; after the strand comes from the register he gives it an additional twist, and by this means the centre yarn becomes one-eighteenth part shorter, the outer yarns from the centre are set up proportionably to the centre, and by that means compressing the whole mass, each yarn is brought to a greater degree of tension than when it came from the registering machine, so that a weight being put upon the strand before it breaks, it lengthens as much as it had contracted before, and when it breaks the whole snaps together. He says the patent rope, upon an experiment he tried, bore a weight of 17 tons, 5 cwt. and 1 qr., and that a rope made in the common way, of the same materials, bore only 8 tons, 13 cwt. 1 qr. and 4 lb; and he says the patent rope broke all at once, and the old-fashioned rope snapped on the outside first, then the next yarn, and so on to the centre. He says this is a most important improvement. He says he should have no difficulty in constructing the necessary machinery for making a rope upon Mr. Huddart's plan, by looking at the patent and the specification. That is material to show that the specification is sufficiently explicit to enable a person of skill in the subject, upon reading it, to accomplish the purpose it professes to execute. Some rope of the defendant's manufacture being put into his hands, he says, if this is made upon Mr. Huddart's construction, the yarn that is on the outside at first will be the outside throughout the whole length of the strand, and will be the longest yarn; the second shell will be the next longest, and so on to the centre, which will be the shortest. He says, I know of no other mode but Mr. Huddart's for producing this effect, and in proportion as that is deviated from, the strands will be worse; this exhibits to the eye that regular gradation of length in the different shells which he should expect to find in Mr. Huddart's invention. The external yarn is two inches longer than the piece of strand; the second is somewhat shorter than the first, and taking a yarn out of the third, he says that is half an inch shorter than the second; and taking a yarn out of the centre, he says it is a little longer than the strand, owing to the setting up; and the result he draws is, that he believes this to be made upon Mr. Huddart's method. And I should state that this is certainly what is called *primâ facie* evidence of its having been made by that method; when one sees it agree in all its qualities; when it is produced with a rope actually made upon Mr. Huddart's plan, it is *primâ facie* evidence till the contrary is shown that it was made upon his method, and, therefore, as against him it should seem, supposing this patent in full force and a valid one, it is reasonable fair evidence, in the absence of contrary evidence, to presume that it was made in that way. There is certainly great weight in the observation of the counsel, 'am I to come forward and divulge my mode of making rope from which I reap a great advantage?' Whether it was necessary to have gone that length in proof, does not appear; persons might have been called upon who might not be privy to the making of the strands in the small room; however, whether it puts him to inconvenience or not, the question is, whether it is *primâ facie*, probable, presumptive evidence, in the absence of evidence on the other side, and it is a competent ground for you, if you think the facts bear you out, to form that conclusion upon.

Then a letter is read, threatening to bring an action, and insisting upon seeing the manner in which the manufacture was carried on. The answer to that letter is received verbally. Mr. Rennie put it down in writing: he says, 'after delivering the letter to Mr. Grimshaw, I asked him to show me those parts that he did not generally show. He refused, because he did not show them to others, and because there were several partners to be consulted.' He says, 'I am certain, according to my judgement, that the specimen of the rope sold to Mr. Walker is made upon Mr. Huddart's principle. I know of no other mode but that mentioned in his specification in which it can be done in the perfect manner that this is done; there might be another mode without the perforated plate, by which it might by chance be done; but with it, it will be done with certainty.'

Upon his cross-examination, he says it would be a lucky hit if such a rope was made without the perforated plate; it could not be done otherwise than by chance. He says he thinks this has been set up, or hardened up, according to Mr. Huddart's method, described in the specification. He says he has not seen a model of the machine of 1793 that he recollects; and no model has been shown us of the patent obtained in that year. The object of the patent is a more equal distribution of the strain upon the yarns; each yarn is wound round a separate bobbin. Now the object of this patent, and to be sure the objects of the two patents are substantially the same, both of Mr. Belfour and Mr. Huddart; but it does not follow, that because the ends are materially the same, it is thereon open to the public. It has happened to me in the same morning to give, as far as I was concerned, my consent to the granting of three different patents for the same thing; but the modes of attaining it were all different, and I thought I was entitled to receive them. He says the object of the patent was a more equal distribution of the strain upon the yarns; the bobbins are ranged in a frame at one end of the rope yard, and at the other end is the winch that turns the bobbins; the rope-walk is longer than the strand. The desideratum in rope-making was to keep the yarns separate, and in a certain state of tension before they were taken up into the rope; the twist in the rope-walk commences at the winch; if the yarns were all kept in a state of tension, none of the bobbins would render more than is wanted at the twist; at the superfices more of the yarn will be rendered than at the inner part.

Mr. Rennie dissects a piece of rope made on Mr. Belfour's method; he takes an outside strand, and opens it; the yarn is sometimes inside and sometimes outside; he says that never would happen by Mr. Huddart's mode. He says, 'I consider the bobbin as a matter of course; it is of universal use in all manufactures that consist of threads; the mere bobbin is like lead or iron, but the application of the bobbin with a spring to it appears to me to be a material part of an invention for making ropes.' He then dissects a strand of Mr. Huddart's; the outside yarn keeps its place throughout, and is longer by six inches than the strand; the second shell is not so long as the other by about an inch and a half, and so on to the centre yarn, which is the same length with the strand.

The evidence that has been adduced as to the value and utility of Captain Huddart's mode of making ropes, leaves no doubt that, by whomsoever it was effected, this improvement is a most important one in the manufacture of cordage; but it is material for your consideration, whether it be a new invention, and if it be a new invention, whether this person, in taking his patent, has embraced within it, as essential parts, any thing which was a part of a prior invention communicated to the public before, and to which, therefore, he had no right to any benefit.

On the part of the defendant, no witnesses are called, but it is said that this is not an original invention, and if it is, there is no proof that we have violated it. It is no matter that the two patents profess the same object; the end proposed in Mr. Belfour's invention is to improve the manufacture of ropes and cordage, by making every yarn employed in the composition thereof bear its proper and equal proportion of the stress. The description of the invention of Mr. Huddart is a new mode or art of making great cables and other cordage, so as to attain a greater degree of strength therein, by a more equal distribution of the strain upon the yarns; the one is a more equal proportion of the stress, the other a more equal distribution of the strain.

As to the bobbins, they are not worth mentioning; the springs and the tube are the things in which they should seem the principal originality of the invention consists. It is contended that the springs are not an essential part of the invention: if they are enrolled as an essential part, whether they are so or not, it would certainly go to his patent, because no deceptive things are to be held out to the public; those that are material are to be held out as material; according to the evidence of Mr. Rennie, they are material. He considers that they are material to regulate the tension. Mr. Huddart points out that his mode would be defective without springs. I will read to you first Mr. Belfour's, and then Mr. Huddart's. Mr. Belfour states how the end is proposed to be answered: he says, 'I have introduced four springs into each reel, which springs are marked L, and should be made of iron or steel, about two inches and a half in length, one-fourth of an inch in breadth, and one-eighth of an inch thick in the middle, and smaller towards each end; two of these springs are fixed into each end of the barrel of the said reel in the inside; one end of each spring is fixed fast to the barrel of the reel, the other end is moveable, and is governed by a screw marked M, which, by being turned towards the right, closes the two ends, and thereby fixes the reel faster to the spindle; or being turned the other way, opens the two ends, thereby allowing the reel to move more freely.' According to the greater freedom of the motion of the wheel, or the retardation of the wheel, the greater or less tension is produced. Now Mr. Huddart's specification is this: 'at K a spring is fixed to the wooden arm, by means of a screw and nails, or otherwise; the screw works in the square part of the spindle, by means of which the spring may be made stronger or weaker, as requisite; the other end of which rests upon the globular part of the head of the bobbin, formed for that purpose to regulate the tension of the yarn in drawing it from the bobbin, whilst the spindle is turning in registering the strand.' Here for a moment let us take our stand: the same end appears to be produced, according to my understanding, by the one and the other, to regulate the tension; now if it is a spring to regulate the tension of the yarn, which is essential to be regulated, it does seem to me, but it is for your judgment to say, whether, it is a material part of the invention; if it be a material part of the invention, and relied upon as such, as it should seem it is by both, and if it is the same, then that which has been communicated by Mr. Belfour, Mr. Huddart cannot take the benefit of.

Then there is another matter, with respect to the tube. Mr. Belfour says various other methods may be substituted for the purpose of preventing the strand from twisting until it has received that position the workman wishes, such as pieces of wood with holes bored in them; small machines, divided in a similar manner, or something like to the separating machine before described; or by the external application of a ring or other circular instrument; or any other shape so as to press upon the strand, and prevent its receiving an improper twist, to serve the purpose or intention of the top minor; for unless the strand is regulated in the twist, and kept exactly in the position in which it is to remain, the good effects proposed by this invention will be in a great degree defeated; therefore, it is not of any consequence in what manner it is so regulated, so long as that point is accomplished. Now what Mr. Huddart says upon it, is this: 'This disposition of the yarns is necessary previous to their passing through the cylindrical tube of metal in which the strand is compressed and formed.' He says the tube compressing the yarns, and confining the outer shell to its proper figure, which outer shell compresses the next, and so on to the centre, there cannot be any crossing of yarns, or change in situation; but the whole strand formed close and compact, and no more yarn required from the bobbins than is necessary, according to the situations of the shells, or their distance from the centre. Now the tube does seem to me, with submission to you, an important difference from the mere circle through which it passes, because it keeps it in a degree of confinement for a greater time, and more certainly obtains the end pointed out in Mr. Belfour's specification; the same end is to be obtained, and had the patent been taken for that to be done by a tube, which was before done by a ring or circle, I should have thought the patent good, for that is a distinct substantive invention. It will be for you to consider, whether that which is pointed out in Mr. Belfour's specification will be broken in upon by a tube, which keeps it in a state of confinement for a longer time, and attains the end with more certainty. It is for you to say, for that is the substance of the case, as to the invasion of the patent, whether any essential part of it was disclosed to the public before. If you think the same effect in substance is produced, and that the springs in Mr. Belfour's, by producing tension, obtain a material end in the making of ropes in the way proposed, and that it is in substance the same as in the other, this patent certainly must, upon principles of law, fall to the ground. If you think it is not the same, or if you think it is not material, though we have had the evidence of Mr. Rennie upon its materiality – if you think this patent has been obtained for a new invention, carried into effect by methods new, and not too large beyond the actual invention of the party, in that case the patent may be sustained; but if you think otherwise, in point of law or expediency, the patent cannot be sustained.

Verdict for the plaintiff. Damages, one shilling.

The manufacture of rope could now proceed unchallenged until the patent rights expired, and then the present partners left the firm.

Huddart devised a machine for testing the strength of the firm's ropes which he called a Breaking Machine. As will be seen from the following letter, when the Navy Board wanted to test the strength of Huddart & Co's ropes, in spite of their autocratic attitude, it was not beneath them to seek the use of the manufactory's Breaking Machine, but later they decided to have their own:

Limehouse 5th November 1807

Hon Gentlemen

In answer to your letter of the 3 In^t respecting a Trial on Ropes which you wish to be made on Monday, we beg leave to say our Breaking Machine will be very much at your Service to make any Experiments you may think proper.

Hon Gentlemen
we are your obd^t Servants
Huddart & Co.

To the Hon. Com^s of H M Navy

Hon Gentlemen

We herewith send you the result of three Experiments made in Consequence of your Letter of the 26th July.

The Trinidad Hemp in our opinion had through some means received injury from its appearance we think must naturally have been much stronger than it proved on the experiment.

Hon Gentlemen
we are Your Mo^t obd^t Servants
Huddart & Co.

Limehouse
5th August 1808

Commissioners HM Navy

Experiments on the strength of Cordage.
Tried and Mfs^d Huddart & Co. Breaking Machine
Aug. 1st 1808

Size			From what Hemp made	By whom made	Weight Born in pounds	Weight Born in Tons
1¾	1 Rope	Tarred	Trinidad		1040	9 1 4
1¾	1 D°	White	Trinidad		1456	13 " "
1¾	1 D°	Tarred	Russia	Huddart & Co.	1768	15. 3 4

In 1808 the Board decided to have their own machinery for testing the strength of ropes and the following letter from John Rennie gives them an estimate.

Hon Sirs   Stamford Street June 18th 1808

Agreeably to your request I have estimated the expense of a Machine for trying the strength of Cordage, according to the plan invented by Captain Huddart, but with an Iron Barrel for the ropes – a different plan of ballancing the Levers, and the partes made in general stronger – I will undertake to make the Machine for the sum of One hundred and Eighty pounds Nett.

I have also Estimated the expense of Such a Machine having a Cast Iron frame, & in other respects better finished, & will undertake to furnish this for the sum of three hundred & thirty pounds, if one Machine only is ordered, but if several were to be Made, I could do them for about ten pounds per cent less than if one Machine only was to be made.

I have the honor to be

Hon & Sirs

Your Most Humble Ser.

J. M. Rennie

The Honble The
Commissioners of
His Majestys Navy

In response to this letter the Board gave instructions for the machine to be fixed at Woolwich and a certificate to be issued for £180.

It appears from the following letter of 11 January 1809 that the machine had been ready for some weeks.

Hon & Sirs   Stamford Street Jay 11[h] 1809

The Machine for trying the Strength of Cordage, ordered by your Honb. Board, has been compleated for some weeks; But as it was ordered for Woolwich & the Dimensions having been made suitable to the building at that place where it was to be fixed, My Clerk while I was absent from London did not think it right to send it to Chatham as directed in your letter of the 6[h] Ult., lest the uprights which have been made for Woolwich should not be suitable to the building at Chatham. I mention this for your information, as some alteration may be requisite, should you continue in the resolution of sending it to Chatham.

The Machine being still in my possession, I take the liberty to request you will have the goodness to allow me to retain it a short time longer & to make some experiments with Strength of Bars of Iron under an Inch dia[r]. If you shall be pleased to agree to this, you will oblige me & I shall be happy to furnish you with the results.

I have the honour to be

Hon & Sirs

Your Most Humble Ser.

The Honble Com[s]   John Rennie
of His Majestys Navy.

On this the Board gave the following instructions:

Own the receipt and acquaint him We have no objection to his retaining the machine for the period necessary to make the experiments on the Strength of Bars of Iron, and request he will let us know when he is ready to make the experiments, as We intend to send over our Mechanist to attend them and at the same time to obtain such information concerning the Machine as may enable him to give Instructions for fitting it at Chatham. Minute for Mr. Goodrich accordingly.

Minute made

Lr. 2 Mar to Mr. Rennie to send the machine to Deptford. Deptford Officers directed to forward it to Chatham.

Like all businesses Huddart & Co was not free from disputes over payment as will be seen from the letters of 28 June 1808 and 12 July:

Honble Gent[n]

We have received your Letter informing us that you had directed the Officers of Deptford Yard to make out a certificate at 20/= per cwt. for Manufactoring the Sunn Hemp and in reply beg to acquaint you that the extra charge of three Shillings is the same as paid by the Hon[ble] the East

India Company and that it is only equivalent to the difference of 4 pence in heckling and Spinning between Sunn & Russian Hemp.

> We are
> Honb^{le} Gentⁿ
> Y^r ob^t huble Serv^{ts}
>
> Joseph Huddart & Co.

Limehouse 28 June 1808
To the Honble
the Comm^{rs}
His My Navy.

Honble Gentⁿ

With reference to our letter of the 28th Ultimo we beg to enclose you the accompanying certificate from Deptford Yard for manufacturing your Sunn Hemp into Cordage which we apprehend is made out by mistake at 20/– per cwt. instead of 23/– the Price mentioned in our letter as above and which is the same as paid by the Hon. the East India Company and no more than equivalent to the extra pence of Heckling and Spinning this Hemp.

> We are
> Honble Gentⁿ
> Yr Ob^t humb^{le} Servt
> Joseph Huddart & Co.

Limehouse
12 July 1808

To the Honble the
    Comm^{rs} H M^{ys} Navy.

6 July

Dock & Rope Yard Officers at Woolwich

Messrs Huddart & Co. having applied to us, for an addition of £3 per Ton for manufacturing cordage from His Maj'es Sunn Hemp . . . on the warm registered plan, upon the plea of the difference in labour between the heckling and spinning of that, and Russian hemp; we direct you to give Us your opinion whether such an advance ought to be allowed for the differences in the workmanship.

And even in those days factories were not free from strikes as will appear from the following letter of 23 August 1809:

Hon Gentlemen

In consequence of our Machine for closing Cordage being quite compleat and our preparing to make a Cable Yesterday, our Spinners and various other workmen connected with them, quitted their Work and have not yet given any indication of return.

We have good reason to believe these workmen will not only receive general Employment, but would, were they to require it, procure assistance from the other Spinners.

When we tell you Hon. Board, that it is by no means our Intention to Spin by Machinery & that we have offered our Workmen the same Wages for *Spinning* as they have been in the habit of receiving. In *Laying* we trust your Hon. Board will not deem us intrusive in applying to you – particularly when we assure you that the only object we have in mind, is to make our Cordage perfect, so as to prevent any possibility of difference in the Rope or Cable.

Considering then the object thus attained of great National Consequence we have to ask the assistance of your Hon. Board: and should it not interfere with the public Service, we are of opinion a Temporary suspension of orders to the Rope Makers generally would induce the return of our workmen – particularly if it were known that your Hon. Board approved and would encourage the Machinery.

We are Hon. Gentlemen.
Your Obed^t Servt

Huddart & Co.

Limehouse
23 August 1809.

The Honable Comm
H.M. Navy.

The Board gave the following instructions:

25 August 1809

Own the receipt and acquaint them we shall suspend issuing any more Warrents for Ropemaking at present.

Board

Commee of Stores – Noticed

By this time Huddart had retired from the partnership and there is little point in pursuing its activities further beyond the fact that in 1815 the Admiralty decided to set up their own rope-making machinery as will be seen from the following letters:

Limehouse 12 Aug, 1815

Sir,

We beg to inform the Lords Commissioners of the Admiralty that we have received the following Letter from the Navy Board. –

Navy Office 7th Aug. 1815

Messrs, Huddart & Co,

The very liberal offer which you have made to the first Lord of the Admiralty of the Models of your Machinery for manufacturing Cables & Cordage, for imitation in the formation of a Steam Ropery to be erected in one of His Majesty's Yards, having been communicated to us by the Lords Commissioners of the Admiralty, –

We acquaint you that we are desirous of availing outselves of it; and we therefore request you will permit Mr. Holl the Surveyor of Buildings to this Office, to inspect them as often as he may find necessary, and to take plans of such parts as may be considered elegible to be introduced into His Majesty's Service.

Signed   R Seppings
                  H Legge
                  P Fraser

To the above we replied on the 9th instant.

To The Hon[ble] The Commissioners of His Majesty's Navy.

In compliance with your Hon,[ble] Board's Letter of the 7th ins,[t] and our offer to the first Lord of the Admiralty we shall be glad to see Mr. Holl at Limehouse and shew him every attention in our power. –

Signed Huddart & Co.

But as the foregoing Letters refer only to a verbal communication, at our Interview with the first Lord of the Admiralty in June last.

We desire now to repeat and confirm the offer then made, which was to the following effect – That we would give every possible assistance either by Drawings, the use of our Patterns, or in any other way, which our extensive experience and the ability of our Capt. Huddart enables us to offer towards the erection of Machinery similar to our own, *for the perfect manufacturer of* Cordage in His Majesty's Yards, with this only condition, – that we should *annually make a stated quantity of Cordage for His Majesty's Navy*, thereby assisting to keep our extensive works in Employ. –

We are,
Sir,
Your most obed,[t] Serv,[ts],

Huddart & Co.

Isaac Barrow Esq,[r]

Admiralty comment reads:

Aug 15 Send copy to Navy Board and acquaint them their Lordships do not think fit to enter into any obligation to take rope from Messrs. Huddart.

The Manufactory continued to operate for many years after Huddart had left the partnership in the same way as he had planned it. One innovation was gas lighting from their own plant: Boulton and Watt had done this as far back as 1803.

Writing in 1838 about the eventual fate of the rope-making machinery William Cotton says:

The object in view, when Captain Huddart's beautiful Rope-making Machinery was sold to the Admiralty, was to preserve it, as a lasting memorial of his scientific knowledge and mechanical powers. It was thought that in a National Establishment it would not be subject to those contingencies by the death of Partners, or their retirement, or other circumstances, which, in mercantile concerns, frequently lead to the breaking up of such machinery; and particularly that, which is on a great scale, and more particularly that which is fit only for a large establishment. Huddart's machinery was fixed by the Admiralty in the yard at Deptford, and there was added to it some of the best machinery that had been invented for the spinning of rope-yarn; and under Captain Sherriff, the intelligent Superintendent of the Naval Depot, who had superintended its erection, it would have continued to perform its work in the same accurate and efficient manner it had done at Limehouse. Most excellent drawings of all the machinery, and a very clear statement of its powers, appeared in the 5th Vol. of the Professional Papers of the Corps of Royal Engineers. It is there stated, that 'Captain Brandreth R.E. dedicated much of his time to the investigation of the merits of these Inventions, and whose able report to the Lords of the Admiralty induced Her Majesty's Government to determine on the erection of the Rope-making Machinery in Deptford Dock Yard.'

The determined hostility to Captain Huddart's first and most important invention, 'the register plate and tube', which established his great principle of giving to each yarn its proper length and position, had ceased; and when his patent was out, was adopted in every rope-ground as it had been for some time in the Navy yards. After the proof that had been given at Limehouse of the powers and accuracy of the laying machines, (the largest of which, with only two persons to attend to it had in six days made 10 cables for first-rates for the North Sea Fleet) it was not expected that there would have been any hostility against its use in the Government yards; but it is grievous to think that this was not the case, and has led, not only to the discontinuance of the use of this machinery, which had been admired by every scientific person who had seen it in operation, but to its most wanton destruction, accomplished at a great and useless expense.

Had the Admiralty thought if expedient, from any cause, to discontinue its use, and had it been offered for sale in its complete state, many persons, and certainly the Writer of this letter, would have been disposed to purchase it in order to its preservation; but on his return to London, after a lengthened absence, he was surprised and grieved to hear, that the machinery had been pulled to pieces, every bit of gun metal, wrought iron and steel, separated with great labour the beautiful and costly patterns of the wheels and frame-work destroyed, and to his additional surprise he found, on further enquiry, that the parts of machinery were to be immediately sold by auction, together with a large quantity of other materials, in 13 lots, and that a part of each machine was put into almost every lot, as if to prevent the possibility of their ever being put together again. There was no time for remonstrance, and an order was immediately given by the Writer to purchase every lot, and the machines in this sad mutilated state were again brought to Limehouse, and deposited in a warehouse there. On application to the Admiralty, a large quantity of gun metal, which had belonged to these machines, and which had been sent to Woolwich to be melted, was purchased at the price of new metal, and has thus been secured.

The greater part of the machinery was purchased at the price of old metal, and the cost of the total amount of the lots purchased could not, it has been thought, have paid the expense of the useless pulling them to pieces. It was probably unfortunate that the Rope-yarn Spinning Machinery was sold at the same time for against this there was a strong prejudice on the part of the rope-makers; but this machinery, of recent construction by Messrs Blyth, which would have readily sold in its perfect state, was pulled to pieces in the same manner as Huddart's Rope-Machinery; useless labour having been devoted to its destruction, even to severance of the little steel points from the gun metal in the machines; rendering the whole of little value except as old metal.

Time has not in any way diminished the Writer's perfect confidence in the accuracy of Captain Huddart's Rope-Machinery, and but for the advance of age, and a desire to retire from business and give his attention to other objects, the last Partner of 'Huddart and Co.' would have repaired all the injury so sadly inflicted on the Rope-Machinery, and shewn it, at work again, at Limehouse. Some hope was entertained that the Admiralty would be disposed to reconsider the subject, and the machinery was offered at what it had cost the present possessor, and he would be willing to part with it to any party on the same terms if with a fair prospect of its being preserved.

CHAPTER X

The Conclusion

A bold usurper seized the arms of France;
Pale Victory at his feet crouching lay;
Kingdoms and Empires trembled at his nod;
All Europe bowed beneath his iron sway.
Gentleman's Magazine

CAPTAIN HUDDART'S son Joseph was in partnership with one Robert Porter as factors at Leghorn and Joseph Huddart junior was also the Pro-Consul there. Livorno, or Leghorn as the British called it, had been established by the Medici as the port of Florence to keep foreign traders out of the City. By 1727 the last of the Medici family had died and the Duchy passed to the house of Lorain Hapsburg. In June 1795 having sworn eternal peace to the Grand Duke Ferdinand, Napoleon sent Joachim Murat into Tuscany to seize the goods of the British merchants.

Napoleon arrived at Nice on 26 March 1796 to find a ragged half-starved army into which he breathed new life and, like a gust of wind rekindling a smouldering fire, on 10 April he swept through the mountain passes. By the 23rd he had crossed the Alps and was threatening Turin. He then reduced Piedmont, poured into Lombardy and on 15 April occupied Milan.

The British Navy had been Napoleon's stumbling block in an otherwise victorious war. To call the British a 'Nation of Shopkeepers' – a phrase he had borrowed from Adam Smith – was no punishment, he had to harass those shopkeepers wherever he could lay his hands upon them and Leghorn was the obvious place.

Joseph Huddart junior, as Pro-Consul, had so far as possible to keep the British fleet informed and the following are two letters which have survived, dated 13 February and 16 February 1799, which are taken from Nelson's papers.

13th February 1799.

My Lord

As it would appear from the movements of the French and from the best information that we can obtain, that they have no immediate intention of invading this State, I am desired by a resolution of the British Factory, which had a meeting this Day, to inform your Lordship that they are of opinion that this would be a favorable opportunity for the Convoy now at Palermo, to come here without delay, in order that the Proprietors of the Cargoes may dispose of and realize their effects & the Masters of the Vessells receive their Freights.

Not knowing however how circumstances may change before they can arrive here your Lordship may perhaps think it prudent to order the Merchantmen to Anchor in the Road under the Convoy.

The Honble Lord Nelson,
Etc etc

Johnston Huddart in the uniform of a midshipman. From a portrait attributed to Guan Zuolin of Macao.

Captain Joseph Huddart, FRS. From an engraving by James Stow
after the portrait of 1801 by John Hoppner, RA.

Memorial erected to the memory of Captain Joseph Huddart, FRS
in the north transept of Christ Church, Allonby.

A group of eminent scientists of the late eighteenth century with Captain Joseph Huddart, FRS in their midst. From an engraving by W. Walker and G. Zobel.

Leghorn 16th February 1799

Dear Sir

By a Bark come in from Corsica I have got intelligence that the expedition there is not given up an armed vessel is arrived at Ajaccio, which from the description is a Corvette, but of what force I cannot learn on board of this vessel they were receiving all those of the requisitions that they could get, but great numbers of the Corsicans not liking the business fled into the woods, – General Wallis the present Commander in Chief of the French troops at Lucca came here on Thursday last at which time some vessels were chartered here by the French Agents, but on what service they are to go is not known, I have also learnt that the Garrison of Capraio is to be augmented with 200 Men/100 French & 100 Genoese) and there is loaded on board some vessels now in this Mole about 3000 sacks of Flour, destined for the same place, from these several circumstances I am to believe that the object of the Enemy is Elba, and if so they may perhaps attempt to send over from Viareggio/The sea port of Lucca about 15 miles distant from this/ a number of Men &c to cooperate with the Corsican Armament but this I mentioned as merely my own idea – Elba is so fine an Island that I doubt not they will attempt to get it if possible with regard to Sardinia as they have possession of Corsica they can at their pleasure attack that and without any great preparation as it is well known they have a very considerable party of Friends there –

With regard to other news we have none at present of any importance

I have the honor to be with much respect

Dear Sir

your obliged H^{ble} Servant

Jos Huddart

In spite of the truce that existed with Grand Duke Ferdinand, on 15 October 1800 Napoleon's troops poured into Florence and at Leghorn they seized forty-six English ships, a million hundredweight of wheat, barley and dried vegetables and every penny of British capital in the town. Joseph Huddart and his partner, who had a consignment from Messrs Sargent & Walkden of Hull partly unloaded, gave Captain Hewson, the master of the *Charlotte* carrying their cargo, notice of the presence of the French troops and he hauled out of Leghorn under a British convoy making for Port Mahon, Minorca's largest naval port and at that time held by the British. This was the last Porter and Huddart saw of their unloaded cargo of 2,073 quarters of beans.

Joseph Huddart gives the following account of the cargo:

In the year 1800 the ship Charlotte Captn Hewson was consigned to the House of Porter & Huddart of Leghorn having brought a cargo of beans &c. from Tunis to the consignment of David de Montel of that place. On the 16th October the French suddenly invaded and took possession of Leghorn but the Charlotte had the good fortune to escape in consequence of the notice Porter & Huddart gave to Captain Hewson and went to Mahon with one third of the cargo which remained undischarged together with five brass cannon belonging to the freighter and valued at about 1,000 dollars.

At this time Porter & Huddart had paid to Captn Hewson and by his order for the use and service of his ship about 12,000 dollars which with the customary commission on freight being the sole advantage to the consignee for their trouble, amounted to 12319 – 8 – 11 Leghorn dollars this sum together with the interest thereon would have been deducted from the freight as is usual at Leghorn had it been paid by the freighter to the consignee of the ship and which was alone prevented by the vessel proceeding to Mahon with part of the cargo on board.

In 1801, Porter & Huddart returned to Leghorn in consequence of the peace, having been driven from thence soon after the French took possession, and immediately wrote to the owners of the Charlotte requesting them to furnish Accounts of Sale of that part of the cargo carried to Mahon, in order that they might settle the freight &c. between the ship and the freighter, to this letter they received no answer, they wrote again in July 1802 with like success and again in December of the same year and at last they received a letter dated 20th February 1803 from Mr. Sargent one of the owners with copy of an Account current from Mahon but without any account of sale of the cargo or the guns, so that the freighter became uneasy about it, for by his statement had it been landed at Leghorn it would have rendered him at the price the rest sold for after paying all the freight out of it due to the ship upwards of £1,300 sterling.

Seeing the probability of effecting a settlement between the owner and the freighter on account of the former not sending the necessary accounts on the 16th of March 1804 Porter & Huddart sent the account of the disbursements on the vessel to Mr. Sargent the managing owner and drew on him for the amount but he protested their bill which was returned with heavy expenses.

In March 1805 Porter & Huddart again wrote to Sargent very fully on the subject and drew on him a sum and time but he again dishonoured their bill which also went back with a heavy loss, since that time the state of the continent has been such that all correspondence between Leghorn and England has been so much intercepted that letters seldom reach their destination, but Messrs John Lubbock & Co. in 1806 again endeavoured to induce the owners to pay their demand but with the same bad success.

Mr. Huddart of the House of Porter & Huddart being now here and having received the account continued to the 18th Sept. 1811 at which time the exchange was at 75 in Leghorn, he requests Messrs. Weston & Teasdale will do the needful to secure the interest of this House, in case the owners still refuse to pay, they have abundance of evidence at Leghorn to establish every fact stated above and by sending out a Commission the heavy expense of which must ultimately fall on the owners, every thing can be proved.

Porter & Huddart have made no charge for the heavy loss on their returned bills but they have simply continued the account with interest at 5 per cent altho' the lawful rate of interest at Leghorn is 6 per cent and have reduced the whole outstanding money at the exchange of the day making £1119 – 4 sterling.

Sargent claimed eventually that the net proceeds of the cargo sold at Port Mahon together with the sum paid to Captain Hewson by Porter & Huddart barely covered his freight charges and the ship's disbursements, which were obviously increased by having to go under convoy to a second port. John Lubbock & Co. were Huddart's London bankers and Weston & Teasdale his attorneys, who after taking counsel's opinion at a fee of 10s 6d, advised that the claim against Sargent was statute-barred. The consignee, a merchant of Leghorn having received only two thirds of his consignment, considered that Porter & Huddart must look to the other third for the freight charges.

The loss of his share of £492 17s 8d, the sterling equivalent of 12,319

Leghorn dollars with interest can hardly have caused much worry to Joseph Huddart and but for his partner who had lost everything to the French, he probably would not have pursued the matter to the lengths he did.

Robert Porter assumed Tuscan citizenship to avoid any further harassment which was being meted out to the British on the Continent, but he never recovered financially: in fact, after his death Sir Joseph Huddart, as he had then become, helped his widow with an annuity of £20 a year.

So far Johnston Huddart has been left unmentioned. When the *Royal Admiral* was paid off in 1788, Johnston was appointed on his next voyage to third officer in the *Princess Amelia* but when he returned in 1794 he was in a very delicate state of health, being threatened with consumption from a neglected cold and was advised to try a milder climate.

He decided to join his brother in Italy and travelled to Germany and then on to Italy, but he died at Leghorn on 29 January 1795, at the age of twenty-four and was interred in the burial ground of the British factory, a marble monument being erected to his memory. It was a sad blow for his father, who had already lost his wife and one of his sons, to have another son, who had accompanied him on two voyages, taken away from him.

Joseph Huddart, the son, after the invasion of Leghorn, left Italy and went to live with his father at 12 Highbury Terrace, Islington. One feels that this must have been a solace to his father, who although absorbed in his scientific pursuits needed company. He had been a widower for eighteen years and lost the two sons who had sailed with him and proved their ability to follow in his footsteps had not poor health brought them to an untimely death.

Life at Highbury Terrace was of the simplest order. There lived in the house Benjamin Bulpit and Mary Bulpit; Benjamin was a sort of gentleman's gentleman cum lab-boy, who Huddart had instructed to help him in his astronomical and mathematical pursuits. Apart from this Ben would bring up his master's tea and dinner, join him in eating it and then join him in a rubber of whist. If a friend came to call Ben would attend to his horse or he would undertake any errands which were required. He and Mary were there to look after the house if their master was away on one of his trips to Cumberland or making a survey. When Gale came to stay in 1809 before joining his ship it was Ben who met him on the coach and was his constant companion while the boy stayed at Islington. On 12 April 1809 when Gale joined his ship, the *Earl Howe*, Huddart and Ben went on board together to bid him farewell. There is more of Gale in the succeeding pages.

Huddart was an early riser, usually breakfasting about eight o'clock, dining at one and having tea at five: at eight o'clock in the evening he had supper and went to bed at ten. Apart from smoking, which Huddart was recommended to do as a young man because of a chest complaint, he was moderate in all his habits. In these days smoking would be regarded as the worst treatment the lungs could be subjected to and even in the eighteenth century there does not appear to have been any consensus of medical opinion advocating smoking, rather the reverse. Taking snuff was, of course, more popular and if tobacco formed any medical function it was as an emetic.

Huddart maintained that smoking helped him to think and when his mind was engaged in solving some difficult problem, his pipe seemed to be equally absorbed in reaching a solution, which would eventually emerge in a cloud of smoke. Smoking was his first occupation on rising and his last on going to bed.

Huddart is said to have been a lover of cats and to have had a number of them. But Ben must have found his master easy to cater for as he paid little attention to the quality and regularity of his meals and equally little demand was made upon Ben as a valet seeing that he had a master who paid little regard to his dress. His family said that if a question was put to Huddart he seemed unaware that he had been spoken to and then after a lapse of some minutes, when the remark appeared to have been forgotten he would turn to his questioner with a reply. Although he rarely mixed in society and there were few who really knew him, to those who did and to his family he was affable, good humoured and kind: he would be full of anecdotes about his early days, even tempered and of a cheerful disposition. As a commander we get the impression of his being fair and considerate, but not too easy going. He was a man who knew his ship, knew his crew and above all knew the sea.

One of those who knew Huddart well was his young partner, William Cotton who, after Huddart's death, was one of the trustees of his estate. Cotton recounts of him:

> On one occasion, when walking with a young friend and talking to him on the recent discoveries in Astronomy by Arago, accounting for the irregular motion of the moon, he observed, that every apparent difficulty in lunar observations appeared to be removed; and that, except in the discovery of some additional planet or star, he thought little could be expected from astronomical observation, except to raise our admiration of the wonders of creation, and to exalt our reverence for the Creator.

As one of the Elder Brethren of Trinity House, Captain Huddart took a heartfelt interest in those who had to subsist on the charity of the Corporation. Apart from almshouses a monthly pension list was maintained 'For poor decayed merchant seamen and their widows in indigent circumstances incapable of labour'. The scale of pension was £30 a year for masters or their widows, £20 a year for other officers and £15 a year for seamen. London was divided into districts for distribution of these pensions; two Elder Brethren being in charge of each district.

By 1807 the first patent was due to expire, which included the register tube, the linch pin of the invention, and added to this chains were being used by ships in place of the cables that benefited most from the invention; this induced the original partners to retire. Huddart had by his invention amassed a considerable fortune, part of which he now decided to invest in the purchase of land. While in Anglesey and Caernarvonshire in May 1808 visiting Holyhead in connection with the South Stack Lighthouse he was attracted by an estate – the ancient demesne of Brynkir which was for sale.

For someone who was based in London with Trinity House and the East India Dock Company as his main interests he could hardly make a more outlandish choice than Snowdonia, particularly as this was a part of Wales where many of the inhabitants spoke only Welsh. Possibly he was attracted by the beauty of the Pennant valley, or he may have been influenced by the fact that estates in those days did not often come onto the market. At that time land passed automatically to the heir at law unless a will or settlement directed otherwise, but even then it was invariably devised to the eldest son. There was no probate to be granted for land and no duties to be paid, so it was only where land descended to daughters that it came onto the market, because daughters took equally and needed to realise their shares.

Two years later Joseph Huddart purchased the Wern Estate at Penmorfa and other land in Caernarvonshire and gave the management, in fact the beneficial ownership, to his son Joseph of all his land in Wales. Captain Huddart had sufficient to support him in London without the rents and profits of these estates. The younger Joseph Huddart thus became a country squire of an estate which included land in the following parishes: Llanfihangel-y-Pennant (Brynkir), Penmorfa (Wern), Llanlyfni, Criccieth, Llanstymdwy, Clynnog, Dolbenmaen, Llanaelhiarn and Llanfihangel-y-Tracthan, covering over 7,000 acres. He was now a married man, having married Elizabeth the second daughter of Andrew Durham of Belvedere, County Down on 15 May 1808.

He also built extensively onto the existing house, but without achieving a successful architectural composition: either the original three-storey building should have been the dominant feature or it should have been concealed behind a new facade. But to build in front of an old building at a lower level destroyed the unity of the design. The late Sir Clough Williams Ellis regarded the ashlar finish as not without merit and it is a pity the design did not do justice to it.

Internally, there was a small hall leading into a larger hall, two drawing rooms, a dining room and a library and sixteen bedrooms upstairs. In accordance with the requirements of the times there were extensive servants quarters, stabling and a walled garden. It always has been said that the Prince Regent was entertained at Brynkir during one of his visits to the slate quarries.

On being knighted at the time of the Coronation of George IV, Sir Joseph built a folly to mark the event, which is a feature of the neighbourhood consisting of a gothic tower of six storeys; it is supposed to have been intended as studies for his sons. The intention brings to mind the lines of Milton:

> But let my light at midnight hour
> Be seen in some far distant tower.

Unfortunately only one of Sir Joseph's sons reached manhood, but he had eight daughters to fill the rest of the accommodation. There was so much here that his father Captain Huddart could have enjoyed in his declining years, if only he had made the journey.

Kindness had always been one of Captain Huddart's endearing qualities and the following excerpts from letters written to Mrs Catherine Senhouse illustrate the interest he was prepared to take in her husband's nephew Gale. The Senhouses had, of course, been lifelong friends of his, in fact since his school days. Now Catherine Senhouse wanted to enter the boy for the East India Company's service, although he was only ten years old and fifteen was now the minimum for joining a ship. The letters give us an insight into the process of when and how a candidate was nominated, his interview, his kitting out and finally his joining his ship, which in this case was at Hope, a reach in the river Thames.

As a cadet had to be kitted out in London, Gale had to travel by coach and stay with Captain Huddart at Islington, where his faithful Ben looked after the boy. All feelings of separation which a boy suffers in leaving his home must have welled up in his young mind: the apprehension of being the master of his fate, and the sinking feeling of shyness in a strange world no doubt overshadowed him. Huddart was certainly a well-meaning host, but taciturn, reserved and lost in his own thoughts: at the same time he could give the boy the best advice and send him on his way full of confidence. No doubt in Ben there was a more kindred spirit.

Dear Madam

I received your favor but as I am to set out tomorrow for South Wales Had not an opportunity of making the necessary inquiry, I think as Capt.^{tn} Cumming is lately arived he will not be taken up to go out this Season. However I have requested Capt.^{tn} Harriman to see him & make the Necessary inqueries what had passed between him (Cap.^{tn} Cummings) & Mr. Hall on the Subject of his Nephew's going out, & he has promised to write you as soon as he has seen him. If he go out this Season he will not have much time to remain, & I should think he might be soonest fitted out here with what he may want.

I am	yours Sincerely

Highbury Terrace
16th April 1804 — J. Huddart

Dear Madam

I have rec.^{d} your favor of the 1st Ins.^{t} with the Letters of C. Cuming & Mr. Hall. I have this day wrote Capt.^{tn} Cuming requesting him to advise Mr. Hall when it will be necessary he should be in Town, or me in what Ship he is to proceed in, I observe the Castle Eden late C. Cuming now Capt.^{tn} Colnitt wont leave England before March but untill I know what Ship I cannot advise. I have inquired respecting the Customary Allowance of Passage Money & am Informed it is about £95 to Mess with the Capt^{tn} or about 50 or 60 with the Master, But believe that his Uncle would rather wish him to be in the Former Mess as more respectable. The Service is much altered since I Commanded. I had only £60 Paid by the Company for the accommodation of Cadets at my Table.

It will be necessary to have a Certificate & I will indeavour to procure him a form & send it down to you, but this need not detain him if Capt.^{tn} Cuming should advise him to come up immediately. I shall be happy to render him any advice or assistance & am

Dr Madam

yours Sincerely

J. Huddart

Highbury Terrace
20 Dec. 1804

Dear Madam

Your favor of the 7th Ins.^{t} I found here on my arrival from Cheltenham where I had been about 3 Weeks to try the effect of the Waters, in the removal of a complaint in the Stomach, & for which I hope have received benefit as I have not yet had any return of the disorder.

Respecting Mr. Gale, the Age required for the appointment of a Cadet in the Service of the East India Comp.^{y} is between 15 & 22, therefore may be admitted after Christmas, & proceed in the Ships of this Season, & shall be happy to use my indeavours to procure him a Nomination, upon your advising me that you wish him to take the first opportunity, or by Ships of this Season for India.

I hope to hear from Sir Joseph Senhouse upon the arrival of his Son, how Joseph approves of a Sea faring Life, & whether he wishes to enter into the India Service, if so, probably matters may be so arranged as Mr. Gale may proceed in the Same Ship, if we can procure him an appointment as Cadet.

I am Dr Madam yours Sincerely

Highbury Terrace
15th June 1807   J. Huddart

Dear Madam

I received your favor of the 7.th Ins.^t to which I replied saying that the Age required for a Cadet in the E.I. Comp. Service was between 15 & 22 Therefore Mr. Gale would be admissable after Christmas Day. Since which I have got a Promise of a Nomination for this Season provided you are determined upon his going out, (which I should recommend as the Cadets take Rank according to the List of those appointed for the Season) of which I wish to be informed as early as you can, in order that no inconvenience may attend filling up the Appointment, provided he does not go.

My best respects to Mr. Senhouse Miss Isabella & all inquiring Friends

I am yours Sincerely

Highbury Terrace
29th June 1807   J. Huddart

P.S. I have been promised a Cadets appointment for Mr. Gale by Capt.^{tn} Cotton when he is of age, which as I recolect will be next Christmas.

Dear Madam,

I have received your favor of the 5.th Ins.^t I am sory Mr Gale is not of Age this year, as he cannot be Admitted a Cadet untill he is 15 years of Age. Therefore he must remain a year Longer in England, however I have no doubt of securing a Nomination to stand over, untill he is of age.

I am yours Sincerely

Trinity House

9th July 1807   J. Huddart

Dear Madam,

I duly received your favor of the 10.th Ins.^t since which I caled at Welch Ho. who supply those articles for Cadets, & Marked off with their Prices the inclosed for your Perusal: & any thing which you can supply him with will tend to reduce the outfit. I think he should have 3 Doz of Shirts, & I expect that the Suites he brings with him, will be sufficient untill he arrives in a Warm Climate & I should recommend that he take out Scarlet Cloth Carminised &c to be made up in India as what wanted. The Light Waistcoats I mentioned to Mr. Boash were only intended for Change on his Passage what may be servicable, make up the rest give to the Poor. & he should have a thin couler'd Waistcoat & Pantaloons, which I have Mark'd off 2 as they will wear Longer without Washing, & in warm Climates often Sleep without Covering, in a Waistcoat & Musquetto Trousers. Respecting his Military equipment, I was not a judge & put down what they told me was requisite, probably some things may not be necessary; if I meet some officer who has been in India I will inquire of him, for altho I dont wish him to want any thing that may be usefull, I would avoid superfluities & several of the Articles left out, I imagine he may have, by him, but by perusing the List you will make your remarks,

---

¹ East India House which was at the corner of Leadenhall Street and Lime Street in the City of London.

& when I know what he has with him, the rest may be immediately procured here. I shall be making inquiry at the India House¹ respecting what expenses will be upon his appointment which are the Fees of Office; & also respecting his Passage, & you may expect to hear from me what I should recommend between this & the Middle of December.

In the mean Time
I am yours Sincerely

Highbury Terrace

21 Oct^r, 1808   J. Huddart

Dear Madam

I wrote you about 10 Days ago, inclosing the Company's Resolutions respecting Cadets. I am sory to inform you that I was told that the Directors had resolved not admit any Cadets in future under the Age of 16 years & have this day made further enquiries & find it correct. Therefore Mr. Gale cannot be admitted this Season. I hope his remaining in this Country a year Longer will not be to his disadvantage Capt.^{tn} Cotton has assured me that he will attend to his appointment when he is of Age, I was inquiring respecting his Passage, when I got this Information.

yours Sincerely

Highbury Terrace

10.th Dec. 1808   J. Huddart

Dear Madam,

I hope that it will not be attended with any inconvenience that Mr. Gale remains another year in England, as I am of your Sons opinion that it will then be soon enough for his future benefit, Loss in Rank is the only thing against him, but I hope this will be compensated by his better Judgement. I have received a Letter from Sir Joseph Senhouse saying that his Son had arived safe at Bombay & should the Elphingstone be dispatched home from thence, Mr. Senhouse may be expected home in time to go out the Next Season, which I could very much wish; as Gale would then have a friend & adviser on board & with whom he could mess.

yours Sincerely

Highbury Terrace

11.th Jany 1809   J. Huddart

Dear Madam

As the Certificate of the Age of a Cadet Nominated in the Company's Service requires a declaration of the nearest of Kin I thought it proper to send you the Company's regulations, respecting Cadets.

The Nomination is obtained from Joseph Cotton Esq. & I think of applying for his Passage to Madras in the Admiral Gardiner one of Cap.^{tn} Woolmoor's Ships which is stationed to be in the Downs the 16th Jan.^y – you will see by the Regulations the Least Sum to be Paid, for Passage when accommodated at the Capt.^{tn} or Master Ships & shall be Glad to have your instructions respecting it.

With best respects I am

yours Sincerely,

Highbury Terrace

30th   J. Huddart

Dear Madam

I duly rec.^{d} your favor of the 6 Ins.^{t} & I think that the Certificate of Mr. Gale's Age will do very well if Mr. Senhouse put his Name to it, & I wish to see him as soon as convenient altho a few Days will not be material. I wish to see him fixed in His Nomination & there will be time inough with Ben's Assistance to procure what he may want & inquire for his Passage.

If the Coach came through Highgate, the Coach man may set him down with his Luggage at the Sign of the Cock at the End of Highbury Place, if not he had best take a Coach from the City to my house with his things, or if I am inform'd where & when he may be expected, I can send Ben to meet him, In the Mean time

I am yours Sincerely

Highbury Terrace

13th Feby 1809   J. Huddart

Dear Madam

I am very much Pleased with your young Man, the specimens of his Writing & Drawings are much in his favor, & his disposition & deportment will I doubt not gain respect from his Superiours. I went with him to the East India House the Tuesday after his Arival & he was before the Committee of Directors & approved Since which we have ordered some Necessaries & I have spoke to Capt.^{tn} Eastfield of the Earl Howe for Accommodation at his Table.

It is expected the China Ships will be dispatched from Portsmouth about the 25.th Ins.^{t} & such Ships from India as are arived there; I thought it better he should stay with me a little longer than to send him & his Necessaries down by Land to Portsmouth; & hope to see him on board at Gravesend.

Cap.^{tn} Finally Leaves Town.

Yesterday Mr. Gale & Ben went to Apothecarys Hall to procure a Bottle of Hungary Water & having made a Box for it are now gone with an intention of sending it by the Mail Coach to Carlisle, this Evening; should any disappointment happen he will write you or Mr. Senhouse tomorrow, he has enclosed you a Letter inside of the Box.

The Earl Howe is by appointment to be in the Downs the 11.th April I think she will not be much after the time.

Yours Sincerely

Highbury Terrace

14th March 1809   J. Huddart

Dear Madam,

I duly received your favor of the 3 Ins.^{t} & in reply Capt.^{tn} Eastfield took Leave of the Directors Wednesday & is intending to go down on Monday Next. Mr. Gale is going with his Necessaries to the Company Wharff to be sent down to the Ship at Gravesend, & I think Sunday will be the latest Day he can be here, on which Day I conceive the Ship will be unmooring to leave Gravesend. It is also expected that a Convoy will be appointed to sail from Portsmouth in about 10 Days or a Fortnight, hence your Letter to Mr. Gale may be directed to him Cadet on board the Earl Howe East Indiaman Portsmouth. Mr. Gale told me he brought from Home about 18 or 19 Guineas, he says today he has 9 Guineas Left which should he want any thing at Portsmouth or elsewhere will take with him.

I intend to pay to Capt.^{tn} Eastfield or his Purser £10, to be Paid him at Madras in Rupees or Coin of the Country, in order he may not be in any distress on his first Landing.

My best respects to Mr. Senhouse your Son & Daughter & am

Dr Madam

yours Sincerely

Highbury Terrace

7th April 1809   J. Huddart

Dear Madam,

I yesterday (with Ben who has been his constant companion) took leave of Mr. Gale on board the Earl Howe; Capt.[tn] Eastfield inform'd me on Monday, that he would go on board on Wednesday & expected to Proceed, on Thursday (this Day) from the Hope. The Captain was not on board, but I met him on my way to London, & who I doubt not, will pay attention to your young Man. The Ship is not so ready as he expected, & it may be the end of the Week before she can leave the River, & scarcely be expected at Portsmouth, if the Wind is fair before the Middle of next Week. I dont expect that they will be long detained at Portsmouth, therefore your Letters, wrote early in next week will be sure to meet him.

I am yours Sincerely

Trinity House

Thursday 13th April 1809   J. Huddart

Dear Madam,   Highbury Terrace 1st May 1809

I duly rec.[d] your of the 18th Ult° & am rejoiced to hear of the Birth of your Grandson at Netherhall.

I received a letter from Mr. Gale dated Friday last the 28th Ult.°, wrote while the Earl Howe was under way, & sent on Shore by the Pilot. & the Wind being fair untill this Morning, I expect the Fleet is now clear of the Channel. He seem'd to feel much at Parting, but now writes in Good spirits, & acknowledges the Receipt of your Letter at Portsmouth.

Respecting his Book which you mention he brought it down stairs to me, & said that thought he would leave it, if I thought it would not be of use to him, but did not say you requested to have it, I thought it might be usefull therefore he has taken it with him.

yours Sincerely

J. Huddart

Captain Huddart ended his days at 12 Highbury Terrace; he often talked of visiting Wales to see his estates but demands on his time resulted in his postponing his intention until it was too late and he had to abandon the idea. For some years he had suffered minor complaints. In 1808 he was taking the waters, first at Cheltenham and then at Gilsland in Cumberland, according to two letters written to Mrs Senhouse.

Dear Madam

I have received your favor & am sory to hear you have been so much indisposed during the Winter, & hope you will find your Health improved by the approaching Season altho to this time the Weather has been very unfavourable to invalids. I thank you for your attention & hope to have the pleasure of paying you a visit, & give Gilsland a Tryal, at present I am much better than I have been for more than 12 Months Past, & am under ingagement to go to Holy Head, on the business of the Corporation of Trinity House, whether I shall return here, or proceed Northward, I cannot at present determine.

I desire you will give my best respects to Mr. Senhouse Miss Wood & all inquiring Friends & am

Dear Madam

Yours Sincerely

Highbury Terrace
1st May 1808   J. Huddart

Dear Madam

I have just time to inform you that the Water has agreed well with me & I find my appetite improved, but am sory to inform you that the Water is much worse than formerly, from the quantity of Rain Water & exposure to the Air, I propose returning the Latter end of the Week, in the Mean Time I am with best respects to your Family

yours Sincerely

Gilsland Monday Morn.ᵍ

27ᵗʰ June 1808   J. Huddart

In his latter years Huddart had built up a reputation as a consulting engineer and his celebrity increased with the work he undertook but in his last years he had to decline many requests made upon him and by November 1815 he had become a permanent invalid. On 24 November he made his Will, settling all his estates in entail – an interminable document running into seventeen pages of legal rigmarole providing for every possible eventuality. On 17 May 1816 he added a codicil including the recently purchased farm of Isalt in the parish of Llanfihangel-y-Pennant in the settlement. This purchase was no doubt tied in with the sale of his farm lands in Cumberland, which had been in the family for generations. But he still retained a small piece of land at Allonby which remained in the possession of his son until the time of his death some thirty years later. The following is a letter addressed to his attorney closing the deal written by the Purchaser's attorney who also happened to have the name of Huddart, but was no relation. This sort of correspondence has changed little over the years.

To.
    Mr. James Weston
    Atty at Law
    Fenchurch Street
        LONDON

Sir,

I have this day sent per Coach the Deeds for conveying Captn. Joseph Huddarts Estate to the different Purchasers, which I hope you will receive safe, and find in a State ready for executing by the Vendor (dates only excepted) – description of the Premises somewhat varied from the Draft sent to you, making it more satisfactory to the Purchasers, but in fact no better, the Boundary as before – described Inclosing each Lot every side, consequently the Extent of the Premises was ascertained – notwithstanding the 2d. Day of Febry was Named as the Day of Payment, if in case that had been insisted upon, it wou'd have been rather inconvenient for some of the Purchasers altho' they are all People of sufficient Property for the purpose, and have more money due to them than the Am't of the Vendors Claim, but hope that Capt. Huddart will not be offended at them, as they thought a few days over would not be considered by him any great Object – I apprehend that some blame may be found with me for not furnishing the Deeds sooner, but rest assured that I am not the sole cause of delay which I can easy make appear if required – The Premises now conveyed to Mr. Gustavus Richmond were Purchased by him the said Gustavus Richmond and intended for the Revd. Joseph Richmond of Newnham in the County of Southampton Clerk, his Uncle who is since dead, and it was not known until the Night of the 25th Instant who the Premises were to be conveyed to until a Letter was rec'd. from Mr. Gustavus Richmond, Dated Newnham 21st Inst (where he then was) saying that the Conveyance was to be made to him, which deed you will receive, which amongst other things prolonged the time – I rather expect that Mr. Gustavus Richmond will call upon Capt Huddart on his way to Maryport from Newnham, as he says he will be in London a few Days, his Uncle's Death was the cause of his being at Newnham, there has been other causes of Delay which I think not necessary to name –

I hope the business in London will soon be completed, when done, send the Deeds to Mr. Joseph Huddleston Merch't Maryport who I understand is appointed by Capt. Huddart to Receive the Purchase Money, that I make no doubt you are already acquainted with.

Hoping that Capt. Huddart is fast getting better.

I am
Sir,
your most humble Serv't.

Maryport 30th Janr'y
1816   Thos Huddart

This concludes Huddart's business affairs and the last days of his life are recorded by his son.

This but too well foreseen and melancholy event occurred in November 1815; when, finding his illness rapidly augmenting he made his will, arranged his affairs, and desired that his son, then in Wales, should be apprised of his situation; at this time his appetite had almost left him, his strength was rapidly declining and it was but too evident to his family and friends, that he could not long survive. Dr. Babington, Mr William Blizard, Sir Everard Home, and Mr. Hole, attended him in the most assiduous and friendly manner, but all efforts could only prolong his valuable life a few months.

At an early period of his disorder, when it first assumed a serious aspect, he turned his active and comprehensive mind to the study of the anatomy of the human body, with which he soon made himself acquainted; he kept an exact journal of every symptom of his complaint, and of the medicine he daily took: so long as he entertained any hopes of conquering his disorder, he was indefatigable in seconding the efforts of his medical advisors, but at length his complaint turning to a dropsy, he sunk under it after suffering the operation of tapping twice.

From the commencement of his complaint, he kept an exact registry of his weight, and by weighing every thing he took, together with what he lost, he marked the progressive decay of his system; he ascertained by these means the exact quantity of weight carried off by insensible perspiration and by the breath: these minute calculations astonished his professional attendants, particularly Dr. Babington, who frequently told him that had he originally turned his attention to physic he must have reached the top of the profession.

During his protracted illness his excellent and kind friend Archdeacon Watson visited him frequently, and about three weeks before his death administered the Holy Sacrament to him for the last time.

Twelve hours previous to his decease, he lost in a great measure his articulation, of which however he was not himself sensible. He endeavoured, and appeared very anxious to say something to his son, which neither he nor the attendants could understand; and, imagining that he did not speak loud enough, Captain Huddart exerted his voice as much as his weak state would allow. The by-standers comprehended him so far as to learn that he could hear what was said to him, and that he was surprized he could not be heard by those around him. His son then finding it necessary to apprise him that his articulation was not so distinct as usual, he immediately made signs for paper, pen and ink, and being raised up in bed, he took the pen and wrote, – but alas! the few words he attempted could not be deciphered: after this effort he was laid down again, and from that time he did not attempt to speak.

His illness had been so lengthened, and his sufferings so severe, that his form was very much reduced, and his strength quite exhausted. He had been, through life, accustomed occasionally to weigh himself; his usual weight, from some years previous to his illness, was about two hundred and twenty pounds: in the month of January, seven months prior to his death, he found himself weighing only one hundred and thirty-four pounds; yet, notwithstanding his great bodily weakness, he retained his faculties: he was perfectly tranquil and resigned to the will of his Creator, and breathed his last apparently without much pain, at nine o'clock a.m. on the 19th of August 1816. He had expressed a wish to be buried at St. Martin's Church, Westminster, Where his uncle and family were interred: he desired his funeral might be private, mentioning only a few particular friends only whom he wished to be invited on the melancholy occasion, and on the 28th of August his mortal remains were deposited in the vault of that church.

The following obituary appeared in *The Times* on 30 August following the funeral.

The Times 30th August 1816

On Tuesday last the 27th the mortal remains of Captain Joseph Huddart formerly of the East India Company's Service were deposited in a vault under St. Martins Church in the Strand. He closed a life of unmeasured utility, after a lingering illness of many months, in Christian faith and hope, in the 75th year of his age.

To him the science of navigation owes many notable discoveries and improvements, the result of much personal fatigue and expensive experiments: the world in general is likewise indebted to him for many of the best maps and charts extant; and his knowledge of mathematics and astronomy ranked him in the class, if not upon the level with the first professors of these sciences. Of his skill in mechanism he has left a monument in the machinery for the manufacture of cordage, unrivalled in this or any other country, if we except the steam engine, the work of his contemporary and friend Mr. Watt of Birmingham.

In his figure Captain Huddart was tall and erect, his features were regular, and his countenance strongly indicative of those powers of mind for patient investigation and rational conclusion, which he so eminently possessed, blended with an expression of placid benevolence equally characteristic of that amiable simplicity which so strongly endeared him to those who like the writer, were incapable of appreciating his more scientific qualifications.

Captain Huddart was an Elder Brother of Trinity House, House, a Fellow of the Royal Society. He was born at Maryport in Cumberland.

Appropriately, a white marble monument by Fontano of Carrara was erected to Joseph Huddart's memory in the Chapel of Ease at Allonby where he really belonged, bearing the following inscription:

Sacred to the Memory of

CAPTAIN JOSEPH HUDDART, F.R.S.

Formerly of the
Honorable East India Company's Service,
And one of the Elder Brethren of the Corporation of the Trinity House, London;

HE WAS BORN AT THIS PLACE

11th January, 1741,

AND DIED AT HIGHBURY TERRACE, NEAR LONDON,

August 19th, 1816.

He has left a memorial of his Fame far more lasting than this Monument,
in those numerous Works of Science by which he has done
Honor to his Country, benefitted Commerce,
and improved Navigation.

"Unto whom much is given, of them shall much be required;"

And of him it may be truly said that the pre-eminent powers of his mind, and his
superior acquirements in Mathematics, Mechanics, and Astronomy,
were unceasingly devoted to the services of humanity,

by pointing out a

More Secure Path in the Trackless Deep,

and by increasing the facilities,
and lessening the dangers of those who

"go down to the sea in Ships, and occupy their business in great waters."

*"*THESE MEN SEE THE WONDERS IN THE DEEP.*"*

They were strongly impressed on his capacious mind: he saw and acknowledged
in them the wondrous works of God,
and meekly trusting in the merits of his Saviour,
closed a life of unblemished integrity
in the 75th year of his age.

HIS ONLY SURVIVING SON

Erects this Monument in commemoration of those virtues,
which endeared him in all the relations of
private life.

In 1845, 100 years after the consecration of the original chapel it was demolished and the present church built on the same site with transepts being added four years later. In 1885 the chancel sanctuary arches and choir stalls were added, giving accommodation for 300 worshippers, and this monument is now in the North Transept. In 1906 Christ Church Allonby was created a parish in the gift of the Vicar of Bromfield.

APPENDIX A

Curriculum Vitae *of Joseph Huddart*

Year	Date	
Year	*Date*	
1741	11 January	Born at Allonby where he lived with his parents and later attended the school kept by the Reverend Wilson.
1746		John Huddart, his grandfather, died.
1756–61		Visited his uncle in London, Joseph Huddart senior: took to sea with the White Herring Fishery, first as seaman and later as Master: his father was joint proprietor of a company in the white fishing industry and built a fish curing convenience in which he had a one-sixteenth share.
1762	16 April	William, his father, died. Married Elizabeth Johnston of Coupar.
1763		At sea as Master of the brig *Allonby*. His son William was born.
1764		Master of a coasting vessel belonging to a relative.
1765–7		Master of the brig *Gloria* in the coasting trade: and in trade with Ireland.
1768		Had the brig *Patience* built at William Wood's yard at Maryport. His son Joseph was born.
1769–70		Sailed as Master of the *Patience* and owner of the vessel trading with North America.
1771–2		Visited Sir Richard Hotham in London and offered post of fourth officer in HEICS and declined: continued trading with the *Patience* making voyages to North America.
1771		His son Johnston was born.
1773	24 December	Chartered the *Patience* and joined the HEICS.
1774		Sailed to St Helena, Bencoolen, and Batavia.
1775	October	Arrived back in England and continued trading with the *Patience*.
1776	October to December	Carried out commission for Sir Richard Hotham and returned to London.

1777	26 April	Sailed from Maryport in *Liberty* making a survey of St George's Channel.
	10 October	Entered HEICS.
1778	31 March	His chart of St George's Channel published.
	27 April	Sailed as First Officer in *Royal Admiral* under command of Captain Barrow.
1779		In command of *Royal Admiral*: sailed to Bombay.
1780	January	Returned home.
	June	Sailed for Negapatam.
1781	January	Reached Malabar Coast and put under command of Admiral Sir E. Hughes.
	15 July	Dutch surrendered at Jagginaultporam.
1782	12 October	Sailed from Bombay.
1783	31 January	At St Helena.
	25 August	Returned to England – The Downs.
1784	27 March	Sailed for India and China.
1785		At Whampoa.
1786	12 February	His wife Elizabeth died at Allonby.
	April	Returned to England.
	September	Carried out survey of Maryport Harbour: his Survey of the Tigris was published.
1787	30 March	His son William died at Macao.
	August	Returned to England.
1789		Carried out survey of Scottish Islands.
	December	Received thanks of Whitehaven Trustees for improvement plan.
1790		Carried out survey of Hasborough Gatt and determined longitude of Great Yarmouth.
1791		Elected a member of the Royal Society. Elected an Elder Brother of Trinity House.
1792	28 May	His mother Rachel died at Allonby.
1793	25 April	Granted first Letters Patent for his rope-making invention. Gave Report to Boston Corporation.
1794		Received the thanks of the Hull Commissioners of Customs for his Survey of the Port: his Chart of the Western Coast of Scotland published.
1795	29 January	His son Johnston died at Leghorn. Received the thanks of the Trustees of Swansea Harbour for his suggested improvements. Prepared sailing directions for North Sand Head Lightship.
1796	March	Carried out a survey of St Agnes for a jetty. Carried out a survey of Portsmouth Harbour. Read a paper to the Royal Society. Made a survey of False Bay, Cape of Good Hope. Built an experimental vessel at Maryport.

1798		Made a Director of the East India Dock Company.
1799		Granted his second Letters Patent for the Rope-making invention.
1800	16 February	Partnership of Huddart & Co. formed. Rope-making machinery completed and factory in production.
	3 November	Report made of Leith Harbour.
1801		His portrait painted by John Hoppner, RA.
1802		Survey of shoals at Sunk Lightship. Brought experimental vessel from Maryport to London.
1803	January	Received the thanks of the Director General of Inland Navigation for improvements at Dublin.
1804	4 March	Laid foundation stone of East India Docks. In joint command of Trinity House vessel *Iris*.
1806		Survey for Flamborough Head Lighthouse.
1808		Survey of Holyhead for South Stack Lighthouse. Survey of Howth for a Harbour.
	August	Report on improvements to Woolwich Dockyard.
	September	Visited Portsmouth at the request of the Admiralty.
1809		Purchased the Brynkir Estate.
1811		Purchased Wern and Eithinog Estates. Presented with a cup by R. Harker & Co. bearing the inscription:

> To Captn Joseph Huddart F.R.S.
> in grateful acknowledgment of his
> beneficial exertions in support of the
> Interests of the British White Herring
> Fishery from his Obliged & Obed^t
> Serv^{ts}
>
> Richard Harker & Co.
>
> Allonby March 1811.

1812	August	Received the thanks of the Admiralty for his work in connection with Sheerness Dockyard.
1815	September	His health started to decline. Sold his lands in Cumberland and bought the Farm of Isalt at Brynkir.
1816	August	Died at his home and buried at St Martins in the Fields in his uncle's vault.

APPENDIX B

Portraits and Engravings depicting Captain Joseph Huddart, FRS

A three-quarter-length portrait of Joseph Huddart, FRS, shown seated at a table holding dividers over drawings for his invention of the register and the register gauge in front of a terrestrial globe. He is wearing a brown coat with a red collar and gilt buttons engraved with the arms of Trinity House. The portrait was commissioned by his partner Charles H. Turner in 1801 and executed by John Hoppner, RA, and measures 125 cm by 100 cm. It came under the hammer in January 1928. The Institution of Civil Engineers has a copy by Williams presented by James Walker, the President, in 1841.

The Royal Institution of South Wales has a copy measuring 76 cm by 63.5 cm with a document in the left background presumed to be an Act of Parliament which was donated to them in 1896 by J. R. Francis.

A facsimile copy of the original was presented to Trinity House by the late G. W. O. Huddart in 1944 but destroyed by enemy action and a further copy has since been made.

An engraving of the portrait was made by James Stow and another by T. Blood in 1811.

The portrait of Joseph Huddart in the full uniform of a Captain of the East India Company Service illustrated on the jacket was painted in 1785 and is attributed to the circle of Guan Zuolin together with the companion portrait of his son Johnston in the uniform of a midshipman.

A large canvas by Gainsborough Dupont extending the length of the Quarter Deck at Trinity House inaugurating the rebuilding of their premises and depicting of the Elder Brethren and other members of the Court who were Captains Hector Rowe, John Travers, George Burton, Sir Robert Preston, Captains Thomas Brown, Philip Bromfield, William Davis, William Money, Francis Easterly, Gilfrid Reed, Henry Pelly, Henry Rice, John Deffel, Thomas King, John Strachan, Timothy Mangles, Anthony Clavert, John Cotton, and Joseph Huddart. The painting includes David Court, the Secretary, Ambrose Weston, the Solicitor, and Samuel Wyatt, the Architect for the Corporation.

A large engraving by W. Walker & Son of London designed by Gilbert and drawn by F. Skill and W. Walker published on 4 June 1862 showing Joseph Huddart in a group of contemporary scientists taken from paintings done in their lifetime. from left to right these are as follows:

William James Frodsham	1802–1850	Clock-maker
Francis Bailey	1766–1844	Astronomer, FRS
Sir John Leslie	1766–1832	Mathematician
Daniel Rutherford	1749–1819	Chemist
John Playfair	1748–1819	Mathematician, FRS
Nevil Maskelyne	1732–1811	Astronomer Royal, FRS
William Herschel	1738–1822	Astronomer, FRS
Peter Dolland	1730–1820	Optician
Thomas Young	1773–1858	Physicist, FRS
Robert Brown	1773–1858	Botanist
Davies Gilbert	1767–1839	Promotor of Science, PRS

Joseph Banks	1743–1820	Botanist, PRS
Edwart Jenner	1749–1823	Physician, FRS
Henry Kater	1777–8135	Scientist, FRS
William Smith	1769–1839	Geologist
Edward Charles Howard	1774–1816	Chemist, FRS
William Allen	1709–1843	Scientist & Chemist, FRS
William Hyde Wollaston	1776–1828	Physiologist, Physicist & Chemist, FRS
William Henry	1774–1836	Chemist, FRS
Henry Cavendish	1731–1810	Natural Philosopher
Charles Hatchett	1765–1847	Chemist, FRS
Humphrey Davy	1778–1829	Natural Philosopher
John Dalton	1776–1844	Chemist
Henry Maudslay	1771–1831	Engineer
Marc Isambard Brunel	1769–1849	Civil Engineer
Samuel Bentham	1757–1831	Naval Architect & Engineer
Matthew Boulton	1728–1809	Engineer, FRS
Peter William Watson	1761–1830	Botanist
Joseph Huddart	1741–1816	Hydrographer, FRS
James Watt	1736–1819	Engineer
Sir Benjamin Thompson, Count von Rumford	1753–1814	Inventor, FRS
Thomas Telford	1757–1834	Canal Engineer
William Murdoch	1754–1839	Inventor of Coal Gas
John Rennie	1761–1821	Civil Engineer
William Chapman	1749–1832	Civil Engineer
William Jessop	d. 1814	Civil Engineer
Robert Mylne	1734–1811	Architect, FRS
Sir William Congreve	1772–1828	Inventor
Bryan Donkin	1768–1855	Civil Engineer, FRS
Thomas Thompson	1773–1852	Chemist
Edward Troughton	1753–1835	Scientific Instrument Maker
Samuel Crompton	1753–1827	Inventor of Spinning Mule
Charles Tennant	1768–1838	Manufacturing Chemist
Edmund Cartwright	1743–1823	Inventor of power loom
William Symington	1763–1831	Engineer
Alexander Nasymth	1758–1840	Painter & Scientist
Patrick Miller	1731–1815	Engineer
Francis Ronalds	1788–1873	Physicist, FRS
Richard Trevithick	1771–1833	Inventor of the locomotive
Joseph Bramah	1747–1814	Inventor
Charles Earl Stanhope	1753–1816	Scientist & Politician

The Illustration facing page 79 of the Frigates under the command of the Elder Brethren of Trinity House is taken from an aquatint engraved in January 1804 by Wm Daniell of 9 Cleveland Street, London. The aquatint, which measures 69 cm by 43 cm was kindly given to the author by Miss Patience Huddart.

APPENDIX C

The Form of the Log Book used in the Royal Admiral

The Log for Saturday, 10 March 1787 (see p. 190). The ship was approaching the island of Trinidad in the Atlantic, 50 miles off the coast of Brazil.

The ship had been on a course of SW by S for 104 nautical miles and a SW course for 80 nautical miles. It is possible with this data and with the aid of trigonometry to resolve these courses into Southings and Westings, but in practice is it easier to obtain the result from Transverse Tables, which would be given in a nautical almanac.

On a bearing of SW by S for 104, Traverse Tables give a change of latitude of 85.4 miles and a departure of 57.6 miles. On a SW bearing Tables will give for 80 miles a change of latitude of 56.6 miles and a departure of 56.6 miles. This is based on a right-angled triangle with the ship's course as the hypotenuse.

The Southings total therefore 142' and the total Westings are 114' and these are shown in the third space at the bottom of the log. The latitude reading for the previous day was 16° 14', add to this 142', i.e. 2° 22' to make 18° 36'. In the Log this has been adjusted to 18° 41'. The longitude reading for the previous day was 25° 2'. In a latitude of 18°, which was the latitude of the ship, 57 nautical miles is equal to a degree of longitude, and therefore 114' W is equal to 2° of longitude and this is shown in the space headed 'X Lo' and this was added to the previous day's reading to make 27° 2' in the space headed 'Lo in' (see p. 324). This gave the ship's position by account on 10 March 1787 as latitude 18° 41' S and longitude as 27° 2' W. By observation the latitude was 18° 52' S and the longitude was 26° 5' W.

The extent of nautical miles between meridians in any particular latitude can be taken from tables in a nautical almanac or is arrived at by dividing the nautical miles, in this case 114, by the cosine of the particular latitude, i.e. 18°, which is .951, giving a change of longitude of 120' or 2°.

The space headed 'D' gives the total miles covered in the 24-hour period; this is usually adjusted slightly to give a more accurate record. The space headed 'MD' is the total distance covered since the last point of departure, which is arrived at by adding the figure in 'D' to the figure in 'MD' for the previous day (see Log for 9 March, p. 189). The final space gives the next landfall, which is Trinidad, with its bearing and distance from the position of the ship.

Copy Log – 9 March 1787

SHIP *ROYAL ADMIRAL* from ENGLAND towards MADRAS

H	Courses	K F	Winds	Rem Friday the 9th day of March 1787
1	S b W½W	6 2	SE Fair	
2		6 3		
3		6 3		
4		6 3		
5		6 3		
6		6 3		A Pleasant Trade & fair Weather
7		6		Employed as before
8		6		
9		6 3	Departed this life	
10		6 5	Allen Scott seaman	
11		7		
12		6 5		
1		6 5		
2	W b S	7 4	Squally	
3	SW	5 3		
4		6		
5		6 4		
6		6 4		
7		7 2		
8		7 2		
9	SSW ½ W	6 4	Commited the Body of	
10		6 4	the Deceased to the deep	Latitude Obs 16° 19′ S
11		6 4		Lo Chron 24. 45 W
12		6 4		Therm 78°
		157		

Course	D		MD		X Lo	Lo in	Bearing & Distance
S 23° W	157	S154′ W61′	538′	16° 14′	1° 3′	25° 2′	S 48 W 109 Leagues

Copy Log – 10 March 1787

SHIP *ROYAL ADMIRAL* from ENGLAND towards MADRAS

H	Courses	K F	Winds	Rem *Saturday the 10th day of March 1787*
1	SW b S	8	SE b E Cloudy	
2		8		
3		8		A Brisk Trade & fair Weather
4		7 2		A.M. Washed the Gun Deck
5		6	Squally	Bent the Bower Cables
6		6 3		
7		6 5		
8		7		
9		7 5		
10		7 5		
11		7 5		
12		7 5		
1		8 2		
2		8 3		
3	SW	8 2		
4		8 2		
5		8 3		
6		8 3		
7		8		Latt Obs 18° 52′ S
8		7 3		
9		7 2		
10		7 3		Lo Chron 26. 50 W
11		7 5		
12		7 5		Therm 78°
		184		

Course	D		MD	Latitude	X Lo	Lo in	Bearing & Distance Trinidada
S38½ W	181	S142′ W114′	652′	18° 41′	2° 0′	27° 2′	S 57 W 56 Leagues

APPENDIX D

An Account of the Rebuilding of Trinity House after Enemy Damage taken from The Times for Monday, 10 August 1953

NEW BUILDING OF TRINITY HOUSE RESTORATION AFTER WAR BOMBING OPENING BY THE QUEEN IN OCTOBER

The new building of Trinity House on Tower Hill, to be opened by the Queen on October 21, will bring together again all the departments of the corporation that have been dispersed since their old home was virtually destroyed from the air in the last war.

Trinity House has a triple function as lighthouse authority, pilotage authority, and administrator of corporate charities and estates. At present the pilotage service has its headquarters at Ibex House, in the Minories; the lighthouse and corporate services are in Ocean House, Great Tower Street. As it happens, close under the windows of Ocean House are the ruins of another bombed building. They are on a site once occupied by an older Trinity House – built there in 1660, consumed in the Great Fire of 1666, rebuilt, destroyed again by fire in 1715, and removed to Tower Hill in 1795. Disaster through fire was clearly no new experience in the story of Trinity House when incendiary bombs rained on the City on December 29, 1940.

ISLAND SITE

The former Trinity House comprised a main building faced with stone, built in 1793, and an adjoining brick building erected a year or two later. Both were designed by Samuel Wyatt, probably assisted by his brother James Wyatt. Before the war the Brethren of Trinity House owned other property on the same island site, and used some of it as supplementary accommodation. The total destruction of a large warehouse on the north side enabled them to acquire the freehold, and the whole island site is now theirs. Another warehouse is still occupied; when its lease has expired it will probably make room for an additional building harmonizing with the rest of Trinity House.

At the end of the war Professor A. E. Richardson was called in to advise how best to adapt the site for the new offices. The fine classical front of Samuel Wyatt's original building – which was scheduled under the Ancient Monuments Act – had fortunately been saved, and much interior detail was recorded in photographs. Professor Richardson's design has preserved this facade and he has restored the ceremonial rooms and other interior arrangements so far as possible as they were before. To the east he has added a new wing in place of the old brick building, and on the north, along Savage Gardens and Pepys Street, has provided a modern office block architecturally in keeping with the other buildings. The work has been carried out by Trollope and Colls, Limited.

The east wing is faced with stone up to the first-floor level. Above that it is brick, embellished with carvings of the arms of Trinity House, between the arms of Henry VIII, who granted to Trinity House at Deptford Strond its first charter of 1514, and those of the Duke of Gloucester, the present Master. On the roof is a decorative

191

weather-vane, a gilded ship of the eighteenth century. The courtyard railing with its late eighteenth-century lamp standards is back in place, with the addition of unobtrusive apparatus along the kerb that will allow Trinity House to share in the pleasant modern custom of floodlighting buildings.

ELEGANT ROOMS

Internally, the Wyatt building as restored and the new wing will take their place with the handsomest of London buildings. Room after room delights the eye by the combination of perfect proportion with elegant detail. A few incongruous nineteenth-century accretions, swept away in 1940, will not be restored. The court room, for instance, in which hung a heavy mid-Victorian chandelier, now has reflected lighting from lamps concealed in the coves. On the other hand, though the whole building is centrally heated, the principal rooms still have marble fireplaces, either contemporary ones assembled from other places or a replica of the room's original fireplace.

The entrance hall and the main stairway with its beautiful wrought-iron balustrading, which was completely destroyed in 1940, have been restored exactly as before, but it is not yet possible to decorate the plasterwork of the semi-dome above the stairs and the adjoining wall, which contained work in grisaille by Rigaud. The pictures that used to hang here were taken away for safety before the fire and are being rehung. In particular, a portrait group of the Merchant Elder Brethren in 1794, a painting of heroic size by Gainsborough Dupont, is being stretched, cleaned, and repaired to resume its old position on the wall of the quarterdeck – the name by which the first-floor landing has always been known.

The east wing now contains the corporation's library hall, which runs the full length of the former brick building and is reached on the first floor by the extension of the quarterdeck. The library hall has a musicians' gallery, and its books are housed in built-in bookcases hidden under panelling along the walls. In the east wall are three windows of stained glass. The middle window, a new one designed by Mr. Francis Spear, shows the arms of the corporation, and Mr. Spear has also rearranged in the side windows medallions containing the arms and merchant marks of Elder Brethren of the sixteenth to the eighteenth-century, which had been removed before the fire. On the ground floor of the wing are the corporate offices.

Note: On election the Elder Brethren were presented with a copy of the Charter granted by King James I. Joseph Huddart's copy printed in 1793 was given back to Trinity House in 1958.

INDEX